SOUVENIR A. Y. P. EXPOSITION, SEATTLE, 1909

Carnation
The First 75 Years
1899-1974

Carnation
The First 75 Years
1899-1974

JOHN D. WEAVER

Books by John D. Weaver

FICTION

Wind Before Rain
Another Such Victory

NON-FICTION

As I Live and Breathe
The Great Experiment
Warren: The Man, The Court, The Era
The Brownsville Raid:
    The Story of "America's Black Dreyfus Affair"
L.A.: El Pueblo Grande

JUVENILE

Tad Lincoln: Mischief-Maker in the White House

Preface

In 1899 E. A. Stuart had the vision and enthusiasm to start manufacturing evaporated milk, a product few people understood and fewer felt they needed. How E. A. and his associates made "The Milk from Contented Cows" one of America's best known products —expanding sales, distribution and manufacturing facilities across North America and the Free World—is a story rich in Americana. It is also a case history of the food industry and, for members of the now vast Carnation family, a personal account of how Carnation arrived at what it is today.

E. A. Stuart gave his business all his energy and devotion, but Carnation was never a one-man company. At every point in its development it was blessed with people who had the particular talent or skill needed to move ahead. Masters of organization were joined by others with the power to lead. There were men and women of ingenuity when ideas were needed and those endowed with dogged persistence when results were slow in coming.

These are the people who built Carnation and these are the people to whom this book is dedicated. Our only regret is that limitations of time and space made it impossible to record the individual contributions of so many.

Chairman of the Board   *President*

Los Angeles, California
September 6, 1974

Table of Contents

Part I   **Coming Of Age, 1899-1919**

      1. The Founding Father 11

      2. A Small Foot In A Large Door 20

      3. Carnation Coast-to-Coast 31

      4. The Overseas Milk Route 42

Part II   **The New Generation, 1920-1948**

      5. Changing Of The Guard 59

      6. Meanwhile, Back At The Ranch 66

      7. "Contented! With You With Me
             I'm Contented." 81

      8. End Of An Era 92

Part III   **The Explosive Years, 1949-1974**

      9. Growth In The Sun 108

     10. The Instant Revolution 123

     11. What's New? 136

     12. Taking Care Of Business 157

     13. The World Marketplace 173

     14. Milk & Honey 185

     15. The Cow Jumped Over The Moon 201

          Chronology 223

          Facilities: Past & Present 229

          Index 245

Part I

Coming Of Age
1899-1919

1
The Founding Father

*"Solve your problems,
don't let them lick you."*
E. A. STUART.

DURING A LONG LIFE that linked the memory of Abraham Lincoln's assassination with the bombing of Pearl Harbor, nothing ever came easily to E. A. Stuart. In his boyhood on an Indiana farm, when he was bedded down with "inflammatory rheumatism," his Quaker parents had watched him fight his way back to life from a death-like coma, and in middle age, after three business ventures had come to unhappy endings, his friends in Los Angeles had watched him light out for the Pacific Northwest to embark on what appeared to be the least promising enterprise of all.

With no experience in the dairy industry, the 42-year-old grocer had entered into an agreement with a business acquaintance to "share and share alike" in the operation of an evaporated milk plant located in an abandoned hotel at Kent, Washington, fifteen miles south of Seattle. Neither partner knew how to make evaporated milk. They depended on the process of a crusty Swiss, who had patented "a certain new and useful Improvement and Apparatus for Preserving Milk." Production would come to an abrupt halt if, at any time, John Meyenberg took a notion to quit.

In the early morning hours of September 6, 1899, neighboring dairy farmers started driving up to the condensery, delivering some 5,800 pounds (2,744 quarts) of fresh milk. It was converted—only Old John knew exactly how—into fifty-five cases of evaporated milk. Each case contained forty-eight cans, and, to avoid paying ransom to can-making patent-holders back east, each can had been made by hand.

Unfortunately, they developed a distressing tendency to swell and leak. Once air got to the milk, it soured. Never one to let anything go to waste, E. A. sold the milk from his "bloats" to local dairymen, who diluted it with water and fed it to their calves. When his supply outran their needs, he bought two hundred hogs and fattened them with his salvaged milk.

No one in those early days had any words of encouragement except Tom Yerxa, the partner who had steered him into evaporated milk and, as specified in their agreement, had left him in "full charge and control of said business." After the company had dropped around $140,000 in its first year and a half, Yerxa was ready to sell out. E. A. gave him $5,000 as a down payment against a purchase price of $45,000, and agreed to assume Yerxa's half of their $65,000 debt. Thus, on a spring day in 1901, E. A. Stuart found himself sole owner of the Pacific Coast Con-

11

John B. Meyenberg, center, inventor of the milk evaporating process, with E. A. Stuart, left, and partner T. E. Yerxa in front of the Kent plant, circa 1900. Boy is Meyenberg's son.

densed Milk Company.* He also found himself $105,000 in debt.

* * * * *

"Two things were very firmly fixed in my mind," E. A. wrote in 1912, looking back on the company's beginnings. "One was supreme faith in the quality of my product. The other was that evaporated and sterilized milk as I was then preparing it, as the Pacific Coast Condensed Milk Company, with some improvements, is today preparing it—Carnation Milk as it is known in the markets of the country—would eventually be one of the largest single articles in the grocery business."

Twenty years later, in the depths of the Great Depression, when E. A. relinquished the presidency of Carnation Company to his son Elbridge, the editor of *The West Coast Trade* pointed out that Carnation Milk, with a daily production of more than one million cans, was "as much a staple on the shelves of the grocery store as salt or sugar." The modern retailer, as predicted by E. A. long ago, had replaced the old fashioned milkman.

"Carnation Company has today arrived at an enviable position; it is the leading producer of a brand of evaporated milk in the United States, which in turn means in the world," he reported to his board of directors in his February 22, 1932 letter of resignation, written at a time when he was sinking deeper and deeper into the hushed, shadowy world of the deaf and the blind.

A few years earlier, when serious trouble with his eyes first developed, he had gone to a Seattle hospital for some tests. Afterwards, Carnation's liaison with the dairy industry, George S. Bulkley, sat with him while his eyes were being bandaged. He had never seen E. A. so shaken.

"He held my hand, trembling. 'George,' he said, 'what am I going to do? I won't be able to work or see my cattle and my horses.

*The name was changed to Carnation Milk Products Company in 1916 and shortened thirteen years later to Carnation Company.

I never had a hobby in my life, never even went fishing. What am I going to do?' "

Once he was blind, he thought, he would live in total blackness. Instead, he was agreeably surprised to find he could see "visions like the sun shining in trees." He continued to keep a close watch on the company, threshing out major decisions with Elbridge. When the board of directors met at his Los Angeles home on North June Street, he could distinguish some of its members because they were short and stocky (Al Hartwick) and others

because they were tall and rangy (Big John Wilkinson). The directors left the meetings with freshly cut carnations from his greenhouse.

E. A., confronted for the first time with a hobby and the time to indulge it, wasn't satisfied to putter about a potting shed, working with ordinary cuttings rooted in ordinary soil. Instead, he rigged up hydroponic plant beds and fed his carnations a scientifically blended solution of nutrients. A retired director of the company has never forgotten "the sturdy, three-foot stems and the big, heavy centers, four inches in diameter." E. A.'s carnations, like his cattle and his horses, had to be outstanding. He had never settled for anything less than the best.

*　*　*　*　*

"I used to tell Father that the only reason he wanted me to be President in 1932 was because he knew we wouldn't make a profit that year," Elbridge H. Stuart liked to recall with a smile, secure in the knowledge that

Opening day at the Kent plant was September 6, 1899. Farmers delivered milk on the back porch and employees assembled on the balcony to have their picture taken.

once the company had started making money in 1901 it had ended up in the red only three times (1909, 1920 and 1932).

During Elbridge Stuart's years as president (1932-1957) and as chairman of the board (1957-1971), Carnation supported the research required for the introduction of such new products as Coffee-mate and Instant Breakfast, developed overseas operations on six continents and, through such carefully selected acquisitions as Contadina and Trenton Foods, grew to be one of the country's largest food processors. Sales rose from less than $33,000,000 to more than one billion dollars a year, and through it all Elbridge Stuart went his own quiet, modest way, shunning publicity.

"I'm biased," admits his longtime associate and successor, H. Everett Olson, "but in my opinion he was one of the greatest executives that I've ever come in contact with. He would delegate authority, but in delegating it, he never felt that he himself had lost the responsibility for that authority. He was a fearless man, could be very tough, but also very mellow, very gentle. Like his father, if you made a mistake and admitted it, that was the end of the matter, but he was a man you never wanted to lie to.

"I never knew anyone with such a memory. It was tremendous. He was not a trained accountant, and I am, but he could read a statement just as well as I could. He was not a trained engineer, but he could go through a plant and fifteen years later he would know where every piece of machinery was, where every door was. He never had to refer to a blueprint. It was amazing.

"He was in some ways a shy man, but in the meetings we had in this office we always knew where he stood and he always wanted to know where we stood. He invited opinions, and he was not at all autocratic. He was not a picky person. He didn't spend a great deal of time trying to undo things that were done. The past was the past. He was always looking at today and the future, always thinking, always planning."

Elbridge grew up in E. A.'s thrifty, hard-working, plain-speaking image, keeping the same watchful eye on the most minute details of the company's operations. He dreaded speech-making, but when forced to it, acquitted himself with grace and good humor. E. A., on the other hand, delighted in addressing a gathering of jobbers or cattle buyers. He was a born salesman, his son a born executive. Both were men of considerable dignity, somewhat formal and reserved in manner, even with each other. In letters brimming with a father's love for a devoted son, the signature at the bottom of the page was invariably a businesslike "E. A. Stuart."

"It gives me no end of happiness that I am blessed with a son who is capable of carrying on the work for which I laid the foundations," E. A. wrote Elbridge on January 4, 1941. "I hope that in years to come when you reach the point that you feel you are no longer able to actively direct the organization, you may be able to experience the happiness that I have in having one or more of your sons to take up the reins, and I feel confident that this will be the case."

Dwight, the youngest of Elbridge's three sons, was seven years old when his father assumed the presidency of the company. Exactly forty-one years later, on February 22, 1973, five months after Elbridge's death, Dwight Lyman Stuart was elected president of Carnation Company, the fifth in its history.

*   *   *   *   *

His father had taken it for granted that, before his sons started to work for Carnation at the bottom of the company ladder, they would go back to his old school, at Andover, Massachusetts, and prepare themselves for Yale. The two older boys, Hadley and Fullerton, had other ideas. Elbridge's hopes came to rest on his youngest son.

"I went there for three years," Dwight recently reminisced, "and then, for various reasons, I got kicked out. I had to go back to Milwaukee and get on a train with Dad. We were three nights and two days getting to Los Angeles, the worst train ride I ever took. I kept looking around, trying to find someone to talk to. The day we arrived, Dad was

E. H. Stuart was president of Carnation when he took this family group photo. From left, Hadley, Nan (Mrs. E. H.), Mary (Mrs. E. A.), E. A. Stuart, Fullerton and Dwight.

going to the office, so he said to E. A., 'Now you talk to this grandson of yours. I'm disgusted with him.'

"That noon we had lunch together and he said, 'I'm supposed to have a talk with you,' and I said, 'I figured there'd be a talk coming up.' He said, 'Well, let's go outside. We can talk out in the garden.' And then he said, 'Do you smoke?' I was seventeen and in those days you weren't supposed to smoke at that age. I didn't know what to say to him, but I knew I couldn't lie to that guy, he'd see right through it, so I said, 'Yes.' He said, 'What do you smoke?' and I told him, 'Cigarettes.' 'Ugh,' he said 'What about smoking a cigar with me?'

"We went out to the garden and smoked our cigars. He said, 'You know your father is very mad at you, but don't worry about it. He'll get over it. The important thing is what do *you* want?' I told him I was going to go back to summer school, but I said, 'Chances are I'll be put back a grade, and if that's the case I'm not going back to Andover.' He said, 'Well, you make up your own mind. I'm not going to tell your father I told you this, but you do what *you* want to do.'"

The conversation between E. A. and his grandson took place in the summer of 1941. That fall Dwight registered as a senior at Garfield High School in Seattle. After his graduation, he put in a year at the University of Washington and then enlisted in the Navy. When the war ended, he returned to the University of Washington, took a degree in journalism (Class of 1947) and collided head-on with his father by announcing his decision not to go to work for Carnation.

"Dad went through the ceiling," Dwight says, "so I told him I'd go to work for the company for a year and try it out. I started as a trainee in the Fresh Milk and Ice Cream Division, and at the end of a year I quit. There was a very deep falling out."

For the next year or two he served as a manufacturers' representative for the West

Coast franchise-holder of a number of soft-goods lines sold through hardware and department stores. In selling such oddments as ironing board covers and kitchen utensils, young Dwight developed confidence in his abilities as a salesman and, at the same time, discovered that selling was his forte.

"It was stimulating," he once told the editor of *The Carnation* (February-March, 1966). "This is true for anyone who really enjoys being a salesman. When you start out to make a sale, your adrenalin starts pumping and you're like a horse at the gate."

One day, having proved to himself what he had set out to prove, that he was a first-rate salesman who could make it on his own, he got to thinking about Carnation Company.

"Let's swallow a little pride," he said to himself, and, without a word to his father, he got in touch with the vice president in charge of sales, applied for a job and went to work for the company in Los Angeles, where Carnation had established its World Headquarters on its fiftieth anniversary in 1949.

* * * * *

E. A. Stuart never lived to see the nine-story white building on Wilshire Boulevard, but his restless spirit permeates the unostentatious offices. His eye is on the fallen paper clip and the light left burning after hours; and the warmth of his approval radiates across the top-floor dining room where the heads of his corporate family gather for their midday meal, drinking fresh milk instead of dry martinis.

"It's like having lunch with Horatio Alger's grandchildren," remarked a recent visitor from the East, who had never seen so many executives assembled at high noon without a drop of liquor in sight.

"Carnation has grown into a billion-and-a-half-dollar-a-year, multi-national company, but it has managed to hold onto something of the intimacy of a small town, turn-of-the-century family business," says a young product manager who came to Carnation a few years ago, after defecting from a midwestern corporation where, he says, "I never laid eyes

16

The Five Presidents of Carnation

ELBRIDGE AMOS STUART, founder
President, 1899-1932
Chairman of the board, 1932-1944
Born: September 10, 1856 on a farm near Greensboro, North Carolina
Died: January 14, 1944 in Los Angeles, California
Partner in retail store in El Paso, Texas, 1881-1894
Partner in wholesale grocery store in Los Angeles, California, 1894-1899.

ELBRIDGE HADLEY STUART

President, 1932-1957
Chairman of the board, 1957-1971
Born: November 9, 1887, El Paso, Texas
Died: September 16, 1972, Los Angeles,
  California
Ph.B., Sheffield Science School, Yale Uni-
  versity, 1911
Joined Carnation 1911; vice president,
  1916; director, 1918; executive vice presi-
  dent, 1926. President, General Milk Co.,
  1930-1965.

ALFRED MILLS GHORMLEY

President, 1957-1963
Born: July 23, 1896, Moscow, Idaho
Died: January 30, 1965, Los Angeles Cali-
  fornia
Joined Carnation as assistant herdsman at
  the Washington farm, 1915; vice presi-
  dent and director, 1933; assistant to the
  president, 1951; vice chairman of the
  board, 1963.

H. EVERETT OLSON

President, 1963-1973
Chairman of the board, 1971-
Chief executive officer, 1968-
Born: November 1, 1906, Chicago, Illinois
B.B.A., Northwestern University, 1927
Practicing C.P.A., Illinois, 1927-1931
Joined Carnation as assistant controller,
  1931; treasurer, 1948; director, 1950; vice
  president, finance, 1954; assistant to the
  president, 1961.

DWIGHT LYMAN STUART

President, 1973-
Born: September 27, 1924, Seattle, Wash-
  ington; U.S. Navy, 1943-1946
B.A., advertising and journalism, Univer-
  sity of Washington, 1947
Sales representative, housewares, 1948-1950
Joined Carnation in sales, 1950; director,
  1960; vice president, 1962; senior vice
  president and assistant to the president,
  1967; executive vice president, 1971.

Alfred Ghormley, center, manager of Carnation Farm, presides at E. A. Harrison's presentation of cup to Glen Gooding, captain of winning baseball team. Occasion was an office picnic, July, 1920.

on the chairman of the board and saw the president only once—in an elevator. I hadn't been at Carnation two weeks, though, before I found myself face to face with the chairman and the president, making a presentation for a new product."

"It gives us an opportunity to evaluate the young man as to his abilities, how articulate he is, how well he's thinking, his judgment, his astuteness," explains Chairman of the Board Olson. "His recommendations are not always accepted, but we attempt to explain to him why they aren't. We don't shut him off cold.

"We have always had in this company an open-door policy for anyone who wants to see any of us. Our doors are not closed, our telephones are open, and the lines of communication are very short. We can have prompt meetings, and it doesn't take us three or four weeks to make a decision.

"We have not had many levels of management. We have not seen the need for that. The sooner any one of these people in a meeting can get to the top, the better all of us are. We don't hear the information at second-, third-, or fourth-hand. We hear it direct. It's much more satisfactory for getting the facts we need in order to reach a decision."

Bill Dobson, who retired in 1972 as head of the company's foreign operations, was somewhat taken aback in 1939 when he went to work for Alfred M. Ghormley, who was then general manager of Carnation's Fresh Milk and Ice Cream Division.

"I was a graduate of Harvard Business School," Dobson says, "and I'd been trained to look at organization charts to find authority and all that sort of thing. I'd go to Ghormley about every six months with a bunch of organization charts. He was always polite and friendly, but he never paid a bit of attention to my suggestions. He was steeped in the company's philosophy of letting the cream rise to the top. They didn't care if somebody crossed lines of authority once in a while and stepped on a few toes. They felt that the guy who could do the job would take it over."

Ghormley's own career underscores Dobson's point. In the summer of 1915, when he was 19, he worked as a hand on E. A.'s farm east of Seattle. Seven years later he was managing the farm. By the summer of 1924 he had seventy-five men helping him look after Carnation's world-famous herd of registered Holstein-Friesian cattle. To E. A.'s delight, his young manager could rattle off the name of every animal over the age of ten months and, in most instances, its ear-tag number as well.

"Alfred Ghormley is about the best example I know of how a young man can get to the top if he sticks to the job and works," E. A. remarked in 1924, when the warm, friendly youth was on his way to becoming Carnation's third president (1957-1963).

* * * * *

Among financial writers and security analysts, Carnation has such a reputation for being close-mouthed that the editors of *Forbes* (January 15, 1974) likened the task of applying to the company for information to "phoning a sphinx."

"When we have something to say, we say it to our stockholders," explains S. A. Halgren, a retired senior vice president, and the *Forbes* article went on to add that "Carnation's return on equity is a respectable 14.5 percent, vs. 13 percent for Foremost-McKesson and 10 percent for Borden."

In the spring of 1974, when Carnation announced its first public debt offering to United States investors,* the sale of $50,000,000 in 25-year debentures, it received the triple-A rating of the country's two major credit rating companies, Moody's and Standard & Poor. Only one other food company, Kraftco Corporation, has been given the highest ranking of both services, a distinction shared with four other companies, General Electric, General Motors, Ford and Procter & Gamble.

"Carnation's financial reports have long broadcast that the dairy products and pet foods concern is 'clearly a premier operation,'" noted the *Wall Street Journal* (April 19, 1974). "The company has posted profit increases for twenty-one consecutive years and rising sales the past nineteen years."

Art Detman, Jr., writing in *California Business* (July 19, 1973) attributed Carnation's success to four major factors: "One, quality products. Two, an imaginative new product development program. Three, an aggressive marketing program that is keyed to the needs of the supermarkets. Four, a no-frills internal management policy." He traced the high quality and the lack of management frills to the company's early days. He might also have added the aggressive marketing program. It, too, is part of E. A.'s legacy.

"The problems of today in manufacturing and marketing are more intricate than those of a quarter of a century ago," he said in 1927. "But the problems of that time in their inexperienced setting required everything we had. We had to do the pioneer thinking and planning. We had to blaze trails."

Talking to a group of grocers in 1962, Paul H. Willis, Carnation's vice president in charge of advertising, referred to E. A.'s career as an inspiration to everyone concerned with marketing.

"Not only was he an effective personal salesman, but he also possessed that rare faculty for recognizing a market opportunity and knowing how to cultivate it."

Senior Vice President Henry Arnest, who helped build one of the food industry's finest sales organizations during his more than forty years with the company, is fond of describing Carnation as "the largest small company in the world." His eighth-floor neighbor, Senior Vice President Robert D. Kummel, smiles and adds, "Top management is concerned not only with reference to broad issues, but day-to-day issues as well. To that extent, we may be a small company, but, on the other hand, we think big. We get involved up here on this floor, and if you're going to be involved with details, you're also going to be involved with the people who handle the details."

"I've been impressed by the company's tremendous respect for the individual rights of others," says Arnest, who attributes the tradition to the four generations of Stuarts with whom he has been associated. "You feel the presence of the Founder here. It's as though he had passed his hand over our heads."

19

*The company had about $115,000,000 of long-term debt outstanding at the time, but it had been placed either privately or in the Eurodollar market.

2
A Small Foot
In A Large Door

*"As the business grew, I often
heard my father say that the company
was only in its infancy and that it had
a great future. Even just prior to
his death in 1944, he was still
of the same opinion."*
ELBRIDGE H. STUART, 1968.

Stuart & Sutherland grocery store in El Paso.

BY THE TIME he died, January 14, 1944 (he had expressed but one regret—he wanted to go up in an airplane), E. A. Stuart had become "a legendary figure" to the younger men of the Evaporated Milk Association, and dairymen here and abroad remembered him as a leading breeder of Holstein-Friesian cattle. His farm in Washington's Snoqualmie Valley had set more records than "any other breeding institution in the world," *Hoard's Dairyman* noted, and the editor of *Holstein-Friesian World*, mourning the loss of "a great and noble man," paid tribute to "his lasting contribution to the development and progress of America."

Born in Guilford County, North Carolina, September 10, 1856, he was the seventh son of a staunch Union man who left the South at the outbreak of the Civil War, even though "it cost him fully 90 percent of all his possessions." The family settled in Indiana. When they came to sign up for a new Quaker

Meeting membership after having moved from one farm to another, the boy asked to have his name changed from Amos Elbridge to Elbridge Amos. Seventy years later he was still fretting over the possibility of having offended his father by making the request.

"During the busy summer season," he wrote toward the end of his life, "my father would get us boys up early by coming to the stairway and calling to us to get up as it was time to do morning chores, and oh how

sleepy we were and hated greatly to have to get up, but we knew unless we acted promptly Father would be there at the stairway calling again. Hence we learned by experience to respond to his early call.

"Some of us boys would feed, curry and harness the horses, while others would go to the pasture and drive in the milk cows so that they could be milked before breakfast. Well do I remember when it became my lot to go and drive in the cows, and I can assure

you that many mornings when the pasture was heavily covered with dew, my bare feet would become very cold, and if it was my good fortune to find some of the cows lying down out in the pasture, I was very glad to have them get up so that I could stand on the spot where they had been lying in order to warm my feet. When the cows had been driven home and the boys had milked them, we would then be ready for breakfast by five o'clock."

He attended a one-room, red-brick schoolhouse, and later transferred to Spiceland Academy, where he got as far as what would today be the eighth grade. To help pay his way, he sawed wood for the schoolhouse stoves and was graduated with a firm grasp of bookkeeping, "which has proven to be one of my greatest assets in carrying on my business, as that knowledge enabled me to keep my own books as well as to be able to check over work which any bookkeeper working for me might do."

When he was fifteen, E. A. left home ("I did not especially fancy the hard work on the farm"). He and an older brother, Addison, scraped up $300, some of it borrowed from their father, and went into business in Indianapolis, selling farm produce on a commission basis. A few months later, both partners were taken ill, and the firm went broke. E. A. kept a record of its debts and eventually managed to pay them off.

After still another recurrence of inflammatory rheumatism, this one in Richmond, Indiana, where he had been driving a delivery wagon, E. A. decided to head west, determined to find a healthy climate "or else die in the attempt." He was still on crutches when he hobbled into Lawrence, Kansas, where another brother, Jehu, practiced medicine. E. A. went back to high school and toyed with the notion of becoming a doctor, but changed his mind after watching Jehu perform an autopsy. In the meantime, he had discarded his crutches and never again was he laid low by inflammatory rheumatism.

Not long after he turned twenty-four, he seized an opportunity to borrow $3,000 and,

21

in partnership with a friend, Henry Sutherland, he opened a general store in El Paso, Texas, a squat, lawless, adobe town about to strike it rich as a railroad center. In its first fifteen months, Stuart & Sutherland cleared $4,600 and moved from a tent to a red-brick building. The partners decided to devote their new digs exclusively to the grocery business.

In the fall of 1883, as E. A. told the story in the memoirs he dictated in his old age, he made a business trip to New York and slipped up to Rutland, Vermont, one weekend to look in on the parents of an El Paso friend, Amos Horner. While he was talking to the elder Horner, a young lady came into the parlor and was introduced as their daughter, Mary.

"This was surely a surprise, as I was not aware that my friend in Texas had a sister living with her parents in Rutland," E. A. declared, and for once his legendary memory had betrayed him. Among his son's papers at the time of his death in 1972 was a two and one-half page handwritten letter E. A. had addressed to Mary Jane Horner six months before his trip east. He wrote it on April 15 and waited three days before he mailed it.

"Through the introduction, which I presume your brother and sister have given you of me, I take the liberty of writing you this short note, knowing that it is not entirely a proper thing to do. I hesitate doing it for fear that you may feel indignant towards me. But through the assurance of your brother, that you would not feel so, I take pleasure in making your acquaintance by letter when it is

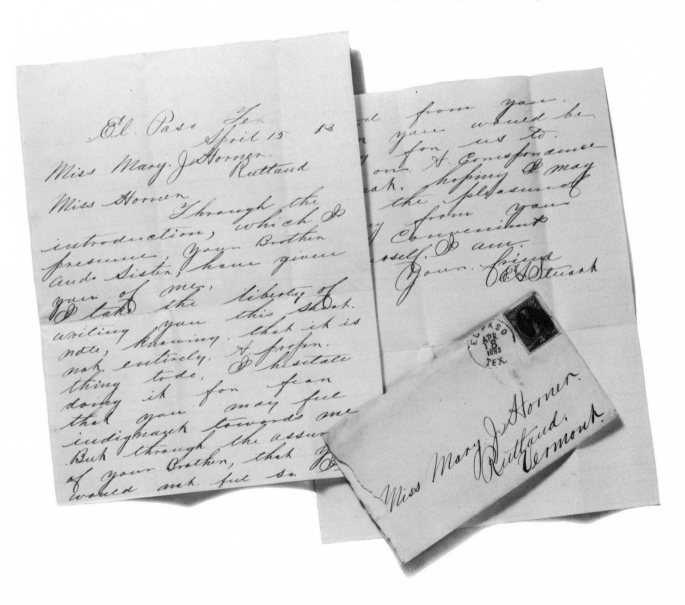

not my privilege at present to make it otherwise. Those of us that have been West a few years find ourselves doing that at times, where if we had been East, would not think of doing so, and I expect you will think this is one of those acts.

"I for one say that it is, though I cannot say I never heard of such a thing being done East for I have, and that they have proven to be very pleasant acquaintances for both parties, and if you should think it a proper thing to do I should be pleased to have a word from you whether you would be willing for us to carry on a correspondence or not. Hoping I may have the pleasure of hearing from you when convenient to yourself, I am

Your friend

E. A. Stuart

When they met in Rutland the following October, E. A.'s weekend in Vermont

E. A. and Mary Stuart
on their 50th wedding anniversary.

stretched out to two weeks. By the time he left Mary, they had come to an "understanding." He returned for another visit the next spring and that fall, on November 13, 1884, they were married.

"Mrs. Stuart and I lived together to celebrate our fiftieth anniversary and almost five additional years," E. A. wrote in his memoirs. "We were blessed with a son born November 9, 1887 and a daughter born August 25, 1893. She was a great companion in various ways throughout all of those years."

* * * * *

While the Texas storekeeper was courting the Vermont schoolteacher, John B. Meyenberg was turning his back on Switzerland, disgusted with the failure of the Anglo-Swiss Condensed Milk Company to take advantage of the process he had worked out for producing unsweetened evaporated milk. Meyenberg stalked ashore in the United States in the spring of 1884 and that fall, just twelve days after E. A.'s marriage, the temperamental Swiss inventor was granted two patents, one for the apparatus he had contrived, the other for the process by which it was to be put to use.

Patents in hand, he made his way west to the rich dairy country around St. Louis, Missouri, settling in the town of Highland, Illinois, amidst a colony of Swiss farmers. He helped form the Helvetia Milk Condensing Company early in 1885 and on June 18, after fussing over the construction of the special machinery he needed for his process, he had the satisfaction of seeing fresh milk flow into the world's first evaporated milk plant. Later that year a Helvetia salesman dropped in on E. A. in El Paso, sold him on the merits of his Highland brand of evaporated milk and left with an order for one hundred cases.

Some of the cans were still on E. A.'s shelves two years later when his son was born. Not altogether pleased with the baby's progress, E. A. decided to try Helvetia's unsweetened condensed milk on him. Improvement was so marked that the delighted father ordered another hundred cases.

E. A. moved his family to Los Angeles in

23

March, 1894, and spent the next five years in the wholesale grocery business. In the summer of 1899, having disposed of his interest in Craig, Stuart & Co., he was looking around for something to do with himself. Tom Yerxa, a former wholesale grocer from Minneapolis, was looking around for something to do with his loose money. They ran into each other on a streetcar and Yerxa suggested they get together and go into evaporated milk. He knew a bankrupt condensery they could pick up for $5,000 and he also knew a Swiss inventor who had a process for making the stuff.

John Meyenberg had long since left the Helvetia Milk Condensing Company.* After winning a gold medal at the World's Columbian Exposition in Chicago, he had moved to Buena Park, California, and started manufacturing his unsweetened condensed milk under the brand name, Lily. He agreed to sign on with E. A. and Yerxa, but once he took over the operation of the Kent condensery, he was so secretive about his process that for the first two years E. A. was in the business, he had no clear idea how to evaporate and sterilize milk.

"He became fearful that we might learn his secret and wanted to quit," E. A. wrote of Old John. "That would have put us in a very bad predicament, so I finally prevailed upon him to teach the sterilization process to my late nephew, Harry H. Stuart, for which I paid Mr. Meyenberg $25,000."

The company thought so highly of the Meyenberg secrets that key production men were placed under $25,000 bond "not to disclose, communicate or divulge the said secrets."

* * * * *

Before he could take his canned milk to market, E. A. had to give it a name. Two thousand unlabeled cases piled up at the condensery while he pondered the problem. He was thinking of a flower of some sort and,

to catch the customer's eye, he had decided on a red and white label.

"I wanted a flower which a child could easily remember in connection with the red and white label, so that if he did not remember the brand name he could describe how the can looked," E. A. recalled in later years.

At the time he was trying to come up with a brand name, his contemporaries were joking about the bride who cooked with a can opener. Her mother, like her grandmother before her, had done her own preserving, working from season to season, from strawberries and blackberries to tomatoes and but-

E. A. Stuart's ledger shows his expenditures in the early days of Pacific Coast Condensed Milk Co.

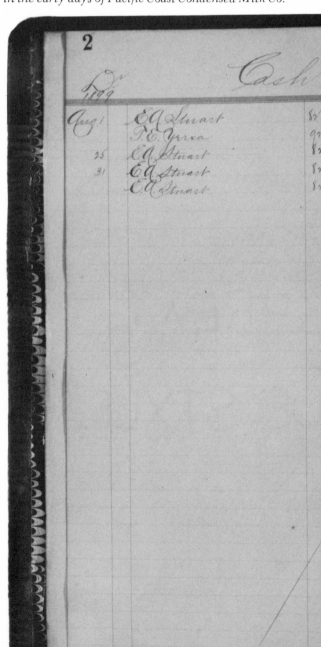

*Helvetia, meanwhile, had introduced its popular Pet brand in 1896. Later, through reincorporation in Illinois (1923) and Delaware (1925), the name of the firm was changed to Pet Milk Company.

24

ter beans, from cucumber pickles to peaches and pears. In the fall she had picked apples and left new-moon slices to dry in the Indian summer sun. At the country store, making her way past loafers huddled around the pot-bellied iron stove, she had bartered eggs, chickens and butter for sugar, salt, flour, molasses, tea and coffee.

Her daughter had traipsed off to the city and stacked her kitchen shelves with packaged cereals, bakery bread, store-bought jams and jellies, canned fruit, vegetables and meat. Dr. John T. Dorrance, whose uncle had gone into partnership with Joseph Campbell, had come up in 1897 with a method for condensing soup and Henry J. Heinz (E. A.'s match in thrift and industry) had parlayed his homemade horse-radish into some fifty-odd products, including his celebrated tomato ketchup (1876) and cider vinegar (1880). Thanks to the Uneeda Biscuit people in Chicago, soda crackers no longer came from open, fly-specked barrels. Now they were available in tidy, moisture-proof packages.

The modern woman bathed with Ivory Soap, breakfasted on Kellogg's Corn Flakes or Post's Grape Nuts, cooked with Royal Baking

The first label of Pacific Coast Condensed Milk Co.

Employees soldering cans in the capping room
of the plant at Mt. Vernon, Washington, in 1907.

Powder, bought Arrow collars for her husband, doctored her young with Chas. H. Fletcher's Castoria and administered to her own unmentionable needs with a dollop of Lydia E. Pinkham's Vegetable Compound (it contained eighteen percent alcohol). She had, in short, come to live in a brave new world of brand-name merchandising.

Cleanliness being next to godliness, it is hardly surprising that providence had dictated a brand name to Harley T. Procter, who, with the Gamble family, was peddling something called White Soap when on a Sunday morning in 1879 his minister called on the congregation to join him in reading Psalms 45:8. Harley reached the passage, "out of the ivory palaces, whereby they have made thee glad," and his heart rejoiced, but neither the Procters nor the Gambles would talk business on the Sabbath, so he had to wait until the next day to bring them the glad tidings of their soap's new name.

Adolphus W. Green, casting about for a brand name for his packaged soda cracker in 1898, thought along classical lines. He rather liked Pherenice, a Greek word that sounded like "very nice" and signified thirst. "Too difficult for the masses," his advertising agency reported, and countered with a list of suggestions which included "Taka Cracker," "Hava Cracker," "Usa Cracker," "Uneeda Cracker," 'Takanoo Cracker" and 'Whata Cracker." Mr. Green ran a red pencil under "Uneeda Cracker," and, to give his product more class, dubbed it a "biscuit."

E. A. stumbled across a brand name for his red and white cans of evaporated milk while walking down First Avenue in Seattle.

"I passed the store of a cigar jobber in whose window I saw a great pile of cigars and on the end of those cigar boxes I noted the most absurd name I ever saw for a cigar—Carnation. The absurdity of calling a cigar Carnation struck me very forcibly, but led me to know that I had at last found a name for my milk."

* * * * *

Grocers and housewives, then as later, did not always grasp the difference between "condensed" and "evaporated" milk. Both were produced by evaporation in a vacuum pan, removing from half to two-thirds of the water contained in fresh milk. Under the process patented by Gail Borden in 1856, sugar had to be added as a preservative. This was the sweetened condensed milk (up to forty percent sugar) that had slaked the thirst of Union soldiers on the road to Appomattox Courthouse. Under the Meyenberg method, patented in 1884, no sugar was needed. His unsweetened evaporated milk was preserved by sterilization under intense heat.

Thus, E. A.'s ten-cent, sixteen-ounce cans contained nothing but pure, fresh milk, he explained when he took to the road selling Carnation from a six-pack sample case. Housewives, however, could not be disabused of the notion that something must surely have been added to give the evaporated milk such a heavy, creamy consistency. To make matters worse, grocers hesitated to surrender shelf space to an unknown local label. Advertisements in Seattle newspapers featured Borden's Eagle Brand ("has stood first for forty years"), manufactured by a newly reorganized company and named for the man who had patented his process "for the Concentration and Preservation of Milk" just three weeks before E. A.'s birth.

"I always carried samples of Carnation," he remembered with satisfaction, "and would open my own and my competitors' cans and let the grocer compare the contents. Mine always looked creamier and tasted sweet, while my competitors' had separated and sometimes tasted bad. On this demonstration sometimes I was able to sell six cans."

At first the company made its cans by hand (the can-makers shared the second floor of the Kent condensery with the Meyenberg family), but in 1901 E. A. was able to buy his own can-making machinery. Another production headache cleared up when a plant foreman devised a can-filling machine capable of handling two dozen cans at a time. Once it had been built and installed,

E. A. noted, "we considered ourselves really in the evaporated milk business."

To test the staying qualities of his product, he loaded two cases on a sailing vessel bound for Japan. Months later, when the ship docked at Yokohama, the evaporated milk was transferred to another vessel heading back to Seattle. When it arrived, E. A. opened a can and, to his delight, found the milk unharmed.

"By this time we were beginning to have a little business up in Alaska among miners and trappers. I had to know whether freezing would have any bad effect on evaporated milk, so I took what was left of those two cases that had sailed almost around the world and placed them in the ice plant at Seattle and froze it several times. When the cans were opened, the milk was still perfectly smooth and in good condition."

E. A.'s 12-year-old son, Elbridge, spent his vacation on the waterfront, counting the cases of milk consigned to Alaska, and his father was pleased with his report on Carnation's increasing share of the Gold Rush market. From time to time, word filtered back to the company's Seattle office that thirsty prospectors, breaking open a can of Carnation Cream, occasionally found bits of butter floating on the surface. They took it as evidence of the evaporated milk's purity.

To E. A., however, it was an as yet unresolved production problem. He put an end to the separation of butterfat globules on December 30, 1905, when he paid a French inventor, A. Gaulin, $2,000 for a machine designed "to prevent the rising of cream on the milk and the transformation of said cream into butter." It was, as far as he knew, the first homogenizer to be put into service in the United States.

By 1906, the company had developed and dropped its first new product, a baby food called Sanipure; acquired three more condenseries, one in Oregon (Forest Grove), the others in Washington (Chehalis and Ferndale); shown off its wares at the Lewis & Clark Exposition in Portland, Oregon; racked up its first year of net sales in excess

This 1907 photo shows the first Carnation office, established in the Pacific Block in Seattle in early 1900s. Roll-top desk in foreground belonged to L. R. Hardenbergh. Man behind center light cord is W. C. Cross. E. A. Stuart had private office.

of one million dollars, and hit on the Carnation slogan. As with other historic merchandising catchphrases, it had cropped up unexpectedly, bursting on E. A. with joyful surprise, like first love.

* * * * *

Ivory Soap's arithmetical slogan surfaced one day in 1882 when Harley Procter was totting up some laboratory reports from college professors and discovered that his product's modest assortment of impurities consisted of uncombined alkali (0.11 percent),

carbonates (0.28 percent) and mineral matter (0.17). By subtracting the total, 0.56 percent, from a perfect score of 100 percent, he concluded that Ivory Soap was "99 44-100 percent pure."

Henry J. Heinz was riding Manhattan's Third Avenue El in 1896 when he noticed a shoe company's car card advertising "21 Styles." It set him to counting the number of different things his factories were processing. He got as far as fifty-nine, but some irresistible force kept drawing him back to fifty-seven. At the next stop, he sprang from the train, hurried off to a lithographer's and had a street car card designed to proclaim the virtues of his "57 Varieties."

"I myself did not realize how successful a slogan it was going to be," he later admitted.

Not for a moment did E. A. question the value of Carnation's slogan. The pearl beyond price dropped from an unlikely oyster one day when he was in Chicago working on the advertising campaign to be launched in the coming year, 1907. Helen Mar, a young copywriter in John Lee Mahin's agency, sat across from him at the conference table, captivated by his description of the dairy cows roaming the lush green valleys of Washington and Oregon, grazing on "tender grasses," quenching their thirst with "pure sparkling waters" and taking their ease in the "shade of luxuriant trees."

"Remembering my lectures in medical college," Miss Mar wrote long afterwards, "and recalling that milk produced under conditions of mental and physical ease is more readily digested, I involuntarily exclaimed: 'Ah, the milk of contented cows.'"

"There," said E. A., "is our slogan!"

The producers of Pet Milk were not impressed. "It is the perfection of the process, not the psychological state of the cow that creates a superior product," Helvetia snorted, thus evidencing—in the words of Martin L. Bell, the company's historian—"a complete failure to grasp one of the basic principles of consumer marketing." Within a year Carnation was outselling Pet.

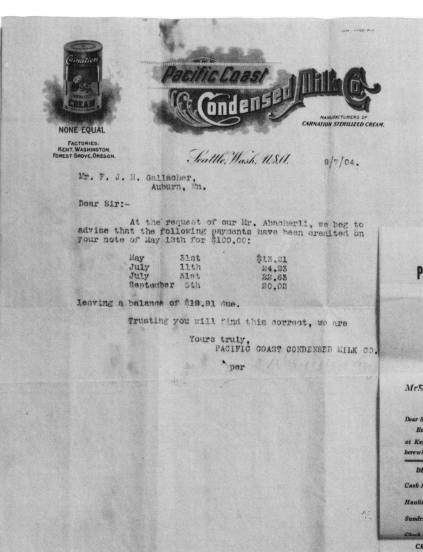

Early correspondence and statement of account with Pacific Coast Condensed Milk

3

Carnation Coast-to-Coast

*"The distinction of having a milkman from the
Pacific Northwest, serving his customers day by day in towns
on the Atlantic, the Gulf and the Great Lakes, is one of those
miracles of modern trade expansion and development
in utilizing the resources of the nation."*
National Magazine, 1909

TOOLING ABOUT THE COUNTRYSIDE in his new 1907 Pierce Arrow roadster, top down to enjoy the sun (an associate remembered him as "a fast and hard driver"), E. A. Stuart must have marveled at how the world had changed in his fifty years. Like millions of other restless Americans who had left the farm to try their luck in the city, he had come to take for granted such modern miracles as the telephone, the talking machine, the electric light and the woman suffragist.

With the appearance of the horseless carriage on farm-to-market roads, it was possible to enjoy the best of both worlds, to live in the country and shop in the city. The country store E. A. had known as a boy, having lost its cracker barrel to Uneeda's packaged biscuits, now found itself smack in the path of the motor car. The gasoline pump would come to symbolize the new era. Old customers would make use of it on their way to town to buy store bread, canned fruit and vegetables, bottled vinegar and ready-made shirtwaists.

"You have a car, I see, but no bathroom?" remarked a Department of Agriculture investigator to a farm wife.

"You can't go to town in a bathtub," the lady replied.

By 1909, when the first Model T Ford rolled off the assembly line, E. A. had crisscrossed the continent, installing Carnation Milk on store shelves from San Francisco to Boston. He had proceeded with characteristic caution, waiting until he had achieved what he considered a satisfactory distribution in one market ("I mean about 65 percent") before moving on to fresh territory.

Once he had established Carnation in the three Pacific Coast states, he lit out for Texas, where he found the going extremely rough until he linked forces with Mart Ebeling ("a 100 percent Carnation salesman"). In New Orleans, a house-to-house canvass turned up a discouraging attachment to sweetened condensed milk, but a local buyer, impressed by the "remarkable job" E. A. had done, predicted he would eventually "reap a bountiful harvest." He moved on to Kansas City, only to be warned by an old friend that any attempt to sell Missourians milk from West Coast cows would be taken as "an insult to local producers." He lined up a broker, shook hands with every wholesaler and retailer in town, and headed for home, with stopovers in Nebraska, Wyoming and Montana.

"I was real sick after that trip and had to remain in bed for about two weeks," he re-

Ad in Kansas City Star of November 20, 1908.

At the turn of the century, most cities had no bacterial standard for milk.

membered, but he had put his red and white cans in national distribution.

"The fame and merit of Carnation Milk has spread eastward from coast to coast," Flynn Wayne reported in *National Magazine* (November, 1909) after making a pilgrimage to Carnation country. He came away from the bustling, immaculate condenseries a convert to E. A.'s concept of the "Modern Milkman" (he also seems to have picked up a lyrical phrase or two).

"The Modern Milkman with his Carnation badge is bringing to homes in all quarters of the globe a pure, sterilized milk direct from cows grazing upon the grassy slopes which never lose their garb of green," he wrote, and took particular note of the "vexing problem" of providing safe, wholesome milk for the country's major cities. "Here comes a simple solution, extending the parcel idea to this package age."

* * * * *

E. A. was not only a grocer ("I had been in it for twenty years or more"), but a farmer's son as well. It was the grocer who came up with Carnation's brand name, seized on its slogan and proceeded to hawk the product with all the lively modern arts of advertising and promotion; but it was the farmer's son who drove his rig (and later his four-cylinder roadster) out into the back-country to line up the company's milk supply and make sure it met his exacting standards.

"One of the most important things I soon discovered," he wrote in his memoirs, "was what I had learned as a boy on the farm milking cows, namely, that the milk should come from healthy cows, the udders be free of any ailment, cows should be cleaned before milking and the cow barns should be kept clean. . . ."

E. A. was as strict with his own plants as with his milk-suppliers' barns. He swooped down on condenseries unannounced, poking about dark corners, checking pipes, filters, pans and sterilizers. Tipped off to a surprise inspection late one night, a plant manager hopped out of bed, threw on some clothes, darted off to the condensery, hosed it down, locked it up and crept back home, only to learn next morning that E. A. had not been taken in.

"George," he said, "I almost caught my death of cold last night on your wet floors."

Oldtimers delight in quoting the letter a general superintendent hurried off to a plant manager at Sparta, Michigan.

"You say that two cockroaches were in the kitchen? For God sakes, don't let them get together!"

* * * * *

E. A. began preaching the Modern Milkman gospel of sanitation at a time when the national conscience was finally responding to the realization that King Herod had slaughtered fewer innocents than the contemporary milkman. If the babies on his route managed to escape or survive tuberculosis, diphtheria or some dread fever (typhoid, scarlet, undulant), they were likely to be carried off in July and August by the summer sickness. It appeared on death certificates as "infantile diarrhea," and it could

be traced directly to homicidal carelessness in the handling of milk.

Cities found it less difficult to control their water supply, which generally came from a single source, than their supply of milk, which came from thousands of cow barns and, on its way to the nursery, passed through an incalculable number of different and not always clean hands.

"Your milkman uses a strainer," Dr. George W. Goler, Rochester, New York, health officer, pointed out in *Charities and The Commons* (August 4, 1906). "Why? He uses a strainer to strain out the large particles of filth. The smaller particles and the soluble filth, of course, find their way through the strainer into the milk that we feed children."

Dr. Harvey Washington Wiley, the crusading chief chemist of the U. S. Department of Agriculture, liked to warn mothers that milk was not only an ideal food for their babies, but for bacteria as well. Left in the summer sun for a few hours, it could produce millions of bacteria per cubic centimeter.

33

Carnation's first 24-sheet billboard.

Even if they turned out to be harmless for adults, they could "prove extremely detrimental" to infants. Their milk "should contain less than 10,000 bacteria per cubic centimeter."

Most cities, however, had no bacterial standard for milk, and those that had enacted such ordinances had bowed to the pressures of greed and ignorance, setting dangerously high levels—250,000 in Milwaukee, 500,000 in Boston. The average count, John Spargo informed readers of *The Craftsman* (June, 1907), ran well into the millions. "Five million, or about twice as many as average sewage, is not uncommon," he declared, and went on to suggest that "the science of milk production and distribution is as yet in its infancy."

*　*　*　*　*

Dr. Wiley, the hulking, articulate dynamo in the fight for a federal pure food and drug law, was ridiculed by the *New York Sun* as "chief janitor and policeman of the people's insides," but the ranks of his supporters multiplied like bacteria in a warm glass of milk. The people's insides, they argued, could no longer tolerate the assaults of unscrupulous canners, meat packers, distillers and patent medicine quacks.

To the distress of ethical food processors and pharmaceutical firms, the hustlers were using formaldehyde to preserve milk and deodorize overage eggs, coloring coffee with burnt umber, larding their canned sausage with borax and peddling cure-alls so heavily laced with alcohol that a zealous federal official, charged with the responsibility of keeping the government's wards sober, had ruled Indian reservations off-limits to one such panacea, the ubiquitous Peruna.

Pure food and drug bills in various forms had been kicking around the United States Capitol for four years when, in the late spring of 1906, it became apparent that, with President Theodore Roosevelt's belated and grudging support, the reformers would finally get some sort of legislation through Congress. The argument was clinched not by a word picture of the white hearses making the rounds of the milkman's route every summer, but by a demonstration staged on the floor of the House of Representatives by an indignant gentleman from Kentucky.

"Here is a quart of alcohol [holding it up]. It will eat the intestines out of a coyote. It will make a rabbit spit in a bulldog's face. It is pure alcohol, and under the skill of the rectifier he will put in a little coloring matter and then a little bead oil [illustrating]. I drop that in it. Then I get a little essence of Bourbon whiskey, and there is no connoisseur in this House who can tell that hellish concoction from the genuine article; and that is what I denounce."

One week later, on June 30, the pure food and drug bill was signed into law. It put Carnation and its competitors to the trouble and expense of changing labels, substituting the word "milk" for "cream" (by law, cream now had to contain 18 percent butterfat), but it also performed a lasting service for both the evaporated milk industry and the consumer by imposing uniform standards on a product that had varied widely in quality. E. A. helped work out an agreement between federal officials and manufacturers providing for minimum requirements of 7.8 percent butterfat and 25.5 percent total milk solids.*

Application of the new law to the producers of evaporated milk was so heavily slanted in favor of dairymen with Holstein herds that E. A., operating in dairy country populated largely by Jersey, Guernsey and Durham cows, dispatched a field man to Wisconsin and Michigan to pick up some young purebred Holstein bulls. Sixty-five were brought into Carnation's Pacific Northwest territory and sold at cost or less to neighboring dairymen who could scrape up a modest down payment.

"This lot of bulls apparently was the first shipment of purebred Holstein cattle to the Pacific Coast," E. A. liked to recall.

*　*　*　*　*

*In 1940, for obscure bureaucratic reasons E. A. never figured out, the standard was changed to 7.9 percent butterfat and 25.9 percent total milk solids.

He began to think of establishing a dairy farm of his own. As he traveled around Washington and Oregon, he kept an eye out for "land suitable for dairying, and fairly close to a condensery." He took a fancy to 1,200 acres sprawled within fifteen miles of his Monroe, Washington, plant, but the land was divided into four tracts and he succeeded in acquiring only three of them, some five hundred acres in all. He told Lewis D. Hardenbergh, his top executive, to keep looking. For expert advice, Hardenbergh turned to a White River cattleman, Jack Ross.

The following year, 1909, while in the East on business, E. A. received a telegram from Hardenbergh: HAVE FOUND FARM ON THE SNOQUALMIE. ROSS RECOMMENDS. E. A.'s reply was a terse BUY IT.

The 360-acre ranch, thirty-five miles east of Seattle, cost $11,000, "including feed in the barn for cows during that winter," E. A. noted. Not until a year or so later did he get around to visiting the place.

"I surely was surprised and disgusted at its appearance. I simply made up my mind that it was a disgrace for E. A. Stuart to own a herd of cows like that and to be connected with a place in such a condition. So I made up my mind to start some improvements."

Timber and brush had to be cleared ($40 an acre), stumps had to be blasted from the ground with dynamite ($145 an acre) and wing dams had to be built to hold back the Snoqualmie River. Meanwhile, he had picked up another five hundred acres, including the hill land where he eventually

35

Had E. A. Stuart seen the ranch before he bought it, Carnation Farm might have had a different location.

located the main farm buildings. None of them had been built in the summer of 1910, when Elbridge first saw the farm.

"It was wet, foggy and rainy that summer," he remembered. "The only plumbing was a couple of Chic Sales out in the backyard."

* * * * *

In that same year a banker ("later I learned he was connected with the Borden people") came to E. A. with an offer to buy out his company. They were one million dollars apart when Elbridge came down to New York from Yale to spend the weekend with his father. E. A. told him about the banker's proposition and Elbridge put an end to the dickering with a nine-word question: "Father, what would I do if you sold out?"

The following March, while Elbridge was winding up his work at Yale, E. A. dropped in on the Mount Vernon, Washington, condensery. Bill Cross, the superintendent, was back east getting married, so E. A. was shown around by Jack Norton, a personable protege he had taken away from Armour & Co., and was about to promote to general superintendent of the new midwestern condenseries.

That night, while they were chatting in the lobby of the Windsor Hotel, they were joined by the company's chief engineer, W. N. MacBriar. Inevitably, the conversation got around to the new farm, and E. A. started talking about the barn he intended to build on the hill, where his cattle would be safe from the snow-fed waters of the Snoqualmie.

"As usual," MacBriar reminisced many years later, "E. A. had very definite ideas as to just how this barn should be built and where it should be located."

MacBriar got hold of some cross-section paper, sketched a section of the barn and was commissioned on the spot to build it. Thus began a close, seventeen-year working relationship at Carnation Stock Farms, during which E. A. insisted on knowing "where practically every nail and plank" went into each new building. In the early days, the two men bunked in the old ranch house down on

36

E. A. Stuart loaded brokers on a train to show them his new condenseries in Wisconsin and Illinois in 1911.

the flat, with no heat other than the living room stove.

"We used to warm up downstairs," MacBriar said, "and run like hell upstairs and jump into cold beds."

Next morning, they would both be up at 5:30, have breakfast at the mess-house, and devote the daylight hours to working in the fields. That night E. A. would insist on sitting up until midnight, laying out the work schedule for the following day. By the time he edged up to the stove, drawing in the last of its warmth before darting upstairs, he would appear to be "tired enough to stay in bed for a week, but the next morning he would be just as fresh as a daisy and ready for the day's work. His recuperative powers were remarkable."

The big feed barn and three milk barns were ready in December, 1912, enabling the farm to take care of more than two hundred and fifty cattle. The first purebred Holsteins (eighty-four cows and a bull, Dutchland

Governor Sir Collantha) had been bought that summer from Clinton Brown of Porterville, California. The following year E. A. decided to dispose of all his grade cows and dedicate the farm to purebred Holsteins.

"The dairymen in the Northwest needed better animals in the way of Holstein blood to help them make the dairy business a profitable one," he explained. "This in turn would assist the Carnation Company in carrying on their business."

* * * * *

In mid-February, 1913, after taking a clinical look at Pacific Coast Condensed Milk Company, a Seattle investment analyst turned in an eighteen-page report to Sam Hill, a wealthy Quaker who had lent E. A. $50,000 to help tide him over the crucial weeks following his split with Yerxa and had then gone on to invest $200,000 in the company. Now he was thinking of putting in another $200,000.

"It does not have sufficient possibilities to make it a good gambling proposition," the analyst reported. "If it pays, it never will pay big."

Hill disregarded the advice and fifteen years later, when he disposed of his Carnation holdings, he turned a profit in the neighborhood of $1,000,000.

"So much depends upon educating the public and making a demand for the product," the analyst had pointed out, underestimating E. A. Stuart's ability to awaken the public to its need for Carnation Milk.

In the fall of 1911, when he was mulling over the message he was about to deliver in the company's first national advertising campaign, E. A. decided to show off Carnation's four new condenseries in Wisconsin and Northern Illinois. He had established operations in the Middle West because freight rates "made it almost prohibitive to manufacture milk on the Coast to be shipped east." Fifty brokers and manufacturers' representatives were bundled aboard a train in Chicago and taken on a four-day tour. MacBriar was waiting at the Berlin, Wisconsin, depot when the Carnation Milk Special made its first stop.

"The train pulled in about 7 A.M.," he later recalled, "and the first man off was E. A. Stuart. He could hardly wait for the train to stop. I remember that he wore a golf cap and my first impression was that here was a man who was all business and an active leader, and expected everybody around him to follow his leadership. He wasted no time in checking into various matters such as steam connections for heating the train and preparations for breakfast. Breakfast was to be served at eight o'clock and he was insistent that everybody on the train attend it promptly."

Some of E. A.'s guests, Mac discovered, had set up a bar in the baggage car ("whenever there was any suspicion that he might be prowling around, the bar immediately closed and disappeared from sight"), but, hangovers notwithstanding, everybody made it to the breakfast table on time. An hour later they assembled on the second floor of the condensery, where "E. A. was master of ceremonies, organizer and leader."

The "old grocer," as he called himself, kept badgering his guests for suggestions as to how his 1912 advertising campaign could best serve the retailer. Up until now he had limited his advertising to newspapers, billboards, barns and streetcar cards in localities the company was equipped to supply. In the coming year, however, he planned to spread the good word about Carnation Milk in the

crooned one advertisement, and another offered mothers a chance to "Avoid Milk Worries" at no financial risk: "Order a 10¢ can of Carnation Milk from your grocer, and if you find that Carnation Milk does not please you better in every way than fresh, raw milk or any other evaporated milk or condensed milk, write us and we will cheerfully refund your money and postage."

Copywriters bore down heavily on Carnation's contented cows ("Carnation Milk cows

By 1919 Carnation was advertising in the nation's leading magazines.

pages of such family institutions as *Ladies' Home Journal*, *Saturday Evening Post*, *Woman's World* and *American Sunday Magazine*.

"Connect your store with all this advertising," Harry Stuart, the company's secretary, urged the nation's grocers, and went on to remind them that the Carnation Milk campaign was hitting a combined circulation of 11,354,000 at a time when people were not only "paying the most serious attention to the contamination of fresh milk," but were also "studying the high cost of living."

"Reduce your household milk bill,"

live where the grass is sweetest, water clearest, air the purest"), stressed the product's convenience ("You can travel with the baby without the bother and risk of carrying bottles and obtaining raw milk at different places"), called attention to its versatility ("use it in coffee, upon cereals, in custards and all desserts") and, most important, its purity and safety ("it contains no cane sugar—nothing but good, pure milk . . . Ask your doctor").

"To the ordinary man, evaporated milk and condensed milk are synonymous," noted *Good Housekeeping* (October, 1914), and

Carnation's model condensery introduced evaporated milk to visitors at the 1915 Panama-Pacific Exposition in San Francisco.

went on to warn mothers that the sweetened condensed milks "are less apt to be sterile than the unsweetened variety. The sugar, which is present in larger amounts than the milk solids themselves, serves as a preservative, and thus the necessity for complete sterilization is avoided."

Carnation set up a model milk condensery at the 1915 Panama-Pacific Exposition in San Francisco, and a couple of million visi-tors got a chance to sip the product, look at contented cows and examine the process by which their milk was evaporated, hermetically sealed and sterilized. In a full-page advertisement in the *Saturday Evening Post* (August 7, 1915), readers were urged to visit the exposition and see for themselves why Carnation was "the *safe* milk for summer."

To keep its name before the public Carnation not only spent heavily on advertisements, but also managed to get free space in the daily press by making news. In the summer of 1916, William Warwick and his wife left Seattle in a one-and-one-half-ton General Motors truck loaded with a ton of Carnation Milk consigned to a jobber in New York. The highly publicized trip represented another first for Carnation, the first commercial cargo to be hauled across the continent by motor. It was also the first time the young driver had operated a truck.

The Warwicks left Seattle in their makeshift mobile home on July 10 and reached New York on September 9.* "A terrible, black, muddy nightmare," Warwick called it, but newspaper readers got the company's message. After bouncing across country roads for two summer months, Carnation Milk was delivered to the shelves of Manhattan grocers as fresh and pure as the day it had been canned.

The profitable production of a reliable, unadulterated canned milk had been made possible by John Meyenberg, who died in 1914, just as the industry based on his inventiveness was about to be caught up in a wartime boom. No one will ever know how

many country club Casanovas and bobbed-hair flappers lived to dance the Charleston and guzzle bathtub gin from silver flasks only because their mothers had reared them on canned milk evaporated and sterilized by the process this temperamental Swiss had patented thirty years before Archduke Francis Ferdinand was done in at Sarajevo.

* * * * *

"We are living in the age of the greatest war," a canning industry spokesman commented toward the end of 1914. "We are reading of the wonderful raids of the submarine, of the hawklike antics of the aeroplane and dirigible, of the immensity of the Krupp siege guns, and of the usefulness of the automobile as an instrument of war; but now that the first grand rush has been checked, I am willing to predict that ultimate victory will not rest with aircraft or submarine, automobile or siege gun, but with the ease of access of supplies of food."

American chow lines got a first-hand look from Colonel William R. Grove of the Quartermaster Corps, United States Army, in the fall of 1917. He told American canners about his visit to the French front when they assembled in Boston for their annual convention the following February.

"Tin plate and soldering iron," he was happy to report, "have made it possible to

*They camped along the way, spending thirty-one days actual driving time. When the trip was reenacted fifty years later by four skilled drivers hauling seventeen tons of Carnation products in a tractor-trailer, it took three days.

Unloading in New York after cross-country trip.

Christian Herald ad, July 1912

BABIES PROVE
that Carnation Milk is *super-digestible*

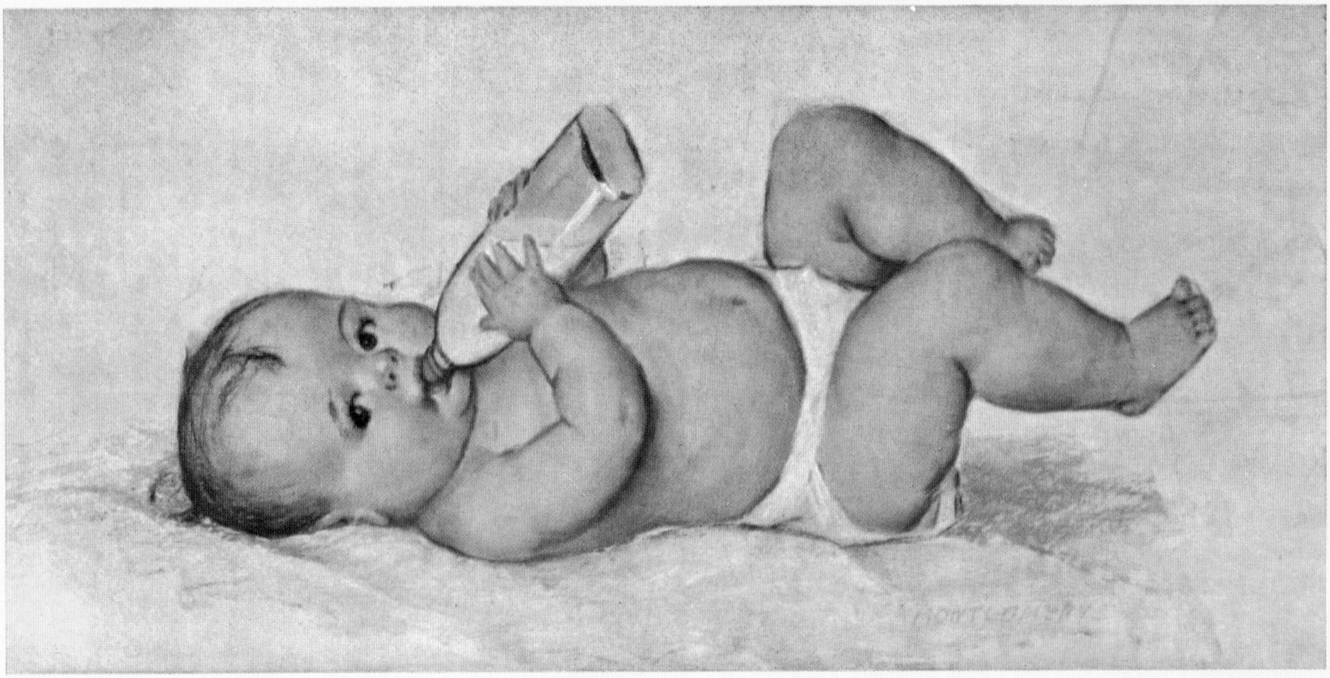

And wonder-working recipes reveal that it's better for *cooking* too

BABIES in homes and babies in hospitals. Babies in cities and babies on farms. Babies in limousines, babies in flivvers . . .

They all prove that Carnation Milk is *super-digestible*—that it agrees with many babies who simply can't digest raw, pasteurized, or boiled milk.

Carnation is being prescribed by noted baby specialists. It is being used in famous hospitals and clinics. Authorities find it nourishing, in every way—*dependably rich in vitamins and minerals.* And perfectly safe. And admirably uniform in composition.

Amazing, isn't it? Think of being able to get milk like that at any grocery!

The ideal cooking milk

Carnation is the same fine unsweetened evaporated milk that you have always known—milk from selected, inspected herds—with only water taken out and *nothing* added.

It is super-digestible because heat treated, and because a process called "homogenization" makes the fat globules one thousand times tinier, far easier to assimilate.

This same process works magic in *cooking!* It makes food smoother, finer in texture and consistency. It improves flavor. Just try Carnation in cream soups and sauces, in custards, in dressings, in cocoa—you can *taste* the smoothness and richness.

Write for these booklets

Besides, you can use this double-rich milk as cream for coffee, fruits, and cereals. You'll like it—the economy too.

There are so *many* things to learn about this modern milk. Two new booklets will interest you—"Baby-Feeding Simplified" and "100 Glorified Recipes." Both are free. Write to Carnation Company, 1040 Carnation Bldg., Oconomowoc, Wis.; or 1140 Stuart Bldg., Seattle; or Aylmer, Ont.

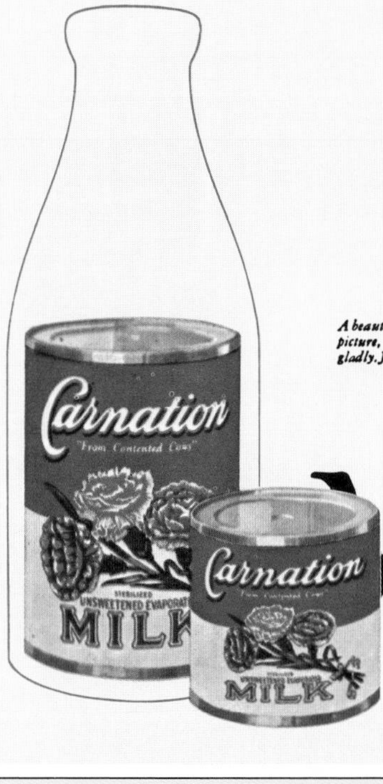

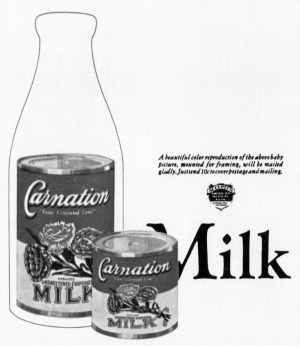

A beautiful color reproduction of the above baby picture, mounted for framing, will be mailed gladly. Just send 10c to cover postage and mailing.

ACCEPTED AMERICAN MEDICAL ASSN

Carnation Milk

"From Contented Cows"

Copyright, 1931, by Carnation Co.

WORLD'S LARGEST-SELLING BRAND OF EVAPORATED MILK

Ads in 1931 featured drawings of babies

LIFE
Belle of the Ball
—eats her milk, too!

Who could resist such food! Icy cold . . . satin smooth. Light as a cloud—if clouds were peppermint flavor.

Wise mothers know it's easy to solve the dessert problem. Simply make desserts you *want* them to eat! Milk-rich desserts from nourishing, digestible Carnation Milk. Desserts that say "Party!" to the young—but whisper "Healthful" to mothers. Because it's just as good to *eat* milk solids as to *drink* them.

Carnation is fine whole cow's milk, with nothing removed but part of the natural water. It has extra enrichment with "sunshine" vitamin D. You keep all the milk values, when you cook with Carnation. Actually get *double* values, when you use it undiluted.

Milk dawdlers go for delicious creamed soups and vegetables, as well as desserts, made with Carnation. Every time you cook with it you're fitting right into the Government's Nutrition Program . . . saving money . . . saving time.

Line up a convenient row of red and white Carnation cans in the pantry. They'll turn the trick for you!

PEPPERMINT MOUSSE

1 tall can Carnation Milk, undiluted
½ cup white corn syrup
2 egg whites
Few grains salt
1 cup finely crushed peppermint stick candy (4 oz.)
(For deep pink color—use vegetable coloring or cinnamon drops.)

Chill milk thoroughly. Whip until very stiff. Beat in the syrup, egg whites and salt quickly. Stir in the candy and pour at once into cold freezing trays. Yield: 2 quarts.

FREE! 48 pages of milk-rich recipes, and menu suggestions for all ages. Full of helpful hints and delicious, healthful dishes that help the whole family *eat* milk. Send a post card with your name and address for your copy of "Growing Up With Milk." Address Carnation Co., Dept. L-13, Milwaukee, Wis.—or Toronto, Ont.

TUNE IN THE CARNATION "CONTENTED HOUR" MONDAY EVENINGS, NBC NETWORK

IRRADIATED
Carnation Milk
"FROM CONTENTED COWS"

American Milk Products' first plant in Germany, a condensery in
Neustadt/Holstein (upper), and first plant in Holland at Schoonhoven (lower).

give the soldier of today a widely varied and healthful diet, whereas there was given to his predecessors in arms not much more than 'salt horse' and scurvy."

Every twenty-four hours, along with his meat (225,000 pounds of bacon, 1,500,000 pounds of beef) and potatoes (750 tons), the doughboy's daily diet consisted of 130,000 cans of tomatoes, 36,000 cans of corn, 24,000 cans of green peas, 2,500 cans of stringless beans, 1,800 cans of cabbage, 7,500 cans of peaches, 3,000 cans of pineapple, 1,000 cans of pumpkin and 2,200 cans of apricots. He washed it down with 275,000 cans of milk, condensed and evaporated.

Now that it had plants in the Middle West as well as in Washington and Oregon, Carnation could supply its new customers in training camps at home and trenches abroad without having to stint the housewife shopping at her corner grocery store. Helvetia, the manufacturer of Pet Milk, was less fortunate. Not only had Carnation opened more plants (six to Helvetia's four), but its condenseries in the Pacific Northwest also enabled it to deliver evaporated milk at a lower price to the major markets of Idaho, Utah, Arizona and Texas. Finally, as Dr. Bell notes in his history of the Pet Milk Company, *A Portrait of Progress* (1962), Carnation was "unquestionably outmerchandising the Pet product."

Helvetia was forced to surrender its western market to Carnation. It was a difficult decision, Dr. Bell writes, but "there was almost no alternative. Even had the inclination existed to do so, it would probably have proved impossible to build or acquire West Coast condenseries during the war. It was vital to protect the nearby markets at a profit, for by 1911 Carnation was already producing in Wisconsin and Illinois. With reluctance, then, but probably unaware of the full impact of the decision, Helvetia halted shipments to West Coast brokers...."

Only fifteen years had passed since E. A. Stuart, plodding from door to door, had watched Helvetia's salesmen outsell Carnation thirty-five cases to one.

When E. A. Stuart began his eastward expansion, he built this new condensery in Berlin, Wisconsin.

Filling machines in Oconomowoc, Wisconsin.

4
The Overseas Milk Route

*"Perhaps the most dreadful and far-reaching effect
of the war has been the blight it has cast
upon the young. Without milk the young may
indeed live for a time, but they can
not prosper. It is the one indispensable food."*
SAMUEL HOPKINS ADAMS, 1919

WHEN SAMUEL HOPKINS ADAMS visited Europe at the end of what President Wilson called "the most terrible and disastrous of all wars," he found the Continent "full of sick and wounded whose prime necessity in the line of food is milk." The Germans had done away with 2,000,000 cows in France, 1,100,000 in Belgium, he reported in *Delineator* (June, 1919).

"Every child in this region is a foster-child of American canned milk," Adams was told by a welfare worker in Northern France. As for Belgium, the small, ravaged country had been "kept alive" on canned milk from the United States. In the last four years exports had skyrocketed from 16,000,000 pounds to 530,000,000 pounds. At the same time, its use on the home front had increased so markedly that some prophets foresaw the day when Americans would turn from the hazards, high cost and inconveniences of fluid milk to this handy, economical, germ-free product.

The wartime shortage of fresh milk had prompted the Nestlé and Anglo-Swiss Condensed Milk Company (the two concerns had merged in 1905) to cross the Atlantic and line up some forty American factories to manufacture its products. It had also acquired an interest in the John Wildi Evaporated Milk Company and Hires Condensed Milk Company. With their twenty-seven plants, these two companies were able to produce considerably more canned milk than the American market could absorb. Nestlé and Anglo-Swiss hoped to dispose of this surplus to European consumers who had grown accustomed to using canned milk during the war.

"But," Jean Heer writes in *The First Hundred Years of Nestlé* (1966), "when the armies were demobilized and the government food supply departments closed down, one by one, there was no corresponding flood of civilian orders for preserved milks—products which, for four years, had been indispensable to millions of men."

Carnation Milk Products Company, awash in a peacetime surplus of evaporated milk, responded to the Nestlé invasion of the United States by taking advantage of the Webb-Pomerene Act of 1918, which enabled American companies to pool their resources for joint ventures abroad without running afoul of antitrust laws. Carnation got together with Pet Milk Company and formed

42

Four tourists at the Palace of Frederick the Great in Potsdam, circa 1926:
(l to r) Otto Lagerfeld, Glücksklee sales manager; E. A. Stuart; A. W. Pidwell,
general European manager; and P. R. McKee, vice president and secretary.

the American Milk Products Company to sell milk in foreign countries, but not in the United States and Canada, where the overseas partners would continue to compete in the marketplace. The export company was chartered April 5, 1919, with a capital of $1,500,000. Carnation owned sixty-five percent of the company, Pet thirty-five percent.*

E. A. scurried off to Europe on the Mauretania, promised to send Belgium's King Albert a couple of his finest Holsteins, invited Queen Marie of Roumania to drop in on him if she ever passed his way (sure enough she did), set up American Milk Products Company headquarters in Paris, with a German branch office in Essen (later moved to Hamburg), and came home with an empty Carnation Milk can retrieved from a trench in France.

*   *   *   *   *

"We banked on Carnation 'over there,' "

*Its name was changed to General Milk Company on December 26, 1930. Carnation bought out Pet's interest on January 21, 1966, and, in view of overseas diversification, renamed it Carnation International on May 12, 1972.

remarked a clean-cut American aviator, seated at table with an elderly couple, presumably his parents, in a full-page *Saturday Evening Post* advertisement (March 1, 1919), a cup of coffee in one hand, a can of Carnation Milk in the other. "Carnation," he told the folks, "was like a letter from home."

Jack Adler, a real-life Fourth Division infantryman from Cincinnati, Ohio, stumbled across Carnation Milk one summer day in 1918 when his outfit's rations had run low. Twenty-five years later he shared his story with the company.

"We raided a German machine gun nest and after capturing the crew, I searched one of them and found a can of Carnation Milk in his pocket. I never had liked canned milk, but on this occasion I was so hungry that I could have eaten a raw cow. With my bayonet I punched a hole in the can and drank it raw, and after I came back to the States nothing would satisfy me in the milk line but Carnation Milk."

Starry-eyed readers of *Photoplay* (April, 1919) were relieved to learn from a Carnation advertisement that one of their favorite screen heroines, Marguerite Clayton, who was about to "spend the year being photoplayed throughout the war-ridden sections of France and Belgium," would ward off homesickness by packing "several cans of Carnation Milk in her trunk."

* * * * *

their milk to neighboring cheese factories, were suspicious of the newcomers. They paid a good price—nobody disputed that—but, unlike the cheese factories, where milk was weighed in full view of the farmers, the condensery's processing procedures removed it from view. The rumors floating around the countryside amused William Keys, a con-

44

During the war Carnation had fallen in love with the Wisconsin town of Oconomowoc (River of Falling Waters) huddled between two lakes, Fowler and La Belle, in the rolling green milkshed of Waukesha (Home of the Fox) County. The company built a large condensery in the town in 1914, acquired property for a stock farm on its outskirts the following year and, in March, 1918, began making cans in what the *Oconomowoc Enterprise* called "one of the leading can factories in the country."

Local dairymen, who had been selling

tented Carnation milk supplier. As he explained to readers of the *Enterprise*, he had heard the stories before.

"A few years ago when the same company built at Richland Center," he recalled, "I owned a dairy farm six miles from that city. There was a good cheese factory one-fourth mile from my farm. I was loath to see it close for want of patronage and was not the first to pull away from it, neither was I the last; but before the season was half over, it closed, also nine-tenths of all other factories within a radius of seven miles of the condensery."

"Just wait till they get all the factories out of business, then they will fix us," skeptics had predicted, and some had gone so far as to insist that within two years the condensery would be turned into a brewery.

Instead, Keys pointed out, the condensery's daily purchases of fresh milk had shot up from 60,000 pounds* to 225,000 in four years, and "at the same time a number of cheese factories had reopened and were taking in at best from 10,000 to 12,000 pounds of milk per day. . . . The fact is the condensery created an incentive for farmers to keep more and better cows and practice more intensive farming."

With this in mind, Carnation established what it called its Eastern Farm at Oconomowoc. The star of its foundation stock, the company announced in January, 1915, would be a $25,000 Holstein bull, Johanna McKinley Segis. His dam, Johanna De Kol Van Beers, had set a record of 40.9 pounds of butter and 663 pounds of milk in seven days, and no cow of any breed had ever come up to her 120-day record of 541 pounds of butter and nearly 10,500 pounds of milk. One of her sons, King Segis Pontiac Chicago, had sold for $20,000. This calf, the *Enterprise* reported, was "the highest priced dairy animal ever sold at auction."

In the bosom of the Carnation family, where he was cherished for traits other than a cavalier disregard for the value of folding money, no one seemed a less likely candidate for the role of the dairy industry's biggest spender than E. A. Stuart. On June 8, 1918, however, cattlemen in a tense, smoke-filled Milwaukee arena tossed their straw skimmers in the air and yelled themselves hoarse when the Carnation president, bucking a buyer representing the president of Morton Salt Company, acquired a six-month-old calf from Canada and, in the process, shattered all existing records for the purchase of dairy animals.

Before the bidding got underway, a young Wisconsin county agent named Merton Moore predicted the calf would bring

*Note: 2.15 pounds of milk equal one quart.

$5,000. One or two others thought it might go for as much as $10,000 because his dam, May Echo Sylvia, had achieved world-wide fame as the only cow ever known to have produced 152.1 pounds of milk in a day, 1,005.8 in seven days and 12,899 in one hundred days. Moore's former dairy science professor at the University of Wisconsin, A. C. (Oostie) Oosterhuis, had his doubts about this astonishing feat.

"No cow can carry 152 pounds of milk between two legs day after day and keep up," he was still insisting sixty-five years later. He had a hunch the test had been rigged in some way, and he had learned from the young Canadian who had milked the cow that her udders hung so low to the ground she couldn't be milked with a pail. "He told me he milked her with a dishpan."

In E. A.'s opinion, May Echo Sylvia was "the greatest Holstein living," but some months earlier he had passed up a chance to buy this particular calf of hers for $35,000. He came to the Milwaukee auction prepared to go as high as $25,000 and started the bidding at $10,000. It quickly leaped by increments of $5,000 to $50,000, whereupon two of the five bidders dropped out. Another bidder gave up at $75,000, leaving E. A. and Joy Morton's agent in contention. At $101,000 the Morton man balked and E. A., making a lavish gesture, promptly upped the ante $5,000 (he could have got by with $500). The calf was his for $106,000.

"SHALL I SEND YOU MONEY TO COME HOME?" Elbridge wired his father from Seattle.

"I only wish you could have been present when that calf was sold," E. A. replied a few days later. "Never saw such excitement over any sale at public auction."

Mr. Morton, he added, had offered to take the calf off his hands for the full purchase price, but he had declined. For a man who was still squeezing mileage out of a 1907 Pierce Arrow roadster, risking a broken arm every time he cranked it up for a spin around his Snoqualmie Valley farm, the purchase seemed strangely extravagant, but it was worth a couple of million dollars in free advertising, and, E. A. reminded Elbridge, "The breeders of the United States from now on will know that Carnation Stock Farms is on the map."

* * * * *

The $106,000 bull failed to live up to his owner's great expectations and died as a three-year-old. Aside from his publicity value, however, Carnation King Sylvia returned $86,000 in calves, $50,000 in insurance. The real star of the Carnation Stock Farms turned out to be a creaky, ill-marked, ill-tempered reject with an incongruously regal name, King Segis Tenth. His blood flows through the veins of some of the greatest milk cows on earth. He cost five dollars.

E. A. enjoyed telling the story of how he acquired his celebrated bull by chance in 1915, when he closed a deal with George B. Leighton of Boise, Idaho, for eighty-five Holstein-Friesian cows, whereupon the seller casually remarked that he also had an old bull he would be happy to throw in free, if E. A. would take him away, then and there.

"I peeped through a crack in the solid board fence enclosing the lot in which the bull was staked. Just then he started bellowing with rage, stamping the ground as he evidently realized someone was looking at him. I thought the bargain was a pretty hard one, as I did not care to attempt to go in there to put a staff through the ring in his nose. Finally I found a man who would do it for five dollars.

"I told him he had the job and the five

E. A. Stuart, left, and M. J. Norton, right, with $106,000 calf.

46

dollars if he could catch the bull, put the staff in his nose ring, lead him out and tie him to a certain post. He consented. A staff is a pole about eight feet long with a hook on it to catch the ring in the bull's nose. The man had quite a hard time. Finally, he managed to work the bull up close to the gate and by cleverly handling the staff he was able to put the hook into the bull's nose-ring. If you ever saw a mad animal, that bull was one."

Five years later, King Segis Tenth had sired, among other notable offspring, Matador Segis Walker, the 1920 Pacific International Exposition's grand champion ("one of the most sensational bulls of the breed," declared the *Holstein-Friesian World*). The old bull had thirty-five daughters in the Car-nation herd and the fairest of them all, Segis Pietertje Prospect, had just produced more milk in one year than any cow of any breed in the animal's recorded history.

* * * * *

C. Y. Baker, who had paid three francs a can for Lait Carnation as an American tank corpsman in France, dropped in on the Oco-nomowoc farm after he got home from the Great War. He was somewhat taken aback by the admonition posted on a yellow card above the entrance to one of the big barns: ALWAYS SPEAK TO A COW AS YOU WOULD TO A LADY. The rule, he discovered, was religiously enforced.*

"When taken over by the Carnation Company several years ago," Baker reported in *The Carnation News* (July-August, 1919),

*"I am a milk machine," E. A. Stuart wrote in *The Prayer of A Contented Cow* (circa 1919). "I ask only for proper food and care and I will produce rich, pure, sweet milk. . . . I must have good food from rich pastures. I must have pure water and I must have plenty of fresh air. . . . Please do not swear at me and do not strike me. I like to be petted often. Kind words also will help make me happy and contented."

King Segis Tenth, mean and ugly, sired world champions.

"the Oconomowoc property had been used by a millionaire horse fancier as a breeding farm for Kentucky thoroughbreds. All stables and buildings are of concrete construction and built so as to admit the greatest possible amount of light and air. Warmed by a modern heating system, the buildings housing the Carnation herds are far more comfortable in the winter season than many a city apartment."

There were about two hundred head of registered Holstein-Friesian cattle living in contentment on the Wisconsin farm and another four hundred in Washington's Snoqualmie Valley, C. A. (Al) Altwegg, superintendent of the Oconomowoc condensery, explained as he showed Baker around the Eastern Farm. The cows in both herds, Al added, were put through official seven-day tests to make sure they produced a prescribed quantity and quality of milk and butterfat.

"Our main interest throughout in these stock farms is not only to make them success-ful as breeding establishments," he continued, "but to be able to furnish dairymen in the different districts in which our condenseries are located high grade bulls to cross with their grade cows. We are simply 'casting our bread on the waters.' By improving the breed of cattle in the farmer's herds, he will increase the average production of milk and butterfat from his herds, and we will obtain greater amounts of pure, quality milk for our condenseries."

Professor Oosterhuis, a Holstein-Friesian scholar, traced the history of the big, handsome, black and white cattle back to 300 B.C., when they were known to have been grazing in the lowlands of the Netherlands province of Friesland. Some were brought to New York by Dutch settlers, but not until the Civil War period were there distinct purebred herds. They were called "Dutch Cattle" until 1871, when they were misnamed by a group calling itself the Association of Breeders of Holstein Cattle. Dutch breeders, annoyed at having their cattle falsely credited to the province of Schleswig-Holstein, responded eight years later by setting up a Dutch-Friesian organization. Finally, in 1885, the two groups merged to form the Holstein-Friesian Association of America.

"The Holstein-Friesian," Oostie wrote in *The Carnation News* (October-November, 1919), "is the largest of our dairy breeds, cows weighing on an average 1,250 and bulls 2,000 pounds. The tendency in recent years has been to increase the size. The outstanding features of the breed are this large size, their ruggedness and their capacity for feed. This large capacity for feed makes possible the characteristic of high milk production. No other breed has approached them in this respect."

Jack Norton, the personable head of Carnation's eastern operations, lured Oostie away from the University of Wisconsin faculty in 1918. A dapper bachelor with an eye for the ladies, he made his headquarters in Oconomowoc, but as the new director of the company's dairy extension service, he spent

A. C. Oosterhuis,
first director of dairy extension.

most of his time in the field, working with dairy farmers. He spoke their language and they respected his knowledge of dairying.

"The Carnation people got off on the wrong foot when they first came here," Oostie recalled recently, long after he had bought Carnation's Eastern Farm, subdivided it and kept a green knoll for his own home. "They dressed like city people and they acted like city people. At the hotel they expected a clean napkin every day."

Oostie turned out to be such a hit with dairy farmers in the area around Oconomowoc that Carnation asked him to recommend somebody to take over similar missionary work in the Pacific Northwest. He suggested one of his brightest and most engaging students, George S. Bulkley (Class of 1914), who had taught dairy husbandry at Penn State for a couple of years before serving as the college's dairy extension specialist.

George showed up in Seattle in 1919, and until his retirement in 1963, there was no more amiable and articulate spokesman for the dairy industry. He served on the National Dairy Council's board of directors for eleven years and was a longtime director of the American Dairy Association. When he attended its first meeting in 1915, the group had been able to assemble in one small room.

Oostie and George, working with their separate constituencies, not only helped dairy farmers breed more productive cows, but also kept a watchful eye on their handling of the milk they sold to the company. The farmers had to live up to a two-page list of Carnation rules and regulations. Their cows had to be healthy, clean, kindly treated ("no milk will be accepted from cows that are overheated or excited") and kept away from "sour, noxious grasses and weeds."

"If there is any good reason to suspect that the milk has been skimmed, or water has been added to it, or that the milk has not been properly cooled, or has been shipped in unclean cans, such milk will be refused," dairymen were warned.

Among the mementoes George Bulkley took with him into retirement was a letter from a Carnation milk supplier written the day after the Fourth of July celebrations of 1947.

"You returned to me two cans of sour milk," wrote Aurelia B. Parry. "I feel a word of explanation is due. It soured because it was never put into the running water in the spring house.

"We had six guests to come in on Thursday P.M. They did not give me any previous notice and came to spend the 4th. One man brot two small kiddies, no Mother to watch them. I have a Berkshire boar that weighs 700 pounds. These children were from Hamilton, Ohio, and never saw a pig and did not know where the milk came from. They insisted on riding around in the field on 'Berky.' He was never around children, altho he is not cross. I took them both off the boar three times. The Father thot it was cute to call the pig a 'pony.' I was afraid the boar would bight them and it made me just

George Bulkley and friend.

crazy mad. I forgot to do anything about the milk, and thus it goes."

* * * * *

The company changed its name to Carnation Milk Products Company in 1916 and touched a raw nerve in the dairy industry when it came out with a new product called Hebe. In today's ethnically sensitive marketplace, Carnation's product managers and public relations people wince at the mention of the word, even though the name of the Greek goddess of youth is pronounced "Heebee," not "Heeb." What upset short-fused dairy farmers, though, was not the product's name, but its composition.

Making use of a process devised by Carl A. Bowman and Clarence S. Stevens (he joined Carnation and later ran its overseas operations), the new subsidiary—Hebe Company—removed the butterfat from fresh milk and replaced it with coconut oil, thus enabling Carnation to sell its butter and, at the same time, market an economical product clearly identified as "a compound of skimmed milk and vegetable fat." The label suggested it be used "for cooking, baking, coffee."

Hebe came under attack from the same politically active and powerful dairy industry that had fought so long to keep oleomargarine off the American table, even when it meant denying hard-pressed housewives a choice between expensive butter of dubious quality and a pure, wholesome, low-priced substitute. When the sale of Hebe was banned in Ohio, the company filed suit in federal court.*

"There is no claim that the product, or either of its ingredients, is impure or unwholesome," the three-judge panel agreed. They didn't care whether the manufacturers had deliberately set out to practice deception. It was enough that one of their three Ohio wholesalers had delivered Hebe in filling two government contracts for condensed

*Hebe Co. v. Calvert, 246 F. 711 (D.C., S.D., E.D., Ohio, 1917).
**Hebe Co. v. Shaw, 248 U.S. 297 (1919).

milk, and many retailers had freely sold it as such to unwary customers who could not, in the court's opinion, be blamed for failing to "closely scrutinize the label." The case was dismissed.

Hebe carried it to the United States Supreme Court,** where the company's side of the argument was presented by Charles E. Hughes. He lost on a split decision, with Justice Holmes speaking for the majority and Justice Brandeis concurring with two other members of the court in a dissenting opinion.

"The label on the plaintiffs' cans tells the truth," Justice Holmes admitted, "but the consumer in many cases never sees it. Moreover, when the label tells the public to use Hebe for purposes to which condensed milk is applied, and states of what Hebe is made, it more than half recognizes the plain fact that Hebe is nothing but condensed milk of a cheaper sort."

"It is not evaporated milk," insisted the

Three Stuarts on Carnation's 20th birthday: E. A., seated; E. H., left; and Harry.

50

three dissenting justices, "and makes no pretense of being such. It is a food compound consisting in part of condensed skimmed milk. It is so labeled in unmistakable words in large print on the can containing it."

In states where Hebe could still be legally sold, a newly designed label added the warning: DO NOT USE IN PLACE OF MILK FOR INFANTS, but dairy lobbyists were still not satisfied. They leaned on Congress to pass legislation to protect them against the competition of all such products. The Federal Filled Milk Act, adopted March 4, 1923, prohibited interstate shipments of milk in any form which had been "blended or compounded with any fat or oil other than milk fat."

Virtually all of the then forty-eight states adopted similar laws, some of which have since been modified, repealed or declared unconstitutional by state courts. The last time a Carnation lawyer looked into the situation he found that in only one of the sixteen states where filled milk was permitted to be sold had it acquired more than one percent of the fluid milk market, but these dusty statutes designed to soothe groundless fears of competition continue to hobble research and development of new products which might not only be easier on the family budget, but, in this age of dietary anxieties, might also be more in line with what the doctor ordered.

* * * * *

On the morning of September 6, 1919, just four days from E. A.'s sixty-third birthday, he walked into his Seattle office to find his desk overflowing with decorative cards sent in by members of his corporate family, congratulating him on Carnation's twentieth anniversary. The cards bore the message of a company versifier:

> You planted a flower of white
> In Purity's soil. It has grown
> Through twenty long years,
> 'till it stands
> Supreme—on a height all its own.

Carnation now had more than twenty condenseries (the company was still fighting a losing battle to call the plants "evaporatories"), including one in Canada. As E. A. told the story of his acquisition of the Aylmer, Ontario, plant, "a qualified representative" of the company had taken a weekend option on it at the time he arrived in town on Monday, October 1, 1916. He checked out a nearby receiving station, drove around the countryside and, at 11:30 o'clock that morning, he had made up his mind "to buy the plant before noon that day."

Actually, as Carnation's first Canadian superintendent, Jack Coyle, recalled on the twenty-fifth anniversary of the transaction, it involved two plants, one at Aylmer, the other at Springfield, and it was concluded on November 27. Coyle had started work for the company in 1912 as a clerk in Jack Norton's district office at Berlin, Wisconsin. Four years later, on Sunday, November 26, he got a telegram from Norton directing him to present himself at Aylmer the following

51

Men of Early-Day Management

A. M. J. (JACK) NORTON
Vice President and General Manager.

B. LEWIS R. HARDENBERGH
Executive Vice President.

C. MERTON MOORE
Albers' jack-of-all-advertising and merchandising trades.

D. *Condensery superintendents and district superintendents at Carnation Stock Farm meeting in March, 1917: (l to r)* R. A. STUART, JOE CROW, P. G. KINZER, C. R. FARNSWORTH, E. H. STUART, MURRAY STUART, E. O. LAMB, VESTAL COFFIN, HARRY HILL, C. C. BROWN, G. R. SIBLEY, OWEN JONES *and* E. A. STUART.

E. *At Carnation Farms in January, 1923: (l to r)* FRED YOUNG, WILLIAM MATHENY, E. H. STUART, E. A. STUART, H. G. STIBBS *and* P. G. KINZER.

F. PAUL R. McKEE
Vice President.

G. WILLIAM MATHENY
Western Sales Manager.

H. W. N. MacBRIAR
Chief Engineer.

A.

D.

F.

B.

C.

E.

G.

H.

Carnation had been producing in Canada for nine years when this photo of Aylmer plant was taken in 1925.

day. He found E. A. Stuart waiting alongside Norton.

"Mr. Stuart had been considering the Canadian market for some time," Coyle wrote in *The Carnation* (October-December, 1941). "When he came to the point of seriously considering the purchase of the company at Aylmer, he was just as thorough as in everything else. He inspected the plant minutely, of course. But he went further. He drove around the country, looking over farms and herds—he talked to farmers, particularly the patrons of the Aylmer condensery."

E. A. sent word to his strong right arm in Seattle, Lewis R. Hardenbergh, that he was "exceedingly well pleased with the price at which the plants were bought." Both were in excellent condition (they had been appraised in 1914 at $176,000). The buildings were of concrete blocks, resting on solid foundations. The pans, boilers and vacuum pumps were in good shape. Two of the three sterilizers would have to be worked on, but, otherwise, the only thing the company needed to produce evaporated milk of Carnation quality was a couple of Dickerson-type fillers. Jack Norton had already ordered them. Operations began on December 1.

"The coming of Carnation Milk has meant to Canada a new basis of milk supply—and a new high standard," proclaimed one of the resident minnesingers in the employ of Baker Advertising Agency, Limited.

Bilingual texts featured "Lait Carnation —de Vaches Bien Nourries" ("Frais, Riche, Toujours a Votre Portée," "Un Perfectionne-

ment a l'Appret des Aliments," "Il Fait Profiter les Enfants") and "Good Cow's Milk on the Prairie" ("If you spent your childhood on an Ontario farm, you know how wonderfully sweet and rich was the fresh milk from high-grade cows well cared for. That's the kind of milk we use for Carnation Milk").

The two Canadian condenseries were the most easterly of all Carnation plants. Thus, Jack Coyle found himself supplying not only a rapidly growing market in Canada, but Detroit, Cleveland, Buffalo, Pittsburgh, Philadelphia and Boston as well (the canned milk crossed the border free of duty). Easterners were lapping up so much Carnation Milk in the early fall of 1919 that three trains of nearly one hundred cars left Seattle for the Atlantic seaboard carrying more evaporated milk (5,000,000 cans in one instance) than had ever been moved before in a single shipment.

"To have revolutionized the market for the principal commodity of the table—milk —so that increasing thousands of people feel that they may buy it as they want it, in any quantity, of their dealer, and do not have to depend upon the varying quality of the supply from their local milkman, is distinctly a modern achievement," noted *The Carnation News* (October-November, 1919), and enlivened its pages with a quip attributed to the founder's son-in-law:* "You can whip Carnation, but you can't beat it."

*"Wedding bells have seldom pealed their joyous chimes for a larger, handsomer wedding," the *Seattle Times* reported November 18, when Katherine Moore Stuart married Harry Glenn Stibbs.

Mrs. E. H. Stuart driving E. A. Stuart's brown hackney gelding, Seaton Melancthon, winner of 101 blue ribbons. Carnation Stables in Pomona, California, and Carnation Farms became the home of many high-stepping champions once E. A. admitted that his love of fine horses was as great as his love for prize cattle.

Part II

The New Generation
1920-1948

You can dilute the double-rich contents of the tall can until the quart bottle overflows with pure milk

"From Contented Cows"

And nothing to cry over

Spilt milk ... Drop it—it doesn't break. Carry it wrong-side up—it doesn't leak. Keep *lots* of it on the pantry shelf—it doesn't spoil. *Milk in a modern package* ...

Carnation is pure, rich milk (unsweetened), made twice as rich by evaporating part of the natural water—*and "homogenized" to give every drop an equal share of the double helping of cream.*

That, as domestic science experts have shown, is why Carnation imparts superior texture, body, flavor, and richness to all milk dishes —surpassing the best results obtainable with bottled milk ... Try this convenient, economical, *better* milk. Here is an especially fine recipe for your initiation.

Carnation Caramel Custard

2 cups Carnation Milk diluted with 2 cups hot water; ½ cup sugar; ½ tsp. salt; 5 eggs; 1 tsp. vanilla. Caramelize sugar and add to scalded diluted milk. Let remain in double boiler till sugar dissolves. Add this mixture to slightly beaten eggs; then add salt and vanilla. Pour into buttered custard cups. Bake in 225° oven with cups set in deep pan of hot water. This serves eight.

"My Hundred Favorite Recipes"—Write for this unusual little recipe book by *Mrs. Mary Blake.* It is free

CARNATION MILK PRODUCTS COMPANY

940 Carnation Building, Oconomowoc, Wisconsin

1040 Stuart Building, Seattle, Wash. · New York · Aylmer, Ontario

© 1926, Carnation Milk Products Co.

5
Changing
Of The Guard

*"Of all the men that I have trained,
this is the only case in which the trainee
eventually became my boss."*
P. G. KINZER, 1968.

59

IN JUNE, 1922, eleven years after Elbridge H. Stuart had come home from Yale and gone into training under P. G. Kinzer (Carnation's Captain Bligh), the two men sat in a Chicago conference room with E. A. Stuart and Vice President Lewis R. Hardenbergh. On the other side of the table, the Pet Milk Company had fielded its top brass. After two days of dickering, the heads of the rival companies, now overseas partners, worked out a plan to consolidate. Once the Pet people had left the room, E. A. turned to Elbridge and asked him what he thought of the idea.

"If the deal goes through, I'll resign," Elbridge said, and negotiations were broken off that evening.

As a Carnation vice president and director, Elbridge would argue as heatedly with his father as with anyone else in the company, but in their personal relations he displayed the same respect E. A. had shown for his own Scotch-Quaker father. Back in the 1870s, for example, when E. A. left home to seek his

fortune, he took to smoking a pipe. When he came back for a visit, his father would put aside his dislike of tobacco and invite his son to light up. E. A. always refused.

A generation later, long after E. A. had switched from pipes to cigars, his son returned from college puffing on what his father contemptuously called "cigar*eets*," but the young man never lighted one when in E. A.'s company. His father, on the other hand, wasn't above sneaking a cigarette behind Elbridge's back, as Carnation's chief engineer discovered one night in 1914 when he attended a company party in San Francisco.

"They passed the cigarettes," MacBriar remembered, "and I naturally refused one, knowing E. A.'s feeling in the matter. However, when the cigarettes came to him, he took one and looked over at me and said, 'Mac, you take a cigar*eet* because I am going to smoke a cigar*eet* and I am not going home to Seattle and have you say that you saw me

n Ladies' Home Journal, September, 1926.

smoking a cigar*eet* unless I can say that I saw you smoke one also.' Probably he did not wish me to go home and tell his son Elbridge that I had seen his father smoke a cigarette because, although Elbridge hated cigars, in those days he always had to smoke a cigar in his father's presence or else not smoke at all."

Elbridge loved and respected his father, but both men were heavily streaked with stubbornness, as they had demonstrated some years earlier when the subject of college had first been tossed into play. E. A. had made up his mind to send the boy to Haverford College, the Quaker school near Philadelphia his brother Jehu and his nephew Harry had attended. Elbridge had set his heart on going to Yale by way of Phillips Academy at Andover, Massachusetts. The two Stuarts took their stand and, true to character, both refused to budge. In the end, as Elbridge's mother had predicted, it was E. A. who came around.

* * * * *

While basement tinkerers fiddled with their 1922 crystal sets and Sunday supplement readers devoured articles on King Tutankhamen's tomb, E. A. bought his first fine horses, a pair of three-gaited mares named Ethel May and Sonia ("While the cow has been very good to me, I think the horse was my first love, because I had to milk the cow") and, on September 10, he observed his sixty-sixth birthday.

Edging toward his Biblical allotment of three score and ten years, he had suffered two abrupt and painful reminders of his mortality. A heart attack had carried off Addison Stuart, the older brother who had been his first business partner, and an accidental fall had killed his nephew, Harry Stuart, at the age of forty-two, the same age E. A. had been when he decided to take a chance on evaporated milk.

At the time of his death, Harry was a vice president of the company he had helped his uncle build. Back in 1903 and 1904, when he was superintendent of the Forest Grove, Oregon, condensery, he had taken charge of young Elbridge during summer vacations,

initiating the boy into the Meyenberg mysteries of the vacuum pan and the sterilizer. In 1911, when Elbridge finished college, his Cousin Harry was one of the key executives in the Seattle office, but E. A. decided that the delicate problem of getting his son started with the company should be handled outside the family circle. The matter was referred to Hardenbergh.

"He debated whether to send me to the Forest Grove, Oregon, plant to work under Mr. P. G. Kinzer, who was always addressed as Mr. Kinzer by the employees," Elbridge later recalled, "or to the Mount Vernon, Washington, plant under Mr. M. J. Norton, who was referred to by everyone as 'Jack.'"

Hardenbergh didn't make things easy for the boss's son. He packed Elbridge off to Oregon to serve an indeterminate sentence under Mr. Kinzer.

* * * * *

Philip G. Kinzer had been working for the railroad for more than ten years when, in the summer of 1908, he stopped off in Seattle to visit his parents. While in town, he looked up a boyhood friend, George K. Spencer, who had gone to work for the Pacific Coast Condensed Milk Company.

"He knew that I was not entirely satisfied with the position I had with the Missouri Pacific, because I felt that the railroad business did not offer sufficient opportunity for advancement," Kinzer reminisced sixty years later, "and that my work required that I do a lot of travelling. For instance, during the twelve months preceding my visit to Seattle, I had spent three hundred and sixteen of the three hundred and sixty-five nights either on board private cars or Pullman cars, or at some hotel, which gave me little time with my family."

Kinzer had a chat with E. A., toured the Kent plant with Hardenbergh and was offered a job. He took it. "After talking to Mr. Stuart," he explained, "I realized that he was developing a business that had fine prospects for growth." He spent the first week of October learning his way around the Mount Vernon, Washington, condensery, and then took charge at Forest Grove, replacing Harry Stuart, who was being shifted to the Seattle office.

In 1913 Kinzer was transferred to Seattle as general superintendent of the western plants, and Elbridge, having served a stint at Mount Vernon as a foreman under Bill Cross (a hard-nosed boss of the Kinzer school), was put in charge of the Everson, Washington, condensery that same year. When he filled out his first salary card as superintendent, Elbridge restrained himself from adding the salary increase to which he was entitled.

"We consider this change as a promotion," his Cousin Harry wrote, February 26, 1913, "and this will authorize you to make out a new card for yourself at the rate of $125 per month. . . . We are confident you will be able to save this increase and more for the company and also want you to know that we appreciate your action in filling in your card when you went there at the same rate which you had been receiving, which was the proper thing for you to do."

* * * * *

Elbridge turned up at his sister's wedding reception in the fall of 1915 squiring a strikingly handsome girl. Jack Norton caught an appreciative glimpse of her as she was leaving the party. Six months later, when he got word that Elbridge and Nan Fullerton had set a date in June to get married, Jack wrote his former assistant a charming letter.

"I feel, from what little I saw of her, that you should be congratulated, and if I knew her better, I would not hesitate to congratulate her upon securing you for a husband. There have been a lot of girls who sat up nights trying to put something like this over, and didn't do nearly as good a job. I want to see her, however, and have a talk with her, because I do not want her to become so infatuated with you that she will spoil you."

They were married June 22, 1916, and Elbridge was indeed spoiled by his lively, fun-loving bride. "A delightful person, a beautiful woman," says Austin Smith, recalling Oconomowoc's *la dolce vita* of Carnation

Club dances and picnics, ice carnivals and lake-fishing. Nan used to worry about Elbridge's long hours at the office. To get his mind off of his work, she would organize impromptu poker games, often sitting in for a few rounds herself. She wasn't as good at the game as Elbridge, who kept track of the cards and could calculate his chances of drawing a fifth diamond. Nan played for fun, Elbridge played to win.

"Nan was a pretty girl and popular, always had a friendly word for the farm hands," says Al Oosterhuis, who half a century later could still remember the day a team of horses spooked and raced across the front yard of the eastern farm, dragging a wildly swaying wagon. Everybody else froze, chilled by the prospect of damage to company property, but Nan laughed and clapped her hands. She was rooting for the runaways.

Elbridge became a vice president of the company in the fall of 1917, not long after he turned thirty. Earlier that year, on July 12, Nan had given birth to a son, Elbridge Hadley Stuart, Jr. The other two boys were named after uncles, Reginald Fullerton (born December 4, 1919) and Dwight Lyman (born September 27, 1924). Louise Smith, Austin's wife, has a vivid, vagrant memory of Dwight in a Peter Pan suit, with a Dutch bob, and she remembers being forcibly struck by his resemblance to his mother, both in appearance and in personality.

Nan and the boys spent their summers on the Washington farm, while Elbridge commuted to the home office in Seattle. In the fall, when school opened, the family moved back to Oconomowoc, where the company had set up its eastern general office in a handsome two-story building regarded by the editor of the *Enterprise* (April 20, 1923) as "not only a credit to Carnation Milk Products Company, but also a great asset to our growing city. . . ."

The city grew abruptly that late-April week-end when, along with a carload of desks, chairs, file cabinets and wastebaskets, the company shipped some one hundred and fifty employees from its Chicago office to the

61

The Oconomowoc General Office—interior view taken July 11, 1917.

headquarters Roy Henszey had run up on a reclaimed swamp. The newcomers, greeted by welcome signs and window displays of carnations, made a "very favorable impression," the *Enterprise* reported (May 4), but fifty years later some oldtime residents had different recollections of that distant spring.

Men who now have trouble climbing stairs remember their resentment when slick-haired dudes from Chicago roared through town in snappy roadsters, whisking their girls off to Milwaukee. Women who have long since adjusted to bifocals and salt-free diets remember the secretaries who be-witched the apple-cheeked youth of Ocono-mowoc with their worldly ways (some even smoked in public) and the Chicago wives who turned up at Carnation Club picnics decked out in hats and gloves and filmy frocks more suitable for a lawn party than for can-stacking contests.

"John Wilkinson's wife came to the ice carnival wearing high heel pumps," recalls a gray-haired alumna of Etta Spencer's sten-ographic pool who was bobbing her hair at the time of the Carnation invasion. "We had a pair of scissors in the ladies' room and we used to go in there and take turns snipping each other's hair. We didn't have a beauty parlor in those days. You had to go to the barber shop and I would rather have died than walk in there with all those men sitting around."

*   *   *   *   *

Original plant in Carentan, France, taken in 1926.

Carnation had come through the 1920 recession at home only to find itself facing new difficulties abroad in its joint undertaking with Pet. The American Milk Products Company was bucking increasingly heavy competition from Holland and England, where low wages and depressed milk prices enabled manufacturers to deliver evaporated milk at a cost well under the going rate of the American product. To compound its overseas problems, the export company learned early in 1923 that France was about to clap a stiff tariff on milk imported into the country after July 1 of the following year.

American Milk Products set out on a frantic search for a suitable place in France to produce evaporated milk. The European manager, an Englishman with headquarters in Paris, sent word back to the Carnation-Pet directorate in America that he had found just what the company needed, a nineteenth century butter and cheese plant in the venerable Norman town of Carentan. Phil Kinzer was dispatched to supervise the installation of twentieth century machinery and equipment.

Bustling into Carentan in October, 1923, he found himself staring up at a magnificent old pile, medieval in style, huddled on the banks of a canal built by order of Napoleon.

An inn on one of the cobbled streets nearby, tradition insisted, had sheltered William the Conqueror when he was polishing his plans to make 1066 a memorable date in England's history. Kinzer, wasting little time on the charms of this den of antiquity, buckled down to the formidable task of converting the old buildings into a modern condensery and can factory.

"My principal problem was that of getting the French employees to do their work the way I felt it should be done," he recalled forty-five years later.

Production began, somewhat haltingly, the third week in June, 1924, just seven days before the French tariff was to take effect. Kinzer stuck around long enough to iron out some of the rough spots (for one thing, the inexperienced crews in the can factory couldn't keep up with the machinery, so he slowed it down), and then headed for Germany, which was about to impose a similar tariff on the importation of milk. He located a desirable site on a canal at Neustadt and, in the fall of 1925, booked passage for the States.

"When I got back," Kinzer told an interviewer in 1968, "Mr. E. A. Stuart asked me if I would take charge of the sales operations in the area west of the Rocky Mountains, in other words, the western division. I protested, saying that I had had no sales experience and didn't feel qualified. His answer to that was: 'You have demonstrated an ability to analyze problems and find a solution. I am certain you will handle sales work successfully.' "

* * * * *

A familiar face was missing from Carnation councils when Kinzer returned to Seattle and resumed his place on the company's board of directors. Executive Vice President Hardenbergh had resigned after having been with the company for more than twenty years. Relations between E. A. and his chief executive had begun to deteriorate in 1923 when Hardenbergh moved to Oconomowoc to take charge of the new eastern general office. Carnation at that time had outgrown its West Coast base, but it wasn't quite ready to leave home.

In this period of transition, the company maintained two general offices on opposite sides of the Rockies, but when a major decision had to be made, there was only one final arbiter and he spent most of his time in Seattle. Such divided authority was costly and cumbersome, Hardenbergh complained. During the course of their arguments, E. A. got the notion that his old friend no longer trusted his judgment. Hardenbergh tried to disabuse him of the idea, but the break had become irreparable and on January 13, 1925, at E. A.'s request, Hardenbergh resigned.

One evening a few months later, when E. A. had worked at his rolltop desk long after everyone else had left the Seattle office, he came home to find Mother had gone out somewhere. He ate dinner alone, glanced at the evening's headlines, and went upstairs to bed. He awakened in the early morning hours, sensing something was wrong. He turned on the light and looked around the room. Everything appeared to be in order until he tested his eyesight. When he closed his left eye, the room went black. "Detached retina," he was subsequently told by an eye specialist. Already deaf, he now found himself half-blind as well.

He had been stricken at a time when his company was going through a managerial crisis following the departure of its executive vice president and its treasurer, George Spencer, who had elected to leave with Hardenbergh. E. A., having ridden out similar storms in his day, kept a firm hand on the company's helm, consulting regularly with Elbridge and with Carnation's general counsel, Paul McKee, the two lieutenants he trusted completely. It was decided to move Jack Norton up to general manager and Elbridge, who had served with him on the Executive Committee for five years, was appointed treasurer and assistant general manager.

"You know what Jack Norton was doing when I first saw him?" E. A. once remarked to George Bulkley. "He was carrying a big quarter of beef on his shoulder in a packing house, but he had a gleam in his eye, a spirit."

Merritt J. Norton had worked his way up to the job of assistant manager of the Seattle branch of Armour & Co. when, in June, 1906, he quit his job and cast in his lot with E. A.'s condensed milk company. He was sent to the Forest Grove condensery to be broken in by Harry Stuart. The following September he was moved to Mount Vernon, where he did field work before he made superintendent. When Carnation crossed the Rockies, Jack was sent east to take charge of the district office.

In the fall of 1926, less than two years after he had been named general manager, Jack found himself caught up in a classic storybook situation. The king was growing old and infirm. A deadly serious, hard-working prince, too shy and reserved to make friends easily, was the legitimate heir to the throne. Jack, a prime minister beloved of the masses, was treated as a son by the old king, but he was not of royal blood. He would not inherit the crown.

Having come to the painful conclusion that he had gone as far as he could go with Carnation, Jack quietly lined up a job as vice president at Borden Company, where there would be no ceiling on his ambitions. On October 15, 1926 he submitted his resignation to E. A. The loss of this surrogate son was a hard blow. E. A. had made his rambling Colonial house in Oconomowoc his home whenever he visited the eastern general office and the Nortons had named their daughter Mary after E. A.'s wife. Elbridge and Nan had felt close enough to Jack to talk of naming their third son Jack Norton, but had changed their minds and given the honor to the boy's Uncle Dwight. Jack had roared with laughter when the couple acquired a new coach dog and decided to call him Jack.*

"It hurts," E. A. wrote Elbridge when he received Jack's letter of resignation.

E. A. expressed his confidence in his son's ability to handle Jack's old job, but Elbridge got a foretaste of the years to come when his father added, "I know you will try and secure my opinion before acting on anything of importance." E. A. not only continued to squint over his son's shoulder, but kept peppering old associates with questions about Elbridge's ability to run the company. The point at issue, it seemed to the older and wiser heads of the corporate family, was not so much a question of whether the crown prince was ready to take over the throne as whether the old king was ready to surrender it.

*Jack Norton died April 3, 1932, a few weeks after Elbridge's elevation to the presidency of Carnation Company. Daniel F. Norton, who had worked in his brother's shadow during their years together at Carnation, had gone to Nestlé with Hardenbergh and succeeded him as president.

65

A Business Tragedy: The directors of Carnation Milk Co. discover a Discontented Cow.

Reprinted from *Life*, February 16, 1926.

6
Meanwhile Back At The Ranch

*"He had many disappointments,
not only in the company, but on the farm,
but he never allowed anything to stop him
from building a fine herd of animals."*
ALFRED M. GHORMLEY ON E. A. STUART

As LIFE CLOSED IN ON E. A., dulling his hearing and dimming his sight, he found sanctuary at the Snoqualmie Valley farm. Even in the long, troubled letter he wrote to Elbridge at the time of Jack Norton's resignation he took time to report on the new buildings ("splendid"), the cattle ("doing good"), the weather ("no more frost") and the autumn work ("some more beets to get in, only day or two more work on them, then only some more hay to haul").

"I think Alfred has done well to keep ahead of work," he added.

Alfred M. Ghormley had been doing well ever since taking a shovel-and-broom job at the farm in the summer of 1915. The quiet, gangling youth (he turned nineteen that July) attracted E. A.'s attention one day when he was showing some visitors around the farm. He asked the manager about the record of a cow Alfred had brought out for inspection. The manager was unable to supply the information. Alfred had it on the tip of his tongue.

When the boy's summer vacation ended, he decided to forego a college education* and stick with his on-the-job training at the farm. It was the kind of work he liked and it paid thirty dollars a month. He slept in the bunk-house his first year and then, assigned to keep the farm's records, he was installed in an upstairs room at E. A.'s bungalow.

"I thought I was a big shot," Alfred later reminisced, "so I started smoking a corncob pipe. One night, going over the records on the porch of the bungalow, I was puffing away, blowing smoke in E. A.'s face—he was deaf, so I had to put my face close to his. He nearly got sick from the pipe smoke. 'Alfred,' he said, 'if you will throw that pipe away, I will buy you a year's supply of cigars.' "

Accustomed to getting up early (in later years he managed to sleep until five or six o'clock), Alfred discovered that the records weren't enough to fill his long work-day. On his own initiative he put his natural aptitude for sketching to use and started taking the markings of the calves. He was promoted to herdsman and, in time, to head herdsman.

*An older brother, Robert, who was graduated from the U.S. Naval Academy in 1906, later commanded the Allied forces at Guadalcanal. A second brother, Ralph, who was studying medicine at Johns Hopkins in the fall of 1915, became a distinguished surgeon at the Mayo Clinic in Rochester, Minnesota. A third brother, Kenneth, received his Bachelor of Letters degree from the University of California, Berkeley, in 1911, did some graduate work in jurisprudence, and became a Carnation executive.

Carl Gockerell (in white) readies "Possum Sweetheart" for a milking by Jack Dempsey and milkmaids.

Although he enjoyed working with cows, he was by his own admission "never a good milker." That was left to Carl Gockerell.

"He was a big ox of a man," recalls George Bulkley, "but never was anybody more gentle with cows."

E. A. recruited Carl from a Guernsey farm in Pennsylvania. When he showed up at the Snoqualmie Valley farm on October 1, 1919 and took charge of Segis Pietertje Prospect (eartag number 221846), a great milker and a great cow had been brought together. They proceeded to make dairy history.

In the pre-dawn darkness of a December morning in 1919, Carl started milking "Possum Sweetheart," as he called the daughter of old King Segis Tenth. Six hours later he milked her again, and again she gave between twenty-five and thirty pounds, more than twice as much as the ordinary cow. For the next twelve months, he milked her four times a day, missing only four milkings in the year-long test conducted under the supervision of Washington State College and the Holstein-Friesian Association.

Carl and Possum Sweetheart started their historic year together in the farm's old test barn. When the mammoth new barn was finished in July, they moved to more com-

modious quarters, complete with running water, but the barnyard prima donna preferred her former digs. Carl didn't argue. He took her back to the old stall.

When the test ended on December 17, Segis Pietertje Prospect had produced as much milk as ten ordinary cows, averaging over one hundred pounds (46.5 quarts) a day for a 365-day total of 37,381.4 pounds, thus beating the previous world's record, set in 1919, by 3,956.4 pounds.

An enterprising press agent hit on the idea of bringing the world's champion cow and the world's champion prizefighter together in order, to quote *Carnation Family News* (May, 1921), "to teach the youth of America (as typified by the Boy Scouts), the importance of drinking more pure, whole milk." In full view of a newsreel camera, Jack Dempsey shucked off his coat, rolled up his sleeves, grabbed an empty pail and set to work milking history's most productive cow.

E. A. was understandably pleased to have set a world's record at Carnation Stock Farms, but, running true to form, he wasn't satisfied. Already he was looking ahead, predicting "new and more startling records of production." In December, 1931, when a man from *Fortune* looked in on the farm, he

67

was amused to find radio music playing softly in the barns during milking time. "The cows," he reported, "don't resent it at all—in fact, they seem grateful. Of the 118 cows in the world that produce 32,000 or more pounds of milk a year, twenty-six were born and raised in Snoqualmie."

* * * * *

Midway in Possum Sweetheart's test, a *New York Times* feature writer noted that "the average yield per cow is 3,800 pounds annually, and if it were not for the purebred cows the average would not be over 1,000 pounds per head."* By replacing scrub cows with more productive stock, the author pointed out, the nation's dairy farmers could feed the same number of animals each day and double their supply of milk each year.

Despite such a strong statistical endorsement of Carnation's breeding program, its Stock Farms had a distressing oversupply of bull calves. E. A. prodded the Chicago office to do something and Hardenbergh turned to the company's leading cowman, Al Oosterhuis, for help. Oostie recommended a former student, Merton (Dinty) Moore. Thus, the company's bull calf sales portfolio was offered to the young Wisconsin county agent who, at the Milwaukee sale several months earlier, had put a value of $5,000 on the bull calf knocked down to E. A. for $106,000.

Moore was interested in the job, but how, he asked, could he possibly sell Snoqualmie Valley calves he had never laid eyes on to breeders he was not likely ever to meet from a desk in a Chicago skyscraper? If the company knew the answer to that question, it would never have hired him, Hardenbergh replied, and installed the young man in an office on the twelfth floor.

He knew next to nothing about Holstein-Friesian cattle when he started his career with Carnation, but before it was done, Dinty Moore had come to be recognized by cattlemen around the world as an authority on the breed. In his innocence at the outset, however, Moore hadn't been hampered by the knowledge that pure-bred cattle were not

*June 22, 1919.

Carnation bull, left, bred to cow, center, produced daughters like one at right for the Maharajah of Mysore. Milk production increased 1000%.

generally sold sight-unseen, especially at the prices commanded by calves from Carnation Stock Farms. Without realizing what he was up to, he revolutionized the industry's selling methods when he launched a direct-mail campaign that sold calves at a brisk clip. In his first two years he brought in about $250,000.

He was working away in his office one day when Hardenbergh burst in with E. A. Stuart. Moore was surprised and flattered that Carnation's president would take time to call on a lowly bull salesman.

"He knew every animal I had sold," Moore recalled. "He, in fact, had set the price on them. He didn't tell me how well I had done, then or later. I was to learn, however, that because he didn't tell me I had not done well, I should feel complimented."

Moore had his first run-in with E. A. when he expressed a desire to visit Seattle and drive out to the farm. "We will let you know when we want you to go to Seattle, Mr. Moore," E. A. snapped, and Moore went home that night muttering to his wife about giving up his job and going back to Madison, Wisconsin, to join the university faculty. Mary calmed him down.

with pictures, which I saw in a haze," he remembered afterwards. "The furniture was dark and shiny. Mr. Stuart rose from behind the desk and greeted me with such warmth that it seemed almost like affection. He had the power to sweep away mountains of accumulated misgivings with a word or two."

E. A. proceeded to quote four lines from Dinty Moore's rhyming saga of a Carnation bull shipped to Bangalore, India, where the Maharajah of Mysore had crossed the aristocratic Holstein with one of his lowly, humpbacked Sindis cows, a draft animal capable of giving about seven hundred pounds of milk a year. Their heifer, born with her father's figure and with the royal blood of old King Segis Tenth in her veins, had grown up to produce more than seven thousand pounds of milk a year. Moore was charmed to hear the Founding Father recite his doggerel:

> And the Maharajah fainted
> Out in Asia, there, they say,
> When he saw Carnation painted
> On the road to Mandalay.

That evening E. A. drove Dinty out to the farm and deposited him in an upstairs guest room at the bungalow. On the floor was the black and white hide of a Holstein bull.

"Carnation King Sylvia," E. A. explained, and left his guest staring down at the $106,000 throw-rug.

* * * * *

E. A. was taking the sun in Palm Springs in March, 1925, when he got a sorrowful letter from Carl Gockerell announcing the death of Segis Pietertje Prospect. As Possum Sweetheart lay dying ("It was heartbreaking the last forty-eight hours to see this grand old cow lying in her stall unable to move hand or foot"), her youngest son, only a few weeks old, scampered about on the other side of the partition in her stall.

"The greatest, most beautiful and nearest human cow that ever lived," Carl wrote.

He had managed to "get to her stall just in time to gather her head in my arms and received one last loving glance as she drew her last breath." After checking with El-

There was another blow-up when E. A. criticized one of Moore's advertisements because he thought it might lead a careless reader to infer that the number of cows at Carnation Stock Farms producing more than one thousand pounds of butter a year was ten rather than seven. Moore exploded at what he took to be an attack on his professional integrity. He fired off an indignant three-page special delivery letter marked PERSONAL, and then sat back waiting for the reply from Seattle telling him to clear out his desk. The letter never came.

"You just don't know Father," Elbridge explained. "There was nothing personal in what he intended or said. What you ought to do is to take the train out there and get better acquainted."

Moore interpreted the remark as an official invitation to do what he had wanted to do for more than a year, drop in on the home office and look around the farm. When he got to Seattle, he had no idea what sort of reception awaited him. To his great relief, he was met at the station, whisked off to the Stuart Building and ushered into E. A.'s presence.

"The large office had four walls covered

Scores of dignitaries attended unveiling of monument to Segis Pietertje Prospect.

bridge, Carl had buried her in her show blanket, because he "couldn't bear to see it on any other cow."

"I want a nice fence placed around her grave," E. A. wrote in reply and started mulling over monuments. It had to be something appropriate, something unique.

Three years later Carl was speechless when, in the presence of such dignitaries as the Governor of Washington and the Mayor of Seattle, he was called on to speak at the unveiling of the larger-than-life size statue of Possum Sweetheart E. A. had ordered placed on a seven-foot-high pedestal near the Carnation Milk Farm office. A bronze plaque paid tribute to the queen of cows:

SIRED BY A KING AND OF PUREST HOL-
STEIN STRAIN, SHE HERSELF BORE SONS
AND DAUGHTERS OF CHAMPION ACHIEVE-
MENT . . . FINEST TYPE OF THE NOBLE,
PATIENT ANIMAL THAT IS MOST JUSTLY
NAMED THE FOSTER MOTHER OF THE
HUMAN RACE. . . .

When Elbridge dropped in on the farm's superintendent and found him drunk, E. A. acted on his suggestion that the man be fired and replaced by young Alfred Ghormley. Two years later, in the fall of 1922, Alfred married a Seattle girl, Elizabeth MacLean, and installed her in the superintendent's refurbished bungalow. In its November issue, *Carnation Family News* expressed "the heartiest wishes of us all for a happy life," but an ominous hint of the pain to come had appeared three months earlier, when the farm's correspondent noted that "our genial superintendent, Mr. Ghormley, has been experiencing considerable trouble with rheumatism. . . ."

Alfred had put the farm in the fresh milk business in a small way, setting up a model plant to provide bottled milk for a limited number of customers in Seattle. In 1926, taking his cue from Alfred's operation, E. A. decided it was time for Carnation to expand.

"He asked me to start buying some fresh milk and ice cream companies on the West

Coast," Phil Kinzer recalled. "We started by buying four fresh milk dairies and one ice cream company in Seattle. That was the beginning of our entry into the fresh milk and ice cream field. During the next ten or eleven years, we bought fresh milk and ice cream companies in Portland, Oregon; Oakland, California; Spokane, Washington; Los Angeles, California, and Long Beach, California. Then, in 1929, our Eastern Office became interested in this expansion program and bought fresh milk and ice cream companies in Wichita Falls, Texas; Waterloo, Iowa; Tulsa, Oklahoma, and Houston, Texas."

In 1931, hard times notwithstanding, Carnation moved into the Los Angeles market by purchasing the Henry Creamery Corporation. The following year it acquired Bothell's, another Los Angeles fresh milk and ice cream company, and thus secured an even firmer hold on what it considered a "big, potential market."

In 1920, with a population of 576,677, Los Angeles had ranked as the country's tenth largest city. By 1930, with a population of 1,238,048, it was fifth, and a downtown lawyer was complaining in his memoirs that when he drove into the central city every morning his vision was "impaired by dust, smoke, and the infinitesimal, invisible excrescences which arise from the crowded and much traveled streets and sidewalks."

One of Carnation's first ice cream stores,
acquired with American Creamery Co. in Oakland in 1929.

Buying dairies such as this in Seattle in 1926
launched Carnation's fresh milk operation.

71

The original Albers & Schneider mill in Portland before 1900.

Albers' charming demonstrators, circa 1918.

* * * * *

Back in 1887, when E. A. and Mary Stuart were strengthening their infant son with evaporated milk, a young German immigrant, Bernhard Albers, had turned up in Terre Haute, Indiana, and gone to work for a wholesale grocer. Two years later he headed west to Portland, Oregon, where he found another job in the same field and started saving toward the day when he could go into business for himself. Bernhard's enthusiastic letters brought four brothers, Henry, Will, Frank, and George, to Portland, and in 1895, with capital of $15,000, they formed the firm of Albers & Schneider. Four years later, the same year E. A. cranked up the abandoned Kent condensery, the Albers brothers bought out Thomas Schneider. The company absorbed the business of the Pacific Cereal Association in 1914, thus acquiring two labels of considerable interest to E. A. Stuart, *Carnation Wheat* and *Carnation Oats*.

Albers' use of the Carnation label had proved worrisome to Carnation Milk Products Company in the weeks following the signing of the Armistice, when Albers Bros. Milling Company was promoting its Carnation Mush, attractively done up in a red-and-white package, with carnations on the label. To make matters worse, one of the Albers brothers had got his name in the West

Albers' famous trademark.

Coast papers when he was accused of making pro-German statements on a train ride from San Francisco to Portland.

"There is a tremendous feeling against Albers Bros. products here on the Coast," Carnation's advertising manager, H. G. Stibbs, advised the Chicago office. "I was told by one man that in Seattle the Albers Company had sold to more than two hundred fifty retailers. The next day, after the report about the pro-German utterances came out in the newspapers, more than half of the retailers in the city handling Albers Bros. products called up their local manager and told him to send for the goods as they did not want to handle merchandise made by a pro-German. Only yesterday I heard of one instance where a housewife returned a package of Carnation Mush to the retailer which had been given to her son when sent on an errand to the grocery store, and she stated that she did not want any of the Albers Bros. products."

* * * * *

The old wartime feelings against Germans had died down in the late 1920's when Carnation and Albers went into their mating dance, but E. A. and his lieutenants hadn't forgotten the patriotic backlash stirred up by Carnation Mush. It was one of the considerations which brought the two West Coast pioneers together. They had grown up side by side, gone through similar struggles to make their way in the world and had come to bear a certain resemblance to one another in their corporate profiles. When Carnation went courting, with Phil Kinzer as matchmaker, it was like setting out to marry the girl next door.

Albers and Carnation had both dedicated themselves to products of the highest quality, and in their restless search for improvements, both had been quick to try something new. Years before the first soybeans were planted in the United States, Albers was experimenting with soybean meal. In 1919, two years before identification of Vitamin D, "the sunshine vitamin," an Albers researcher set to work in a hay barn on the Seattle waterfront to find a way to raise poultry in confinement without touching off an epidemic of rickets. Cod liver oil, he found, could be made to take the place of sunshine.

Albers, in the decade preceding the Carnation merger, made major contributions to the industries it supplied with feedstuffs when its researchers found that charcoal, copra and molasses should be dropped from poultry rations and Manioc meal from feed for dairy animals. The company led the way in providing laying hens with the correct amount of Vitamin A and pioneered in the development of food pellets for poultry and rabbits. A few years after consolidation, Albers came out with a scientifically balanced, pelleted dog food known as Friskies.

"A broad policy of expansion along lines of business closely allied to its chief product and to products merchandized through the same channels of distribution during the last year has given the company a diversity and breadth of interest not entirely covered by the old name," E. A. explained on November 18, 1929, when Carnation Milk Products Company was renamed Carnation Company.

In addition to its expansion in the fluid milk field, with the purchase of dairies in Washington, Oregon, California, Texas, Oklahoma and Iowa, Carnation was expanding the market for its new malted milk powder. It dissolved more quickly than its competitors, didn't stick to the sides of the mixing cup or settle at the bottom of the glass when served and was more economical to use, because less powder was required to provide a rich malt flavor.

"The policy of the company to expand its business by bringing into the Carnation organization companies engaged in the production and distribution of food products will be continued," E. A. reported in a 1929 message to stockholders, the first financial statement the company had ever printed for distribution. It made no mention of net earnings, but the figure was included the following year. After expenses, interest, taxes and depreciation, it amounted to $1,411,632.29.

"Business throughout the country during the past year was harassed by falling commodity prices, impairment of purchasing power and unusually severe competitive conditions," the 1930 annual report declared. "In the face of these serious handicaps, your company was able to increase not only its gross volume of business, but also its net earnings. This creditable showing was made without resorting to a liquidation of labor, but largely as the result of increased efficiency in the operation of every department of your company's business."

The last sentence could be translated: "We didn't fire anybody, but we sure cut hell out of their budgets." Elbridge had proved to be adept (or, as others put it, ruthless) in cutting operating costs to the marrow. The following year a young accountant trained at Northwestern University (Class of 1927) came to work for Carnation in Oconomowoc as assistant controller and quickly caught Elbridge's eye. He, too, could lay a budget request on the operating table, examine it with detachment and cut into it with clinical skill. His name was H. Everett Olson.

* * * * *

E. A., deaf and nearly blind, still presided at board meetings (directors spoke loudly into his left ear), still sat in on important policy discussions and still kept in touch with his old lieutenants, but he was spending more and more time with his horses, leaving the everyday concerns of the company to Elbridge. Finally, in the depressed winter of 1931-32, when Carnation was losing money for the first time in a dozen years, the Founding Father came to terms with time and circumstance.

"One of the most difficult decisions I ever made in my business career," he later wrote.

The abdication ceremony took place in E. A.'s Los Angeles home when his ministers assembled in the North June Street throne room for their February, 1932, meeting. E. A. presented his letter of resignation and was elected chairman of the board and of the Executive Committee. Elbridge, who already had the burdens of the presidency, was given the title.

His sister, Katherine Stuart Stibbs, got the news from their mother and lost no time writing to Elbridge, expressing her confidence that he would "carry on the good work our dear father started thirty years ago." Nan's brother, Reg Fullerton, sent a telegram from New York and followed it up with a letter: "It must be a great source of satisfaction to you—not that you haven't been really carrying the responsibilities of that office—to receive this most appropriate recognition."

"There is not much glory in being a president, but if you are a president, it is a pleasure to associate with others who are so well versed in their line as you are," wrote E. G. MacDougall, president of Libby, McNeill & Libby, and J. E. Rovensky, vice president of National City Bank in New York City, warned Elbridge: "This will in no wise change my attitude towards you in any future poker games. Presidents or vice presidents, I mow them all down. In fact, I prefer presidents—they are more apt to have real money."

"I will have to watch my step," Elbridge replied.

* * * * *

When he succeeded his father as president of Carnation Company, Elbridge was forty-four years old, about the same age E. A. had been when he was struggling to keep the Kent condensery from sinking back into bankruptcy. E. A. had started out with a dozen or so employees. Elbridge had four thousand men and women whose ability to buy ground beef, pay the rent and repair the children's teeth depended on the sale of products bearing the Carnation and Albers labels. In Elbridge Stuart, they had a president who had spent his life training for the job. He had "run the pan" in a dozen condenseries and come to have an intimate working knowledge of the problems of production, distribution, advertising and selling.

"From the start he has had a capacity for

The Good Old Days
in Transportation

E. A. Stuart drove a milk cart in France during an inspection trip to European plants in 1927.

Albers Bros. Milling trucks lined up in front of the Seattle mill in 1919.

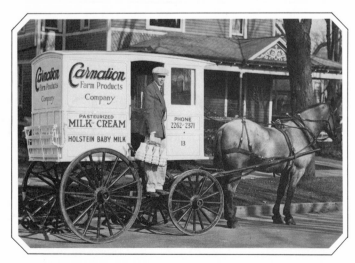

Residents of Waterloo, Iowa, could still enjoy non-polluting home delivery in 1930.

CARNATION MILK PRODUCTS CO.
MANUFACTURERS OF
CARNATION STERILIZED MILK
CHICAGO — SEATTLE

CHICAGO,

December seventh
Nineteen Twenty.

TO OUR PATRONS:

Owing to the increase in use of motor trucks and automobiles over the country roads, we believe that the transportation problem during the winter season can be rendered less difficult if the milk haulers and farmers will use wide truck sleighs in place of the narrow ones which have been in general use for a great many years. This will permit of the use of automobiles and trucks just as soon as the wide track sleighs have broken the road, and will save the inconvenience and trouble experienced during the spring thaw, at which time the snow melts faster in one place than it does in another, which has made it necessary for anybody hauling a load in from the country to use a sleigh as far as possible, and then transfer the load onto a wagon at the edge of town. Such a situation could be eliminated entirely by the use of the wide track sleighs, as the motor truck or farm wagon could then be used for the entire trip.

We understand that your local Blacksmith can widen out the narrow bobs to standard tread at a very small expense to you, and we are satisfied that the saving in time and money, due to such a change, will be more than sufficient to justify the expenditure.

We hope that you will consider this matter very carefully, and take immediate steps to have your sleighs widened to standard tread so they will be ready for use when needed.

CARNATION MILK PRODUCTS COMPANY.

M J N
S A N

Carnation appeals to its milk haulers to use wide track sleighs in December, 1920.

In 1923 Salesman Frazee drove his company car in a parade opening baseball season in Indianapolis.

In 1923 the Cho-Cho car and clowns roared into Texas to introduce Carnation's new product —malted milk chocolate in concentrated liquid form.

Spiffy was the word for Carnation salesmen's 1935 business coupes.

A Ford truck and seven-door coach-in body carried Carnation ice cream in the '40s.

Wholesale fresh milk deliveries in Seattle, circa 1936, were made in this "refrigerated" van with a wet ice bunker.

The company's team of Percherons were used to pull the Carnation entry in the 1932 Tournament of Roses parade in Pasadena.

assimilating ideas, an eagerness to learn, and an ability to sit quietly and listen to the tested opinions of others," Freda Tilden reported in *The Carnation* (March-April, 1934). The new president was "unusually grave, sometimes, for so young a man," she found, and attributed this trait to his attentiveness. He liked to listen "to what others have to say, cataloging it, filing it away in the storehouse of his mind. When his decision on a matter is required, the answer is instantly there—years of experience have taught him most of the answers in the operation of the milk business. . . ."

Ms Tilden visited the Stuarts at their suburban home in River Hills ("a white Colonial house, set in a country of softly rolling landscape"), some twelve miles from Carnation's executive offices in Milwaukee. "Both Mr. and Mrs. Stuart, amazingly young people, one thinks, to have three stalwart sons growing up about them,* enjoy a well-ordered simplicity of living. Elbridge Stuart, removed from the burdens of his office, "becomes a gracious host, whose easy

*When their father assumed the presidency in 1932, Hadley was fourteen, Fullerton twelve and Dwight seven.

naturalness and ready wit create an atmosphere of restful ease."

On weekdays, while Carnation executives lunched at a double table in the cafeteria on the top floor of the Milwaukee Gas Light Building, their employees ate in groups scattered around the room. One day, when five clerical workers—all women—were eating together, they noticed that their new boss had come upstairs for luncheon alone. One of them got up, walked over to the table where Elbridge had sat down and invited him to join them.

"Mr. Stuart promptly arose and carried his tray to the other table," Ms Tilden wrote. "In a few moments he was telling an amusing story of something that had happened the day before, presenting the highlights in a most diverting manner. To the girls who work in the executive office, and whose contact with the president is mainly through other executives by way of reports and statistics, his action revealed an executive laying aside, momentarily, the seriousness of his office, graciously making himself one with his employees, sharing in a highly entertaining way a friendly little incident."

Outside of the circle of executives who played golf and poker with him, only a relatively few members of the Carnation family ever got to see Elbridge in this favorable light. They thought of E. A. as an avuncular tornado sweeping through their offices and plants from time to time, with hand outstretched, his keen eye for detail raking every dark cranny that might harbor a wasted dollar or an inefficiently spent man-hour. Elbridge, coming to power in the depths of a worldwide depression, seemed a rather cold, remote figure who handed down decisions which were, of necessity, often unpopular. E. A. was like a wealthy grandfather who always showed up with a box of chocolates under his arm. Elbridge, to keep meat and potatoes on the corporate table, was the prudent parent who had to cut the children's weekly allowance.

"Our government has certainly been on a spending spree," Elbridge wrote in the last troubled year of Herbert Hoover's presidency, shortly before Governor Franklin D. Roosevelt of New York took to the campaign trail to denounce federal extravagance.

Elbridge had no intention of following the government's profligate example in running Carnation Company. In his first state of the company message to stockholders, he noted that in a year "marked by declining values, by further reductions in the purchasing power of consumers, and by the severest competition that the evaporated milk industry has ever experienced," Carnation had been compelled to omit dividends on its common stock for the latter half of 1932.

"Salaries and wages of all officers and employees were reduced," he added; "various economies in operations were made."

Much of the credit for the economies effected in the Albers milling operations, where the books were stained with red ink, belonged to the self-assured young certified public accountant who had answered an advertisement in a Chicago newspaper and, after being interviewed by Tommy Ellis, Carnation's controller, had gone to work in the Oconomowoc office in December, 1931.

Later that winter, to his astonishment, he was visited by Elbridge Stuart.

"I thought at the time it was quite unusual for the president of the company to want to meet a young fellow who had been employed as an assistant controller," Everett Olson recalled forty-odd years later, and he still had no idea why he was picked to go out to the West Coast and see what could be done to straighten out the tangled affairs of the Albers subsidiary. "Maybe," he speculated, "I was the only one available."

The old order was passing, the new was coming into being. E. A.'s senior field officers, Phil Kinzer and Bill Cross, who had performed legendary feats in the growth of Carnation Company, were totally immersed in the processing, distribution, and marketing of evaporated milk. They were not at home in such strange new areas as daily door-to-door deliveries of bottled milk and the production and sale of cold breakfast cereals and food for calves, dogs, poultry and rabbits. Young Olson had no ties with the company's past. His only commitment was to sound management practices, no matter what the product. He attracted Elbridge's attention at a time when Carnation's new president was casting about for his own Phil Kinzer and Bill Cross.

* * * * *

The Albers brothers, operating plants in Seattle, Portland, Oakland and Los Angeles, had got into the habit of running their own show in their own way, each of them presiding over a separate and equal domain. It was up to Everett Olson, the obscure 25-year-old accountant, to call on the heads of these Balkan kingdoms and remind them that Albers Bros. Milling Company was now a Carnation subsidiary responsible to corporate headquarters in Milwaukee. The rulers had become colonial administrators who took their orders from Elbridge Stuart.

"I ran into some problems," Olson recalls, "but at the age I was, and being somewhat cocky, I was able to put through most of my recommendations."

Instead of having accounting offices and

79

clerical staffs at each plant, as had been the Albers custom, the work was centralized in Seattle, where a new building enabled Albers and Carnation support forces to share a common roof, leaving only a few executives and the western sales management in the Stuart Building. High-level operations were further centralized by transferring P. G. Kinzer and J. F. Douglas to the Milwaukee office. Alfred M. Ghormley, now a vice president and director, was left in charge of Carnation's western operations.

"We who have known Mr. Ghormley since the good old days on the Farm have a fine family interest in him and are glad to see him progress," observed *The Carnation* (July-August, 1933).

Fred A. Young, a veteran of the Carnation sales force, took over responsibility for the sales of Albers cereals as well as Carnation Milk. Years later, in a letter to Glenn Thompson, Carnation's archivist, he recalled that the Albers salesmen were accustomed to

dealing directly with retailers and their "pricing program was not so rigid and definite as the good old Carnation selling program."

"It wasn't easy for the Albers boys to fall in line," Fred continued, "so there were quite a few problems and stumbling blocks along the way, but eventually time and persistence together with more trial and error won out. . . ."

Along with a great many other companies in the Depression years, Albers was losing money when young Olson first looked into its operation. Like a poker player trying desperately to recoup his losses by throwing good money after bad, Albers was making imprudent extensions of credit in order to rack up sales. Its credit policy was tightened and, once it developed new products and backed them with a Carnation-style marketing program, the company began to show a profit. In the meantime, Elbridge had given it a new treasurer—H. Everett Olson.

7

"Contented! With You With Me I'm Contented."

"Dollar for dollar, the Carnation Contented Hour is the most effective program on the NBC today."
A NATIONAL BROADCASTING
COMPANY EXECUTIVE, 1934.

WHILE NEW YORKERS CROWDED into Aeolian Hall on Sunday evening, April 26, 1931, to gawk at the shrunken images of Peggy Hopkins Joyce and Primo Carnera flickering on a six-inch screen set up to receive a broadcast of what the *Times* called "radio talkies," homebodies west of the Rockies tuned in on a new radio program, the Carnation Contented Hour. It ran thirty minutes on NBC Pacific Coast network and its songs were played by Mahlon Merrick's Carnation Vagabonds and sung by a male quartet. The show was an immediate success.

After eight months of West Coast broadcasting, the Contented Hour took its cowbells and its mechanical mooing device to Chicago for its first coast-to-coast broadcast, Monday, January 4, 1932. Glenn Thompson, Carnation's assistant advertising manager, sat in on a dress rehearsal in Studio A of the Merchandise Mart and later took part in the postmortem examination conducted at the offices of Erwin, Wasey, the company's advertising agency.

"Arthur Kudner, who was then top man in Erwin, Wasey's Chicago organization, was all for calling the orchestra 'The Carnation Milkmen,'" Glenn recalls, "but it was felt that the name was hardly dignified enough for an orchestra that was going to broadcast semi-classical music and a program that was going to advertise a quality product such as Carnation Milk."

The conferees decided to go along with the name used on the Pacific Coast, "The Carnation Vagabonds." Ordinarily "vagabonds" would have been a bit racy for Carnation Company, but the word had achieved a certain cachet in a 1929 film, *The Vagabond Lover* ("Men hate him—women love him!" screamed the trailer), starring Hubert Prior Vallee who was, as everyone knew, a Yale man. Not long after the Contented Hour went national, however, the Carnation Vagabonds suffered a sea change and re-emerged as the Carnation Concert Orchestra.

"Again Carnation has led the way, for this is the first evaporated milk company to sponsor a continent-wide radio program," crowed *The Carnation* in its first issue of 1932.

* * * * *

Once the contentment of Carnation cows was aired from shore to shore, Carnation Milk came to the attention of thousands of shoppers who seem never to have noticed the product in their grocery stores or to have

The Contented Hour
1931-1951

The Carnation Vagabonds
made their debut on The Contented Hour,
broadcast on NBC's Pacific Coast Network in 1931.

The full Contented Hour Orchestra, the Carnation Quartette
and chorus, and the Lullaby Lady as they appeared in
Chicago in 1933. Group in front includes
from left, Jean Paul King, announcer; Gene Arnold, narrator;
and Morgan Eastman, conductor.

From left, Tony Martin, Jo Stafford, Conductor Victor Young and Announcer Jimmy Wallington at a rehearsal for the Contented Hour.

Buddy Clark, left, featured baritone on the Contented Hour, with special guest Janet Blair and Percy Faith, musical director of program.

Guest soloist Jane Powell is flanked by (left to right) R. R. Brubaker, Carnation's general sales manager; Buddy Clark; C. W. Chorley, Canadian sales manager; Jimmy Wallington and Ted Dale, conductor.

Dinah Shore and husband George Montgomery help Carnation celebrate its 50th anniversary on the Contented Hour in September, 1949.

read about it in their newspapers and magazines. During an eleven-week slogan contest, nearly 660,000 entries written on the back of Carnation labels (or, to comply with federal requirements, on reasonable facsimiles) poured in on the company's advertising department.

"We knew from the letters that were sent in with many of the slogans that contestants had gone out and bought Carnation Milk for the first time to get the label," recalls Glenn Thompson.

In addition to the condenseries producing Carnation Evaporated Milk in some seventeen states and Canada, the company had three subsidiaries going to market with their own labels. Northfield supplied Minnesota, Iowa and the Southeast. Mohawk shipped its Gold Cross Evaporated Milk to, among others, Kansas City and Cleveland, and also sold its Sweet Clover and Red Cross sweetened condensed milk to New Yorkers. A Fort Lupton, Colorado, acquisition marketed its evaporated milk under two labels, Red Cross and Columbine, while General Milk took care of Europe from plants in France, Germany and Holland.

"Just to think of the Carnation Milk consumed by little delicate babies all over the world is enough to make us feel a keen responsibility in the proper handling of milk," a Bell Buckle, Tennessee, employee wrote *The Carnation* (March-April, 1932). "That thought removes all possible drudgery from cleaning pipe lines and cooling coils."

The beneficial effects of Carnation Milk on the world's toddlers were never long absent from the thoughts of a company founded by a man whose own infant son (and now his successor as president) had been restored to health by evaporated milk, but, unfortunately, the message had been slow in reaching the men and women who could make the most effective use of it—the pediatricians. A 1924 interview with a prominent Chicago pediatrician left a Carnation advertising man muttering to himself.

"He did not have the foggiest notion what evaporated milk was," Charlie Lewis recalled years later. "I had to insist that I didn't mean sweetened condensed milk, and then he thought I must be talking about powdered milk. He had never heard of evaporated milk's being used in infant feeding and said it never would be unless doctors could be persuaded that it was something entirely different from sweetened condensed, which had a bad reputation with the experts."

Missionaries from the Evaporated Milk Association finally converted the experts toward the end of 1931, when the American Medical Association agreed to accept the industry's major claims for its product. Evaporated milk, reported the *Journal* (December 19, 1931), was "more speedily digested" than raw or pasteurized milk and "usually less allergic." It was "the safest milk obtainable" and "equal to pasteurized milk in all important food values." It was "one of the most convenient and economical forms for milk for preparing infant feeding formulas," and in the opinion of "many pediatricians" it was also the "best form of cow's milk" for this use.

Once these pronouncements had come down from the medical mountaintop, Carnation copywriters launched a campaign designed to convince magazine readers that Carnation Milk was more than just another pretty can on chain-store shelves.

"Carnation Milk hasn't changed. . . ." declared a full-page, four-color advertisement in *Ladies' Home Journal* (May, 1932). "But how people's *ideas* about it have changed! No longer is it thought of, by those who know, as a *substitute* for ordinary milk. It is now considered *better*. . . ."

A new word had tiptoed into the text of Carnation Milk advertising copy. The word was "vitamins." Carnation Milk, *Journal* readers were assured, "supplies the same vitamins and minerals that are found in the best bottled milk." In the 1929-32 edition of *Reader's Guide to Periodical Literature* there were three and one-half columns devoted to the subject of vitamins. In the 1910-14 edition, there had been one lone entry.

* * * * *

Ladies Home Journal ad of May, 1931, noted that baby specialists "are now prescribing Carnation Milk."

In the closing years of the nineteenth century, when beriberi was widespread in the rice-eating Orient, a Dutch physiologist, Christiaan Eijkman, produced the nerve-impairment illness in chickens by feeding them polished rice. He could cure the chickens, he found, simply by giving them the hulls thrown away when the rice was polished. He hit on the mistaken notion that the hulls contained an antidote for whatever poison lurked in the polished rice.

Scurvy, as generations of sailors had known, could be warded off by sucking lemons or limes (hence the nickname, "limeys," for British tars). Guinea pigs came down with the disease when fed nothing but dried hay and oats in a 1907 experiment, and recovered when given fresh vegetables. Babies stricken with rickets made miraculous recoveries when dosed with cod-liver oil. No one know how to explain the cause and cure of the diet deficiency diseases until Casimir Funk, a Polish biochemist trained in Switzerland, discovered that to grow and live out their allotted time on earth all God's creatures needed small amounts of certain chemical substances he decided to call "vitamines."*

"The name seems to have come to stay," Dr. Wiley, father of the Pure Food and Drug Law, wrote in the *American Journal of Clinical Medicine* (May, 1919), and went on to suggest that perhaps there was "no point in medicine so confusing and conflicting as the dietaries prescribed by the attending physician in cases of illness, and likewise for children and grown persons as a preventive of disease."

* * * * *

It had been known for centuries that rickets, the bone disease that leaves children bow-legged and knock-kneed, could be prevented and cured by a daily dosage of cod liver oil, but not until 1921 could scientists explain the phenomenon. Cod liver oil turned out to be a rich source of the fourth

85

*From the Latin, *vita* (life), and *amines* (the class of chemical compounds to which vitamines were thought to belong). The "e" was dropped a few years after the word was coined in 1912.

vitamin to be identified. Vitamin D was popularly referred to as the "Sunshine Vitamin" because it is manufactured in the human body by action of the ultraviolet rays of direct sunlight on the skin.

"Modern civilization with its houses and clothes, its dark city streets and its ubiquitous smoke, dust and dirt has robbed us of much of our sunlight," James A. Tobey wrote in *Hygeia* (August, 1933), reporting on a revolutionary development in dairy science which offered the hope that rickets might someday vanish from the everyday practice of medicine.

It was thought to affect half of the children in the country in 1931, when members of the American Medical Association assembled in New York City for their annual convention. Dr. Alfred F. Hess was waiting with a paper reporting his success with a clinical test of a type of cow's milk so loaded with Vitamin D that it could protect a baby against rickets, and if the disease had already struck, it could provide a cure.

Some years earlier, in 1924, Dr. Hess and Harry Steenbock, working independently, had discovered that through irradiation with ultraviolet light certain foods, including milk, could be made to offer protection against rickets. This led to the idea of plying cattle with irradiated yeast to see if it increased the Vitamin D content of their milk. It did and, as Dr. Hess had now demonstrated, the milk worked wonders when tested on one hundred and two babies.

"Not only did it prevent rickets in these babies throughout the winter months when the disease is most prevalent, but the milk cured several cases which were in their incipience when the test started," Tobey wrote, and suggested that Vitamin D milk might "sound the knell of one of the great scourges of mankind, and in that capacity it will be one of the most important factors in the promotion of national vitality."

National vitality needed all the shoring up it could get in the bleak winter of 1932-33, when Carnation's Seattle milkmen started delivering a Vitamin D Certified Milk pro-

duced at the Carnation Milk Farms from cows fed a special ration of yeast irradiated by the Steenbock process, use of which was controlled by the Wisconsin Alumni Research Foundation. The milk was warmly endorsed by local dentists and M. D.'s. One quart, tasting like any other milk, supplied as much Vitamin D as three palate-numbing teaspoonsful of cod liver oil.

* * * * *

In the spring of 1934, when Carnation Evaporated Milk came to be enriched with Vitamin D, the company's Advertising Department went to work with Erwin, Wasey to provide an appropriate setting for the first public announcement. It was decided to engage Madame Amelita Galli-Curci for a special broadcast of the Contented Hour and have her sing the lullaby chosen by the program's followers as their favorite. Brahms' *Cradle Song (Wiegenlied)* won handily, and was duly rendered on the night of June 18.

"With a capacity audience in the studio and millions listening in outside, this special program undoubtedly accomplished its purpose, which was to attract the largest possible audience to hear about Irradiated Carnation Milk," reported *The Carnation* (July-August, 1934).

* * * * *

As one of the poker players Nan Stuart occasionally drafted to get Elbridge's thoughts off of business, Stanley D. Roberts, Carnation's advertising director, was accustomed to figuring odds, taking risks and, if luck was with him, raking in his winnings. In the depths of the Depression, when his stack of chips was running low, he gambled his eroded advertising budget on the theme of infant-feeding. Luck was with him when Professor Steenbock figured out a way to enrich evaporated milk with Vitamin D, and it was with him again shortly before the Galli-Curci broadcast when he clipped and sent to Jack Coyle, Carnation's man in Canada, a *Milwaukee Sentinel* story about a woman in an Ontario town who had just given birth to five baby girls.

"Mrs. Dionne certainly has done her duty

by Canada, so let's try to do our duty by her," Stan wrote, May 29, 1934. "Suggest you send this family two cases Tall Carnation with our compliments."

"We are glad to know that the rare record of Mrs. Dionne was brought to your attention," Jack replied two days later, and reported that two cases of the large-size cans of Carnation Milk had been dispatched to the mother in Corbeil.

On Friday, June 1, before newspaper editors awakened to the biggest human interest story since Lindbergh's flight (the *New York Times* had moved the quintuplets from page nineteen to page twenty-five), E. A. dictated a letter to Stan from his office in Seattle.

"I think you should have your representa-

tive there contact the doctor in charge of this case and sell him on the value of Carnation Milk for infant feeding, and then you should offer to furnish those babies with all the Carnation Milk they might need for the next year."

The letter came to Phil Kinzer's desk Monday, June 4, and he acknowledged it promptly ("I am writing Mr. Coyle again today following the suggestion that you have made"). In his letter to Coyle, Kinzer referred to newspaper reports that the babies were being fed on human milk and raised the possibility that their doctor, Allan R. Dafoe, might not care to make a change, but, he added, "if we could secure their cooperation in using Carnation Milk, under

The Dionne Quintuplets with Dr. Allan Dafoe in 1934.

the formulas prescribed by the doctor, it would indeed be wonderful publicity."

Kinzer talked things over with his seventh-floor associates and decided to send Frank C. Wilson, Carnation's liaison with the medical profession, to Canada. Wilson took a train to Toronto, where he had a pleasant talk with Dr. W. A. Dafoe, whose brother in Callander had made medical history by keeping the quintuplets alive. In none of the thirty cases recorded in the preceding five hundred years had an infant lived out the first hour.

"He courteously, firmly and almost pleadingly advised against disturbing his brother, who has been inundated with hundreds of persons interested in every conceivable infant product—he mentioned a man from California who had traveled all the way to Callander to promote a self-locking safety pin," Wilson reported, and Carnation's Toronto office, acting on Dr. W. A. Dafoe's suggestion, sent a letter instead of an emissary to Callander.

"We understand that the babies are being given breast milk feedings and are gradually gaining," Jack Coyle wrote. "You are certainly to be congratulated upon your success in this most unusual feeding case. We recognize the superiority of breast milk feeding and advocate Carnation Milk feeding only in its absence—this in spite of the enthusiasm for Carnation formulas because of their soft curd and digestibility which are so similar to those of breast milk. . . ."

Some months later, on September 24, E. A.'s offer of a free supply of Carnation Milk for one year was tendered Dr. Allan Dafoe. The letter was referred to W. A. Alderson, a public-spirited Canadian who identified himself in his reply as the "official guardian" of the five babies, with responsibility for "the business part of the Dionne Quintuplet Fund."

"The Dionne babies are still being given mothers' milk which is being received from the Sick Children's Hospital, Toronto," Alderson wrote. "Just as soon as cow's milk is being used, we will be interested in your offer to supply Carnation Milk free for a period of one year. However, it would be necessary to know whether this fact would be used in connection with advertising. We have made many contracts for various lines of supplies and some fair amounts of money have been received, all of which are deposited in the Dionne Quintuplet Fund for the care of these celebrated children."

On November 21 Alderson and Carnation's representatives reached an agreement whereby $3,000 was turned over to the Dionne Quintuplet Fund and a gift of $500 was presented to Dr. Dafoe to help pay for a car (his had been stolen) and a vacation.

"The quintuplets have shown considerable improvement during the last week," Louise de Kiriline, nurse in charge, reported two days after Christmas. "They have been fed a formula in which Carnation Milk constitutes the sole form of milk. The babies are very lively and after having taken their full meal they generally fall contentedly asleep. . . ."

* * * * *

On the same day the quintuplets' head nurse was writing her overdue testimonial (the babies had been on Carnation Milk since November 27), Stanley Roberts, in Milwaukee, was dictating a letter to the Toronto office speculating on "just how we could make the most of our announcement that the Dionne 'quints' were being fed on Carnation Milk." He was leaning toward the idea of using the Carnation Contented Hour as his forum, and he rather hoped Dr. Dafoe would be available.

He wasn't, so the Toronto office made arrangements with Charles Jennings, a news commentator for the Canadian Radio Commission, to go to Callander, see the babies, interview Dr. Dafoe and prepare a report for the Contented Hour. On April 8, 1935, a week before the big broadcast, Carnation distributed to its sales representatives a four-page, red-and-white broadside, with the headlines: DIONNES ON THE AIR! DIONNES IN THE MAGAZINES! MORE CARNATION BUSINESS FOR YOU!

"This is one of the most dramatic events

Theater lobbies across the continent were filled with cans of
Carnation Milk as salesmen built displays to promote a movie on the Quintuplets.

in the history of evaporated milk," the circular pointed out, and called attention to the forthcoming broadcast over a 48-station NBC hookup and to an advertisement (BY APPOINTMENT TO THE DIONNE QUINTUPLETS) which would appear in the May 4 issue of the *Saturday Evening Post*, and also in *Parents*, *Hygeia*, *Good Housekeeping*, *True Story* and *Holland's* (the magazines had a total circulation of over seven million).

"Last November," announced the brief text beneath sepia photographs of the babies, "Dr. A. R. Dafoe started the Dionne Quintuplets on Carnation Milk. Ever since, they have been thriving on it—gaining famously, right along. . . . Many noted baby specialists, you know, prescribe this pure, nourishing, super-digestible milk—irradiated for 'sunshine' vitamin D. . . ."

The response was enough to turn the head of any advertising department. "The great-

est publicity campaign we have ever seen" (Richmond, Virginia). "Nothing short of a complete 'knock-out' " (New York). "Permit me to congratulate you on the scoop" (Cleveland). "The best talking point we have had in a long, long time about Carnation" (Nashville, Tennessee). "We will need no urging to do our part in the spreading of this news" (Philadelphia). "One of the most telling pieces of advertising that we ever heard of" (Wilmington, North Carolina).

*   *   *   *   *

The Contented Hour on April 15, 1935, began as usual with the tinkling of cowbells, a rendition by the quartet and orchestra of *Wait Till the Cows Come Home*, and the sound of synthetic mooing (one of the Dionnes' favorite toys was a Carnation Milk can that mooed when turned upside down and then set right again).

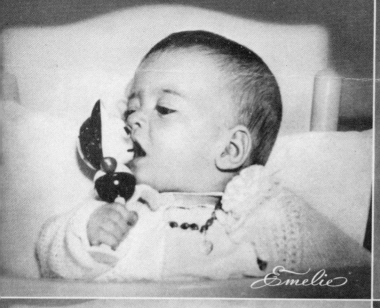

Emelie

Annette

Yvonne

Marie

Cecile

BY APPOINTMENT TO THE

Dionne Quintuplets

Last November, Dr. A. R. Dafoe started the Dionne Quintuplets on Carnation Milk. Ever since, they have been thriving on it — gaining famously, right along. * * * Many noted baby specialists, you know, prescribe this pure, nourishing, super-digestible milk — irradiated for "sunshine" vitamin D. * * * Carnation Company, Milwaukee and Seattle; Carnation Company, Ltd., Toronto.

IRRADIATED
CARNATION MILK

"FROM CONTENTED COWS"

Carnation
From Contented Cows

IRRADIATED
MILK

BY SPECIAL APPOINTMENT

"To the Quintuplets and Canada we dedicate this program," Jean Paul King announced, and Morgan Eastman swung into a Canadian medley (*Vive La Canadienne, Maple Leaf Forever, Alouette*).

"I have just spent an afternoon chatting with Dr. Dafoe in his home," reported Charles Jennings. "He's told me of the drama of that night, when one tired country doctor and a few neighborly assistants were suddenly confronted with a problem that would have taxed the facilities of the greatest city hospital. The babies weren't expected for two months. Nothing was ready. A tea kettle on the stove was the only hospital equipment. Neighbor women took blankets and tablecloths and warmed them in the oven for the babies—whose combined weight was only 11½ pounds. . . .

"Nurse de Kiriline tells me the babies were started on Carnation Milk last November, and that it has agreed with them perfectly. Now here's the very latest! The babies have graduated from the bottle. They're drinking their Carnation out of mugs now—diluted to whole-milk richness. Yes sir, the quints are certainly growing up."

*   *   *   *   *

Again Stanley Roberts was showered with enthusiastic letters. "A ten strike," wrote A. J. Izzard of the Seattle office, and a salesman reported from Duluth that he had "never heard so much favorable 'consumer comment' on any program or advertising." "It has increased our pride in Carnation Milk," wrote a Buffalo, New York food broker. "Very well done and should prove to be an outstanding piece of advertising, not only for Carnation but for the evaporated milk industry," declared Alfred Ghormley, and Frank Wilson, checking in from Toronto on his way to Callander, had some more kind words about the campaign.

"It seems I am getting real chummy with Dr. P. C. Carson, pediatrician, Wichita, Kansas. You will be interested in a comment written in his last letter: 'I have seen the Carnation advertisement on the quintuplets in *Parents Magazine, Saturday Evening Post* and one or two medical journals and I think it is excellently done. The picture of the well-known babies is sufficient to attract one's attention and the advertising part is so very dignified in both message and set-up that one is glad to read it also. I have only commendation for it. I am truly quite sincere both in my admiration for the way the advertisement is done and for the product itself.'"

In Canada, with its long winters and short stretches of direct sunlight, there was an even greater need for irradiated milk. Production began at the Aylmer condensery in January, 1935, but public announcement was withheld until spring, because Jack Coyle could see no point in advertising something he couldn't deliver to snow-bound parts of the country. The news was broken on the April 15 broadcast of the Contented Hour, and two days later fifty-three Canadian newspapers with a circulation of 1,400,000 carried large advertisements announcing "the Improved Carnation Milk, Irradiated for Sunshine Vitamin D."

"All in all, 1935 looks like a big year for Carnation in Canada," reported *The Carnation* (May-June, 1935). "We have irradiated Carnation, the only irradiated evaporated milk with a national sale as yet. We have bigger and better advertising. We have the marvelous Dionne story to tell. And we already have a gain in sales of which the Canadian sales force is properly proud."

On May 27, the eve of the quintuplets' first birthday, the chef at Chicago's Palmer House whipped up a seven-foot cake for the "contented babies." It was put on exhibit at NBC's Studio A and the Contented Hour's audience joined in singing, *Happy Birthday To You.* Someone had come up with an acronym made up of the initials of the five babies, Marie (MAY), Yvonne (YOU), Annette (ALWAYS), Emelie (ENJOY) and Cecile (CONTENTMENT).

91

8
End Of An Era

*"It was 58 years ago today
that Mother and I were married
at four o'clock Eastern Time. While
this is a memorable day for me, my thoughts
have gone back to that happy day and
many other happy years, and
especially to our
Golden Wedding Anniversary in 1934."*

E. A. STUART TO HIS SON,
NOVEMBER 13, 1942.

MORE THAN FOUR THOUSAND members of E. A. Stuart's corporate family were gathered around radios in their homes and in Carnation condenseries, fresh milk and ice cream plants, cereal mills and sales offices on the night of November 12, 1934, when the Contented Hour looked back half a century to the autumn he crossed the continent and married Mary Horner.

"Fifty years ago," recalled the program's announcer, "Chester A. Arthur was President of the United States; Robert Todd Lincoln was in the Cabinet. Life wasn't so complex then. Pleasures were simple and friendly. Radio and movies weren't even dreamed of."

The day after the Golden Wedding broadcast the couple appeared before Dr. Stewart MacLennan, pastor of the First Presbyterian Church of Hollywood, and, in the presence of family, friends and business associates, E. A. and Mary reaffirmed their marriage vows. When they returned to their North June Street home, they found it filled with flowers. Three hundred telegrams and a thousand letters had poured in from around the world.

Elbridge and Nan were on hand for the reception that evening, along with Katherine and Harry Stibbs and their two daughters, Mary and Ethelmae. It was one of those evenings a family comes to cherish with the passage of time, like a group photograph taken before the intervention of death. Katherine would die the following September, as her father entered his eightieth year, and in August, 1937, at the age of forty-two, Nan would slip quietly away in her sleep.

"Seldom does one see two people as closely bound in love and devotion as you and Nan," Alfred Ghormley wrote Elbridge from a hospital bed in Rochester, Minnesota, where he was battling arthritis. "I know this and often thought you enjoyed the happiest married life of anyone I knew—Nan always at your side to help and strengthen you."

As for himself, Alfred reported, he was regaining his strength after eight weeks in bed, but at times he felt discouraged by the slow pace of his progress. Fortunately, his knees now appeared to be all right ("arthritis in one's knees is bad business"). He looked forward to getting away in a couple of weeks for a month or so in the desert before returning to work.

"Hope everything in the business is going

*Shirley Temple holds reins of five-gaited pony
given to her by E. A. Stuart on December 20, 1936. Picture
was taken at Carnation Stable in Pomona, California.*

on quite well," he wrote. "How I hate not to be carrying my end of the load."

The business was, indeed, going on quite well. It had continued to grow and prosper with each new year of Elbridge's administration. In 1933, flying the Blue Eagle of the NRA (National Recovery Administration), Carnation had more employees working fewer hours for higher pay, but, even so, it reported net earnings of $1,762,214, and in the same year it started to build two evaporated milk plants in Ohio and a can factory in Gustine, California.

Two years later it had picked up a couple of new condenseries in Wisconsin, started work on another in Sulphur Springs, Texas, and completed a can factory at Mount Vernon, Washington. Its overseas affiliate, General Milk, had moved into the British Isles, setting up a condensery employing a hundred grateful Scotsmen at College Mains, Dumfries.

By the end of 1938, when Elbridge forced himself to make one of his dreaded public appearances by speaking on the Contented Hour's Christmas show, the company's net earnings were nearly two million dollars and stockholders were looking forward to an extra dividend of fifty cents in addition to their regular dividend of one dollar.

"Glad to advise that Alfred Ghormley seems to be making progress though slow," E. A. wrote to Elbridge after the broadcast ("Your delivery was fine, every word you uttered was clear and distinct"). The change for the better in Alfred's health was quite noticeable in his weekly visits, E. A. thought, and added with pleasure, "He comes to see me almost every Saturday afternoon and we always have a very enjoyable time talking socially as well as from a business standpoint."

When the board of directors met at E. A.'s Los Angeles home in March, 1939, Alfred was present not only for the business sessions, but for the social gatherings as well, and "showed no unfavorable reaction to this strenuous activity," reported *The Carnation* (April-June, 1939). In its following issue,

it carried the good news of his appearance at the Albers sales meeting in San Francisco in May. "His improvement in health was a great happiness to everyone."

Alfred, living with the hope of someday being able to move back to Seattle with Elizabeth and the children, looked on his Los Angeles office as a makeshift arrangement. E. A., sunning himself in his garden, also considered the sprawling, Southern California metropolis as a stopping-off place, not as home. Both men sighed for the giant conifers and the black-and-white cattle of the Snoqualmie Valley.

"The Carnation Milk Farm is a source of particular pride to me for when I acquired it in 1910, the 1,600 acres were virtually all virgin timberland," E. A. recalled as Carnation moved toward its fortieth anniversary; "now most of it is cleared and under a high state of cultivation. The herd of over six hundred head of purebred Holsteins comprises world record cows for conformation as well as for milk and butter production."

* * * * *

At the time E. A. started converting his unpromising acreage on the banks of the Snoqualmie to a world-famous Holstein-Friesian stock farm, no cow of any breed had ever produced 30,000 pounds of milk in one year. By 1936 five cows had rung up records in excess of 35,886 pounds, and four of them were Carnation cows.

To put these figures in perspective for city-bred colleagues, Merton Moore prepared a brief essay for *The Carnation* (April-June, 1936) on the history of man's dealings with his natural foster-mother. Back in the mists of time ("long before anyone ever heard of the New Deal"), Moore explained, cows were designed to produce only enough milk to nourish their offspring. Once the calves were weaned, the cows dried up.

Several millennia later, primitive husbandmen succeeded in breeding cows capable of producing enough milk not only for their calves, but for their owners' children as well. Eventually, through careful selection, cows were developed to the point

94

Jackie Cooper, young screen star, places double crown on
Carnation Ormsby Butter King ("Daisy") after she set world's records
for both milk and butter production in 1936. Cooper is helped by
Carl Gockerell, who milked the champion throughout
the year's test. E. H. Stuart is in background.

where they could manufacture more than 700 pounds of milk a year. By 1936, the average American cow was turning out 4,030 pounds of milk, containing 158 pounds of butterfat. In that same year, a new world's champion in the Carnation herd gave 3,592 pounds of milk, containing 132 pounds of butterfat, in a single month.

Her name was Carnation Ormsby Butter King and she was commonly called "Daisy." Her 365-day record for the production of milk (38,606.6 pounds) and butterfat (1,402 pounds) was set at midnight, February 11-12, 1936. The following Monday evening, as Daisy bedded down in her stall, Carl Gockerell saw to it that her radio was turned to the Contented Hour when Carnation's Vice President Kinzer stepped to the NBC microphone to discuss the achievement. First he was asked to translate 38,606.6 pounds into household terms.

"It is 18,000 quarts," he replied. "That is twenty-four years' milk supply for the average family of four. Or, this cow's one-year butter production would take care of the family's butter needs for twenty-four years also. That is a lot of butter and milk. Just

imagine fifty quart bottles of milk delivered to your home in the morning. That is what this cow averaged every day for a whole year."

Ordinarily a cow's production of milk slows down in the fourth or fifth month after the birth of her calf, and by the ninth month her udder has just about run dry. Daisy's calf had been born on January 28, 1935. A month later (February 27), she had given 123 pounds of milk in one day. At the end of September, when her calf was nine months old, she was averaging 103.4 pounds a day. On the final day of her year-long test she produced 94.4 pounds of milk.

In the presence of Elbridge Stuart, Carl Gockerell and a parcel of press photographers, Daisy was crowned "the greatest cow in the world" by a young movie star, Jackie Cooper. Six years later, with Carl again presiding at the udder, one of the champion's half-sisters in the Carnation herd, Carnation Ormsby Madcap Fayne, set a new record by completing a year's test with 41,943.3 pounds of milk, an average of thirteen gallons a day. Her 1,392.4 pounds of butterfat, however, fell short of Daisy's record.

* * * * *

95

"Capper," as Carl called the new champion, wound up her historic test at 5:30 A.M., May 21, 1942. To celebrate the achievement, E. A. invited some thirty friends and business associates to his Los Angeles home for a "cocktail party."

"The 'cocktail' served was some of the milk taken from her noon milking on May 20th and sent from the farm by air express, arriving at my home that night at eleven o'clock," he wrote in his memoirs. "We all joined in a toast to 'the greatest cow that ever lived.' "

Five years had gone by since E. A. had last set foot on the farm. He still talked of paying it at least one more visit. At times, reliving his years as a Holstein breeder, he must have chuckled at the memory of his meeting with that mean, homely, bargain basement bull, King Segis Tenth, who had sired Carnation's first world champion, Segis Pietertje Prospect. The old five-dollar bull's grandson, Matador Segis Ormsby, had sired the two heifers, Daisy and Capper, who had grown up to set new records.

96

Capper, the current queen of the Carnation herd, had been born to an aristocratic matron, Cascade Madcap Violet Fayne Second, who had just turned nineteen the spring her daughter became the first cow to produce more than 40,000 pounds of milk in a single year. As Madcaps, the new champion and her mother belonged to one of the most remarkable families in cow history.

Their lineage went back to a dairy farm in Washington's Yakima Valley, where William Todd had established his purebred herd with four registered Holsteins, one a cow named Santa Cruz. At the time she gave birth to a frisky heifer, Todd happened to

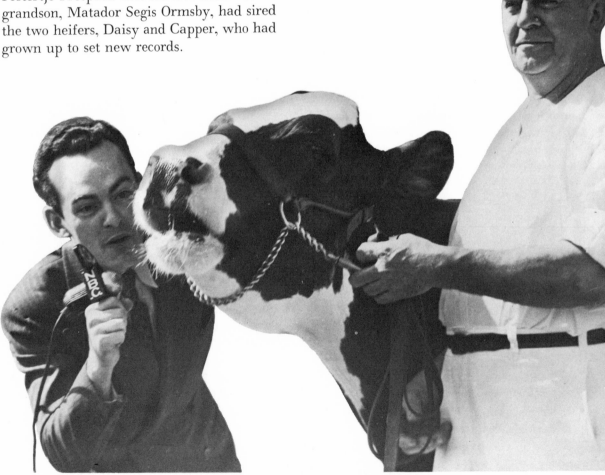

Broadcasting over NBC's National Farm and Home Hour,
Carnation Ormsby Madcap Fayne ("Capper") moos for the audience after
Carl Gockerell, right, milked her to a world's record of 41,943 pounds (May, 1942).

be reading a novel dealing with a harum-scarum character nicknamed Madcap Violet. He named the heifer after the book's heroine.

Madcap Violet's daughter was named for her mother. In due time, the daughter was bred to one of the finest bulls of his day, Sir Johanna Ruth Fayne. Living in the shadow of the Cascade Mountains, Todd named the resultant heifer Cascade Madcap Violet Fayne, thus following the Holstein-Friesian custom of bestowing a first name to identify the herd to which an animal belongs and the others to indicate the family from which it springs.

Cascade Madcap Violet Fayne Second was born April 8, 1923, purchased by E. A. Stuart and brought to Carnation's stock farm. In the spring of 1942, when her daughter succeeded to the world's championship, the old Madcap dowager was still moving sedately about the farm, a historic figure. Merton Moore chose her to illustrate how correct feeding and scientific breeding, as practiced and preached by Carnation Milk Farms, had made the new world records possible.

"This old cow," he wrote in 1942, "has four daughters at the Carnation Farm that average higher than any four daughters of any other cow that ever lived, and others coming on that look fully as good. She is, in fact, the only cow of any breed to have four daughters each with over 1,000 pounds of butterfat in a year. She has had eight daughters and six sons, a total of fourteen offspring in the Carnation herd. Her daughters are not only noted for what they have produced, but for what they have reproduced. Her sons and grandsons head herds in Portugal, Canada, Ecuador, Mexico, and Peru, having been purchased by breeders there to cross on their cattle for improved offspring."

Italy got its first cattle from the United States in January, 1930, when three Carnation bulls and four cows arrived in Rome after a two-month voyage on the *S. S. Feltre*. Eight years later, French dairymen read an astonishing article in one of their leading industry organs. Thirty-two daughters of a Carnation bull servicing the cows on a large dairy farm near Rome had been tested, and on their first freshening, they had produced 63 percent more milk than their mothers. On their second freshening, the figure had shot up to 119 percent.

"They prove that the Carnation bloodline is indeed having an important influence on the dairy industry throughout the world," noted *The Carnation* (July-September, 1938).

* * * * *

The world's dairymen were also benefiting from a new Carnation-Albers product based on a new principle in the feeding of barnyard animals. Merton Moore, who had sat in on the discussions leading to the development of Calf Manna, described it in the fortieth anniversary number of *The Carnation* in the fall of 1939.

"Calf Manna, a product which improves appetite, aids assimilation, and makes the feeds used with it digest better, was developed at Carnation Farms. And today, like Carnation bulls, it is being used in Europe, Asia, Africa, South America, Mexico, and throughout the United States. Any dairy farmer, anywhere in the world, can start with what he has, use a Carnation sire, raise the calves on Calf Manna, and today be more likely to succeed than was the case twenty years ago."

Calf Manna was being used not only to produce outstanding calves, but colts, lambs, kids and pigs as well. Even Moore, who had no need to be sold on the product's merits, was impressed when he visited a Texas ranch and looked at some four hundred and fifty lambs that, at the age of six weeks, had been written off by their owner as a total loss because of their inability to translate food into growth. Then they were given one-tenth of a pound of Calf Manna in each day's ration of oats, corn and molasses (at a cost of one-half cent a day per lamb). Three weeks later Moore looked them over.

"They had been transformed from a bedraggled group of sickly 'critters' to as fine a

The Albers research laboratory in Seattle, shown in 1933,
developed new products which were tested at Carnation Farm.

group of lambs as you would care to see," he reported in *The Carnation* (July-October, 1940). "They were fat and round as butter balls, several of them were almost as big as the ewes."

Perry Workley, manager of the Columbian Steel Tank Company's ranch in Blanca, Colorado, had been showing cattle for twenty years when his steer, Columbian Red Top, was selected as Grand Champion at the 1940 American Royal Livestock Show in Kansas City.

"I would never try to feed cattle without it," he told C. B. (Chet) Batchelder, eastern divisional sales manager for Calf Manna.

* * * * *

In 1929 when Fred Karlsrud went to work for Albers Bros. Milling Company as a sack-sewer, ($5 a day) the company was shipping its limited production of dog food to Alaska.

"It was made of meat meal and gruel grains, and the Alaskans used to cook it with fish," Fred recalled forty-five years later, after retiring as Albers' production manager. "The company was also making a pelleted food for chickens at the time of the Carnation merger, and that gave Merton

Moore the idea of turning out a dog food in pellet form."

Albers researchers started their experiments at Carnation Farms with whatever stray dogs they could outrun in the back streets of Seattle. The mongrels were housed in unsightly, improvised cages with chicken-wire runs. The canine shanties were offensive to the Carnation eye, and the employment of casually bred test animals ran counter to the company's traditions. Within a year, new kennels were flung up and the only dogs in residence were pedigreed Great Danes, Scottish Terriers and Golden Retrievers.

"The new dog food which has been developed after three and a half years of experimental work at Carnation Farm is known as 'Friskies,'" Merton Moore announced in *The Carnation* (January-March, 1936).

"A radical departure in dog foods," Alfred Ghormley explained in the magazine's 1939 anniversary issue, writing as president of Albers Bros. Milling Company. "For the first time Friskies brings owners a cube-type food that is a complete ration for dogs."

The original Carnation Farms Kennels, where the nutritional properties of Friskies products have been tested on forty generations.

Father Bernard Hubbard, Alaskan explorer, was one of the first people to appreciate the convenience and nutrition of Friskies.

One of the new product's most vocal boosters turned out to be Father Bernard R. Hubbard, "The Glacier Priest," who depended on Friskies to fuel the pack dogs that hauled him around Alaska on his research visits to the Eskimos. He usually took along an extra supply for his hosts' dogs.

"Even the bolshevik dogs of Russian Siberia enjoyed them in a big way," noted a Friskies sales official, H. A. Hoffman, writing in *The Carnation* (July-September, 1939).

* * * * *

On September 6, 1939, five days after Hitler's invasion of Poland, Elbridge and his three sons attended the dinner given at E. A.'s home to celebrate Carnation's fortieth anniversary. Speaking for the directors and executives gathered around the table, Phil Kinzer recalled the company's early struggles and E. A. responded by predicting that the company would enjoy even greater op-

A group of old friends interrupted their celebration of the company's 40th anniversary long enough to have this formal portrait taken at the Los Angeles home of E. A. Stuart on September 6, 1939. Seated, from left, J. F. Douglas, E. A. Stuart, E. H. Stuart and P. G. Kinzer. Standing, from left, G. R. Sibley, A. M. Ghormley, J. S. Wilkinson, W. C. Cross and S. D. Roberts.

portunities in the future than in its first four decades.

"I shall make a date with each of you," he said in conclusion. "Ten years from to-day, on the occasion of our Fiftieth Anniversary, I want each of you to be my guest, in my home here in Los Angeles. Don't forget the date—September 6, 1949."

Once the party was over, however, when he was left alone with the afflictions of old age, he may have been less cavalier about his mortality and, perhaps, a shade less eager to shamble through another ten years of sightlessness and the terrible loneliness left in June by his wife's death.

"I know that this season of the year brings you some sad memories of dear Nan and dear Mother as it does to me, especially as it recalls some of the very happy times we had together in the past along with dear Katherine and her family," E. A. wrote Elbridge the day after Christmas, 1940. "I am glad to know that you were being so brave about it and I assure you that I am doing everything possible to carry on."

In a separate letter, dictated the same day, E. A. expressed his gratification "as your father to know that you are directing the organization in such a capable way," and suggested that "1941 should be an extremely active year for business, although we do not know what turn this war situation may take, or whether this country will be engaged in it."

* * * * *

A year and a half after the bombing of Pearl Harbor, when evaporated milk was rationed, the Office of Price Administration explained that it was "the foundation for many of the formulas given by physicians today" and, if unobtainable, its lack "would endanger the health of many millions of our youngest citizens." The babies who gurgled, slept and bawled between daily administrations of evaporated milk formulas turned out to be taller, sturdier and longer-lived than their parents because of the revolutionary changes the second World War brought about in the American diet.

"Soldiers from mountain and farm areas who had grown up on corn pone, fried pork, hot biscuits, and potatoes learned the uses of leafy vegetables, orange juice, and milk," Max Lerner notes in *America as a Civilization* (1957). "The heavy reliance on grains and breads shifted to meats and fish for large sections of the population who had eaten little of either; the reliance on fats and carbohydrates also shifted; the protein content of the diet increased; the words 'proteins,' 'calories' and 'vitamins' came into everyday use. The measure of the change was shown by the fact that vigorous American males—at college and in Army camps—were not ashamed to drink milk: while some called this a sign of the American male's dependence on his mother, the less tortured conclusion is simply that Americans became nutrition-conscious."

While Rosie the Riveter climbed over tail-sections of fighter-bombers, women in crisp white dresses of modest length were taking over jobs in Carnation receiving stations and condenseries which custom had reserved for men. To the distress of male holdouts against sexual desegregation, some of the women were on the receiving porch, carrying out the exacting responsibility of inspecting, weighing and drawing samples of the in-

coming supply of fresh milk. Others were at work on labelling crews and running tests for butterfat and quality control.

"Men who perform these tasks at Carnation are considered skilled craftsmen," noted the editor of *The Carnation* (January-March, 1943). "That the women who are doing these jobs at Carnation are proving to be the equal of the men whose places they have filled is a fine commentary on their work."

* * * * *

Overseas, often hundreds and even thousands of miles from a dairy farm, Americans in uniform were drinking milk from what they called the "armored cow." Army dieticians preferred evaporated milk to cream for use in coffee, Marie Balsey reported in *Hygeia* (April, 1945), not only because it was easier to ship and store, but also because of its nutritive advantages.

"Undiluted evaporated milk contains all the many food values of milk in the same proportion as they occur in the original milk from the cow, but in double amounts. It is higher than cream in the food essentials found chiefly below the cream line, such as protein, calcium and riboflavin.* Calcium and riboflavin are two food essentials which milk products are depended on to provide in the serviceman's diet."

On a March day in 1945, Ms Balsey found when she looked over some of the master menus prepared in Washington for army kitchens around the world, thirty-eight cans of evaporated milk would be needed for every hundred men to be fed. It would be served at breakfast for use in coffee. It would be on the table for the same purpose again at lunch, and would also be used in the gravy made to accompany roast pork and mashed potatoes. For supper, it would turn up in corn pudding, pumpkin pie and cocoa.

Mess sergeants made sour cream dressings for cole slaw with undiluted evaporated milk, sugar and vinegar. An imaginative

101

*Riboflavin, or Vitamin B$_2$, is found in egg whites and in whey, the watery part of fresh milk that separates from the curds in the cheese-making process.

chef de cuisine in the South Pacific came up with sour milk griddle cakes one morning by adding lemon juice to evaporated milk. Having no baking powder at hand, he made do with a mixture of salt and soda available in G. I. toothpowder.

Sergeant Charles Sharples, former superintendent of Carnation's Clarksburg, West Virginia, plant, landed on the coast of Normandy in the summer of 1944 and, as his outfit filed into the ancient town of Carentan, he caught sight of the Carnation condensery and can factory Phil Kinzer had modernized in the early 1920s.

"It was quite a thrill to see all the familiar machinery and equipment," Sergeant Sharples wrote the folks back home. "I recognized the plant the first time by seeing two can elevators standing among the ruins. The boiler room, generator, porch and laboratory were not hurt. They are making butter. The can plant, labelling and heat rooms, as well as sterilizer and filling department, are in a complete ruin. There's about one-third of the old crew working, mostly women . . .

"It's been wet as hell the last couple of days, but believe it might clear up tonight,

102

LIFE *ad, January 10, 1944.*

I'm feeling fine, but am ready to come home any time."

* * * * *

"Our business during the last ten years has progressed to a very enviable position," E. A. told Carnation directors at the board's February, 1942, meeting, the tenth since Elbridge's succession to the presidency. "Ten years ago we thought we were enjoying a really big business, but today you can look back and see that our company was really a very small concern."

Back in 1935, three years after E. A. had stepped aside for his son, Carnation's directors and stockholders had rejoiced at the sight of a net profit of $1,140,211 on combined sales of nearly $45,000,000. Now in 1942, after shelling out $4,165,000 in federal taxes, the company had ended up with consolidated earnings of $2,546,654 on net sales for all units of $112,719,268.

"As the business grew," Elbridge recalled late in life, "I often heard my father say that the company was only in its infancy and that it had a great future. Even just prior to his death in 1944, he was still of the same opinion."

Elbridge's youngest son, Dwight, looked in on the old man one day in the closing months of his life and found him, in his late eighties, bursting with plans for the coming years.

"You know, I can't afford to die," he said. "I've got too much to do."

Among other things, he wanted to dispose of some of the treasures he had laid up on earth. In 1937 he had established the Elbridge A. Stuart Foundation, "the income therefrom to be used for religious, charitable and Christian educational purposes." Four years later, on the fifty-seventh anniversary of his marriage, he broadened its scope by creating the Elbridge and Mary Stuart Foundation to assist "organizations of re-

Dumfries (Scotland) Plant Superintendent D. B. Rogers watches while the Duchess of Kent receives a bouquet of carnations after an official tour of the condensery in 1944.

ligious, charitable, educational, scientific or public welfare nature, including those for the prevention of cruelty to children or animals."

Going over his worldly accounts, preparing to leave with his debts paid and his books balanced, he got to fretting about a niggling lawsuit his attorneys had long ago settled out of court for a few hundred dollars. The cause of the litigation, a welsher named Cox, had blown into El Paso one day with a letter of introduction and asked E. A. to sign the bond he was required to post in order to carry out a contract with the federal government.

E. A. had introduced Cox to two brothers, M. J. and Ernest Kohlberg, who sold tobacco just three doors from his place of business in the Mundy Building. Cox had volunteered to buy his groceries from E. A. and his tobacco from the Kohlbergs, and they had put their names to his bond. Later, after E. A.'s departure from Texas, Cox had failed to make good on his contract and the government had applied to the signers of his bond for satisfaction. E. A. and the Kohlbergs had each been dunned for $553.91.

"Kohlberg Bros.," E. A. recalled shortly before his death, "claimed that I promised to hold them harmless when they signed the bond, but I had no recollection of this and did not consider this correct. Kohlberg Bros. then brought suit against me for $553.91, which they had paid, which, together with interest, attorneys' fees and court costs, amounted to a total of $836.40. Kohlberg Bros., through their attorney, offered to compromise with my attorneys in El Paso for one-half of that amount, or $418.20, which I paid in October of 1905."

Now, thirty-eight years later, the settlement weighed heavily on E. A.'s mind. He had his confidential secretary, Hal Ruddick, dig up his file on the case, and then inquire about the Kohlbergs. Both brothers were dead, and one had left no children. The other Kohlberg, however, had been survived by three children, two in El Paso and one in New York. E. A. dictated a letter to be sent to each of them, along with a personal check.

"Recently," he informed the astonished recipients, "it has been on my mind that Kohlberg Bros. may have sincerely believed that I intended to hold them harmless inasmuch as I introduced Mr. Cox to them. Out of respect to the memory of the cordial relations which existed between Kohlberg Bros. and myself, I have come to the conclusion that I would prefer to discharge any moral responsibility I might have had in this transaction by paying the balance of the Kohlberg Bros.' claim of $418.20 plus interest at the rate of 4% per annum from 1905 to date, amounting to $635.74, making a total of $1,053.94."

"The most interesting and surprising letter that I have ever received," one of the heirs wrote back.

On Saturday, September 4, 1943, E. A. dictated a reminder to Elbridge that Monday would mark Carnation's forty-fourth anniversary. "Little did I think at that time that in the course of forty-four years, the Pacific Coast Condensed Milk Company, as it was known in the early days, would ever attain the record and position which it is now enjoying in the evaporated milk industry. . . ." He expressed the hope that Carnation employees would be reminded of what "the 6th of September stands for in the history of Carnation Evaporated Milk."

In the early morning hours of January 14, 1944, he grew restless, his exhausted body and spirit no longer able to hold off death. In its obituary, *The Western Confectioner Ice Cream News* (February, 1944) pointed out that E. A. belonged "with a group of American industrialists who rose to their zenith in the six decades following the Civil War, men who took the raw products of the country and fashioned them into volume merchandise which could be distributed to the masses of the people. The high standard of American living, a standard beyond anything the world ever previously had known, probably would never have been achieved without courageous and imaginative leaders of this type."

CARNATION COMPANY
1060 STUART BUILDING
SEATTLE, WASHINGTON

E.A. STUART
CHAIRMAN OF THE BOARD

161 North June Street
Los Angeles 4, Calif.
September 4, 1943.

Mr. E. H. Stuart
Carnation Company
Seattle 11, Washington

My dear Elbridge:

Next Monday, the 6th of September, will be
the 44th anniversary of the founding of Carnation Company
and the manufacture of Carnation Evaporated Milk, and when
I recall to my mind the many hardships which I had to en-
counter in starting this business, little did I think at
that time that in the course of 44 years, the Pacific Coast
Condensed Milk Company, as it was known in the early days,
would ever attain the record and position which it is now
enjoying in the evaporated milk industry, and to be known
as the largest seller of evaporated milk under the brand
name CARNATION.

All of this plainly shows that by having a
first class article it has won a firm place among the con-
suming public and has attained this goal under principles
above reproach and handled by high class employees, all of
which is very gratifying to me.

I hope a great number of Carnation employees
will be reminded as to what next Monday, the 6th of September
stands for in the history of Carnation Evaporated Milk.

With much love and best wishes I am as ever
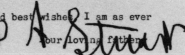
Your loving father,

Part III

The Explosive Years
1949-1974

9
Growth In The Sun

*"Our company's action in establishing
headquarters in Los Angeles is not just a move—
it is a consolidation of general executive
management under one roof
in order to achieve greater operating efficiency."*

The Carnation,
July-August, 1948.

DURING E. A. STUART'S HEYDAY, Carnation's command post was located wherever the Founding Father happened to be at any given moment. By the end of the second world war, the company had long since ceased to be a one man, one product operation, but it had never got around to establishing a home office where policymakers could be quickly assembled. Lines of authority crisscrossed two executive offices (Seattle and Milwaukee) and three division headquarters: Evaporated Milk (Oconomowoc), Fresh Milk and Ice Cream (Los Angeles) and Albers Milling (Seattle), along with the home office of the Carnation-Pet overseas affiliate, General Milk (New York).

"Elbridge Stuart realized that we couldn't operate that way," recalls Chairman of the Board Olson, "but the war came along and all plans for a general office had to be shelved. When it was over, plans were revived and it was simply a question of where the office should be."

"It was decided that it should be located on the Pacific Coast, due to the large investment of the company in that area," Elbridge explained some years later. "The question was whether it should be Seattle, San Francisco or Los Angeles."

"One of the important reasons we decided on Los Angeles," Olson says, "was that it was a good place for advertising. That's where the talent was."

Los Angeles was the nation's most important center for network radio and seemed clearly destined to dominate the new rival advertising medium, television. As for marketing, jet-age salesmen based in Los Angeles could cover the globe in less time than it had taken E. A.'s contemporaries to get around a single state.

"Carnation has purchased an entire city block in Los Angeles on the north side of Wilshire Boulevard, three blocks east of La Brea Avenue," reported *The Carnation* (July-August, 1947).

By January 15, 1948, when ground was broken, temporary accommodations had been found in Los Angeles for displaced executives from the Milwaukee, Oconomowoc and Seattle offices. Elbridge Stuart and his key associates had taken over the Fresh Milk offices in the General of America Building two blocks west of the headquarters site. Fresh Milk had moved with Albers and Evaporated Milk to the new Rexall Building at the corner of Beverly and La Cienega Boulevards. In March they were joined by

La Brea

Wilshire

Highland

In 1949 the new World Headquarters looked like a skyscraper in the largely-residential Wilshire district.

General Milk, its executive feathers still ruffled at having to leave New York.

"Carnation has become a highly diversified and far-flung organization, with business operations reaching into distant corners of the earth," Paul H. Willis, Carnation's general advertising director, explained to the Advertising Club of Los Angeles a few months after the company began operating from its makeshift quarters. "The business itself has become extremely complex, as has the world in which it operates . . . Perhaps to a greater degree than ever before in history, the management of American business must today be keenly sensitive to a fast-changing political, economic and social atmosphere. It is a situation which demands quick decisions and sound decisions."

In decision-making sessions, Elbridge Stuart still consulted his father's two crusty old lieutenants, Phil Kinzer (sales) and Bill Cross (production), but a new breed of col-lege-trained manager was surfacing in the company. Kinzer and Cross represented Carnation's Evaporated Milk past; the aggressive young lawyers, accountants and Harvard Business School graduates represented its multi-product, multi-national future. They would inherit the World Headquarters Kinzer and Cross had helped make possible.

*   *   *   *   *

Everett Olson had been looking after Albers' financial affairs. When Carnation's treasurer decided not to make the move to Los Angeles, Elbridge Stuart tapped Olson for the job. Henry Arnest, who had joined the company in the same depressed winter of 1931-32 ("I was looking for a job, *any* job"), was assistant general sales manager for Albers cereals and pet foods. At the time of the hegira to Southern California, he was happily scanning the trial market reports on a new product, Friskies Canned Dog Food.

Al Halgren, an up-and-coming lawyer in the Corporate Department, had served the company well in Washington during the war, coping with federal agencies in lining up badly needed sugar, trucks, tires and gasoline. Chuck Todd, a chain-smoking, Spanish-speaking lawyer-accountant, was in Mexico watching over the building of General Milk's first south-of-the-border plant. Like so many of the other executives who would eventually acquire eighth-floor offices at World Headquarters, Halgren and Todd had been brought into the company by its prickly, whip-cracking vice president and secretary, Al Hartwick.

"When I came to work for Carnation in 1933, the company's legal affairs were in bad shape," Hartwick recalls. "Every engineer, every plant manager acted as his own attorney. I decided to build not a legal department, but a corporate department. We added people gradually, one by one, until we were doing all the financing for Carnation and handling all of its legal matters, as well as insurance, labor relations, plant safety, the annual report and so on. The Corporate Department grew because of the growth of the company, and maybe the company was able to grow because of the Corporate Department.

"We negotiated the Vitamin D contract, signed up the Dionne quintuplets, handled trademark infringements, anti-trust matters and product liability cases, and our relations with the federal government were such that when our Albers plant in Oakland burned down in the midst of wartime shortages, we managed to have crews at work on a new building in less than a month. And we played an important role in the company's financing policy. If you look at our statements, you'll find some very low interest rate debentures. We could always borrow money as cheap or cheaper than other companies."

Carnation's courtly, highly-respected ambassador to the world of finance, John F. Douglas, was a member of the Kinzer-Cross generation who had been a friend and business associate of E. A. Stuart. They had worked together in the development of Seattle's "Metropolitan Center" (one of the buildings was named for E. A.). After serving for years on Carnation's board of directors, he assumed an active role in the company's affairs in January, 1931. Two years later he was named general counsel.

By the time the decision had been made to round up Carnation's scattered tribes and lead them into a promised land of palm trees and perpetual sunshine, Douglas had stepped aside as general counsel, but was still serving as a director and as chairman of the Finance Committee, preserving the company's traditionally good relations with the banking fraternity. Along with Kinzer, Cross and Ghormley, he was one of Carnation's top six executives. The sixth man was Hartwick, the only vice president of this period who had entered the corporate family after the presidency had passed from E. A. to Elbridge.

In Al Hartwick, Carnation had come up with a boss man as tough and, out of working hours, as charming as Kinzer.

"Before 8 A.M. and after 4:45 P.M., no one was more sociable, witty—if a bit loud and off-color—or tried harder, and more successfully, to please," says one of Hartwick's associates. "He'll never be forgotten as long as one person who worked directly for him remains alive."

Hartwick, in the words of *The Carnation* (Winter, 1970) retired "after thirty-six years of growling, scowling, fist-pounding dedication to Carnation." Like Kinzer, he left behind a bottomless reservoir of anecdote. When Carnation lawyers assemble for luncheon, they still trade memories of traumatizing encounters, laying bare their psychic scars. Of all the stories handed down about the two men, however, none is more revealing of both than Hartwick's own account of his first run-in with Kinzer.

"I'd probably been working for the company five or six weeks," Hartwick remembers with relish, "and Kinzer called me to his office. I stood outside his door for what

110

seemed to me half an hour. Maybe it was only five minutes, or even three. Anyway, I finally got tired of waiting and went back to my desk, whereupon he called me on the phone. He said, 'I asked you to come to my office, didn't I?' and I said, 'Mr. Kinzer, I came to your office. I stood in front of your door.' He said, 'Yes, but I wasn't ready to see you,' and I told him, 'Next time, don't call me till you're ready to see me.'

"He came storming back to my office, bellowing 'I'm a vice president of this company! If I want you to come to my office, you're going to come to my office, and you're going to wait until I'm ready to see you!' I said I wasn't going to stand in front of anybody's door, and suggested we go to Mr. Stuart's office and settle the matter then and there. I was prepared to quit that day and go back to Chicago. Well, we didn't go to Mr. Stuart's office and I didn't quit my job."

To put Kinzer's contributions to the company in perspective, Hartwick likes to recall the early days when Carnation was elbowing its way into the marketplace, inflicting its first bruises on Borden and Pet.

"Carnation wouldn't be what it is today if it hadn't been for Kinzer," he says. "He made those salesmen work day and night, and get their reports in on time, and if they didn't, he'd fire them. He was one of the men responsible for Carnation's success."

Another was William C. Cross, who went to work for E. A. in 1907 and devoted his life to Carnation. Ed Leigh, vice president in charge of the Can Division, has never forgotten his first meeting with Cross. It was brought about by a 1938 Christmas party in Seattle, where Ed's parents got into conversation with Austin Smith, Carnation's general superintendent. Their son had been graduated from Reed College that June, the Leighs remarked, and was looking for a steady job (he'd spent the summer working in a pea factory). Austin interviewed the young man and offered to put him to work if he was willing to make his way to Oconomowoc—at his own expense.

"I don't know why he thinks you should work here," Cross grumbled when Ed showed up to claim the job.

"I was so mad that I made up my mind to show him a thing or two," Ed reminisced years later in talking with the editor of *The Carnation* (Fall, 1972). "At the time of Cross's retirement, I had occasion to mention the incident to him and he didn't even remember."

When Cross retired in 1955, he was succeeded on the board of directors by Al Halgren, whose responsibilities included industrial relations. The manager of the Industrial Relations Department was none other than Ed Leigh.

"Bill Cross was a fantastic individual," Ed says of the bald-headed, square-jawed production chief. "He was hard-nosed, very demanding, typical of the best of his times. He and Kinzer were both one hundred percent evaporated milk men. Sometimes they made life miserable for the young college graduates who came into the company during the thirties and forties, but both of them accepted the fact that modern conditions required younger people, better trained in the formal sense than they had been. They weren't equipped to deal with the problems of the new technology, the new marketplace. They came out of a different world."

*   *   *   *   *

Elbridge Stuart put Carnation's new treasurer, Everett Olson, in charge of the transfer to Los Angeles.

"We moved two hundred and twenty-five people," he recalls, "and only two returned to the place from which they were moved. Everybody else stayed here."

The employees were moved in small groups over a period of sixteen months, from January, 1948, to May, 1949. In one instance, office equipment was crated and shipped over a weekend, so that a normal day's work could end in Oconomowoc on Friday evening and resume in Los Angeles on Monday morning. The company picked up the tab for its employees' moving expenses and hired a local real estate broker

111

*Carnation's first World Headquarters, completed in the summer
of 1949, had room to rent. Four years later it was necessary to extend
the 3rd through 7th floors to full building depth.*

Part of Wilshire Boulevard was roped off to accommodate the crowds attending Carnation's Grand Opening in September, 1949.

Dancing under a tent, employees celebrated both the Grand Opening and the 50th anniversary of the company.

to provide temporary shelter in furnished apartments and company-owned homes until the new Angelenos could find places of their own.

"They did a wonderful job," says Vice President Bob Kohls, who came to Los Angeles as a junior accountant. "They drove us to the airport in Milwaukee and had a car waiting for us when we got to Los Angeles. They had an apartment ready for us to move into, even had food in the refrigerator."

The nation's third largest city was "a little hard to explain," warned *The Carnation* (July-August, 1948). Its downtown district was disappointing, but suburban shopping centers enabled Angelenos to live "a normal life span without having to go downtown." Because of earthquakes, buildings were limited to nine stories (the height of Carnation's World Headquarters). The only exception was the 28-story City Hall. The natives were friendly, lived outdoors and liked to patronize drive-in-restaurants, shoe repair shops, theaters, laundries and markets.

"Except for a peculiar combination of atmospheric haze and some industrial gasses (called 'smog') in the downtown section," the article noted, "Angelenos breathe pure, fresh, country air."

On August 30, 1949, a week before Carnation's fiftieth anniversary, Mayor Fletcher Bowron and Sheriff Eugene Biscailuz turned up at 5045 Wilshire Boulevard for the dedication of the new World Headquarters. Elbridge Stuart and his oldest son, Hadley, formally opened the company's new home by loosening a ribbon tied to the front doors.

"It just goes to show what can happen if you keep your cows contented," Matt Weinstock reported in his *Los Angeles Daily News* column that evening after dropping by to see the new $2,000,000 building towering above the bustling boulevard where he had once hunted rabbits.

Matt, who enjoyed a glass of beer with his midday tacos, was surprised to learn that in 1948 the evaporated milk industry had used as many cans as the country's brewers. He was even more astonished to discover that

"Carnation has its own can company." Like Matt, most of the millions of Americans who used Carnation products every day thought of the company only in terms of shelf after shelf of red-and-white cans of evaporated milk. To the distress of Bob Hare, the articulate new editor of *The Carnation*, they had no idea of "the company's research contributions in the fields of infant feeding, home economics, public nutrition, cattle breeding and stock feeding."

Carnation seized on the consolidation of its executive offices in Los Angeles as a good time to identify its various product lines as members of a single family.

"A new logotype, evolved from the script which had appeared on Carnation Milk cans for nearly half a century, is being used wherever the name appears on products, equipment and buildings (including the large sign, 57 feet long by 21 feet, 7 inches high, atop the Los Angeles Headquarters)," reported *Printers Ink* (August 26, 1949). "The new Glosseal outer wrap for Carnation Corn Flakes (formerly Albers) identifies them as members of the company's family of foods, which was formerly only milk products."

In the mimeographed list of questions and answers prepared for World Headquarters tour guides, it was anticipated that some visitors might ask why the large sign on the building read CARNATION MILK rather than CARNATION COMPANY or, simply, CARNATION. The official reply: "Because it was felt that those words were more descriptive of the most important part of our business."

* * * * *

The dedication of the building coincided with the observance of the company's golden anniversary. In a commemorative booklet, *Fifty Years of Progress*, Bob Hare noted that "twenty percent of American women now buy Carnation Evaporated Milk and every third baby born in the United States is raised on it." Pained by the thought of those eight out of ten American women who weren't buying Carnation Evaporated Milk and of those two out of three babies who weren't drinking it, Bob added that "substantial domestic sales advances are still possible."

In the old Milwaukee days, Big John Wilkinson and Stanley Roberts would have tracked down those statistical holdouts and tried to turn them into Carnation customers, but to the distress of everyone in the company, its Mutt and Jeff team hadn't made it to Los Angeles. Corporate life would never be quite the same without Big John, the towering, captivating Southerner in charge of the sales department, and his affable sidekick in advertising.

The two had become inseparable, sharing hotel rooms and Pullman breakfasts, living out of suitcases for weeks at a time, like a pair of song-and-dance men, working two-day stands at divisional sales conferences. They led the singing, dominated the high-jinks, raked in their share of the poker pots and moved on to the next town, leaving behind a cadre of Carnation salesmen fired up to do battle for increased sales and improved shelf space.

"They were both charming men and lived life to the fullest," recalls Carnation President Dwight Stuart. "I remember them both very well as a young boy when they used to come out to Carnation Farms in the summer in conjunction with Erwin, Wasey's annual presentation of advertising plans for the coming year. This was a real fun get-together. Everybody worked hard in the morning, but the afternoon and evening were given over to fun and games, and the two leaders in that department were Big John Wilkinson and Stan Roberts.

"In the afternoon, it would be tennis and horseshoes. In the evenings, it would be a poker game and Mother used to let us sit up and watch for a while. There would always be a couple of high-rollers in the game, and Dad enjoyed nothing more than sawing them off at the pockets. He was one of the best poker players that ever came down the pike."

Death had broken up the John & Stan act before Carnation decided to make its home in Los Angeles. On a late spring morning in 1945, a few weeks after the fighting in Europe ended, Stan Roberts put in a full day at his Milwaukee office and, seemingly in excellent health, left for Chicago to catch the Monday evening broadcast of the Contented Hour, something he rarely missed. After the show he suffered a heart attack and died a couple of days later. He had spent twenty-seven of his sixty-one years with Carnation.

He loved to tell a story, fill a straight, sink a putt, hook a trout and take in a good movie, but, reported *The Carnation* (July-September, 1945), "he never got far away from his job of handling Carnation advertising," and he was "a perfectionist—an exacting critic whose discriminating sense of verbal and pictorial values could never be satisfied by mediocre performance." His grief-stricken partner stayed on in sales until the late summer of 1948 when the company moved out West.

Ralph Brubaker, general sales manager, took Big John's place on the board of directors. Like his predecessor, he was a born salesman.

"He was very articulate, an excellent public speaker, who always prepared his material carefully and delivered it forcefully and convincingly," says Paul Willis, who succeeded Stan Roberts as general advertising manager. "Having been a graduate of the U.S. Naval Academy, he had a military bearing. He was slim, meticulous in appearance and well-organized in everything he undertook. He was a very gracious man, very persuasive."

As a former naval person, he was accustomed to giving orders and having them obeyed, at work and at home.

"He and his wife bring their two boys into our place," a Los Angeles toy shop owner once told a Carnation colleague of Ralph's. "When they come in with Mrs. Brubaker, they'll spend the whole afternoon fiddling around, trying to make up their minds, but when they come in with their father, he tells them, 'All right, men, you have twenty minutes to pick out what you want,' and twenty minutes later they're leaving the store."

In 1953 P. G. Kinzer, left, turned over administrative responsibilities for the Advertising Department to Ralph Brubaker, center. In 1955 Paul Willis, right, was elected vice president in charge of advertising.

116

* * * * *

In the years before consolidation, Carnation's advertising was fragmented. Different units of the company, with executive offices in different cities, had been spending money for advertising handled by division advertising managers working through different agencies. In some instances, the agencies were located hundreds of miles from the headquarters of the division that manufactured and marketed the products that were being advertised.

Once the company settled into its new home, advertising proceeded along cozier channels. The three division advertising managers, Lawrence Nolte (Evaporated Milk), Walter Mayer (Fresh Milk and Ice Cream) and William Huse (Albers and Friskies), worked under the same roof with Paul Willis, who had come to Carnation by way of the Chicago advertising office of Kraft Foods (he had once been a tenor soloist in the Kraft Chorus).

"His initial plans include the revamping of the Contented Hour to introduce music in the modern manner as an appeal to a more youthful audience," reported *The Carnation* (January-March, 1946), "and the placing of Carnation advertising in the primary women's magazines, where it will reach a larger volume of potential customers."

Black customers rarely figured in the considerations of the white advertising executives who laid out national campaigns at this time, but a black youth on Chicago's South Side was taking a historic gamble that this situation could be changed. John H. Johnson, at the age of twenty-four, had borrowed $500 on his mother's furniture to launch a pocket-size magazine, *Negro Digest*. Three years later, in November, 1945, he plowed his modest profits into a slick new *Life*-size publication he called *Ebony*. It was an immediate hit with blacks.

"Advertisers, on the other hand did not rush to present their wares in its pages," the

This "Carnation Baby" now has 2 of her own!

Yes, the "Carnation Baby" at the left is now **MRS. RUFUS MARSHALL, JR.** ...a "Carnation Mother" who has raised 2 healthy children on Carnation Evaporated Milk. Mrs. Marshall knows from experience why Carnation is so perfect for infant feeding...and every milk purpose.

Give Your Baby Carnation's Extra Advantages

Rich cow's milk...with nothing removed except water...that's Carnation Evaporated Milk. It gives your baby *all* the nourishment of good whole milk, *plus* these very important health advantages:

Carnation is specially homogenized and heat-refined for easy digestibility and perfect uniformity. Each pint is enriched with 400 units of Vitamin D... the "sunshine vitamin." And Carnation is scientifically sterilized *after* it's sealed in the can, to assure absolute safety. Yet Carnation actually costs less than ordinary milk! So be *sure* your baby gets Carnation's extra health advantages.

LISTEN to BUDDY CLARK—every Monday evening over NBC—on Carnation's "Contented Hour."

Ask your doctor about Carnation Milk for your baby

...find out why 8 out of 10 mothers who use Carnation say, "My doctor recommended it."

The Milk Every Doctor Knows

FREE—"Your Contented Baby"—New complete manual by a famous doctor. Carnation Company, Dept. E-109, Los Angeles 36, California.

Carnation

EVAPORATED MILK

"from Contented Cows"

Carnation was an early and regular advertiser in Ebony. *Ad shown ran in October, 1949.*

---

editors recall in their three-volume *Pictorial History of Black America* (1971).

In its infancy, the magazine got a few ads from dispensers of cigarettes, whisky, Lydia E. Pinkham's Vegetable Compound ("Are You Just a Plaything of Nature?"), hair-straighteners ("new scientific way to straighten your hair right in your own home without the ravages of hot combs or strong caustics containing lye") and bleaching creams ("There's no greater beauty prize than a light, clear, smooth complexion").

The tide turned for Johnson's magazine in the winter of 1948-49, when readers were introduced to the merits of such products as Pepsi Cola, Elgin Watches, Zenith Radios, Colgate Toothpaste and Carnation Milk. "Save on Desserts With Carnation Milk," urged an advertisement in *Ebony's* January, 1949 issue, the first any food company had placed with Johnson. Half-page ads continued regularly in succeeding issues. In May, the layout featured black quadruplets reared on Carnation Evaporated Milk. The text called attention to its economy ("costs so little") and its reliability ("the milk every doctor knows").

117

* * * * *

One floor below Paul Willis' office and spilling downstairs onto part of the fourth floor were the new Los Angeles offices of Erwin, Wasey Company, Carnation's advertising agency for thirty years.* Howard Williams, its West Coast director, who played golf and lifted an occasional glass with Elbridge Stuart, likes to tell the story of how his friend became his landlord.

"When the board of directors decided to build the company's general office in Los Angeles, Elbridge sent for me. " 'Howard,' he said, 'I want you to be our tenant.' I wasn't too eager to enter into such an arrangement for fear of having Erwin, Wasey thought of as Carnation's house agency, but I called our New York office and put the proposition to them. They agreed to it, so I

---

*The R. T. Harris agency of Salt Lake City continued to handle the company's evaporated milk brands other than Carnation.

George Burns, Gracie Allen and Harry Von Zell entertain visiting superintendents from the Evaporated Milk Division in 1951. From left, Frank Dowd, James Henry, Gene Lang, Roland Jones, Larry Trammel, Dan Stilling, L. W. Jeffery, James Algeo, Harry McFadden, L. H. Multer, Frank Little, George Bulkley, B. S. Zimmerman, Austin Smith, Ken Susie, R. C. Evans, E. O. Leigh, Ted Lang and Leo Prindel. Carnation sponsored the Burns and Allen Show for 8 years.

phoned Elbridge and told him, 'You've got a new tenant.' "

Elbridge was well into his sixty-second year at the time Carnation took up residence in Southern California. His two oldest sons, Hadley and Fullerton, were part of the corporate family. Fully was working for Fresh Milk and Ice Cream in Texas. Hadley, the crown prince in the Stuart line of succession, had become an assistant vice president and director of the company. Dwight, the young rebel fresh out of college, had struck off on his own, much to his father's distress. The boy, like his grandfather, was a born salesman.

The emptiness left at home now that the boys were gone had been filled by two girls, Ann and Betty, the daughters of Mrs. W.

Kent Ruble of Seattle. Elbridge and Evelyn Ruble had met through mutual friends and in 1945 had been married by the family pastor, Dr. James W. Fifield, Jr., of the First Congregational Church of Los Angeles. Four years later Elbridge decided that once Carnation's new general office was formally opened he would take Evelyn on a business-vacation trip.

For the business part, he invited Bill Cross, who knew everything worth knowing about the production of evaporated milk, and two of the top executives of the Carnation-Pet overseas operation, Lowell Wilson and Bill Stott. They would accompany him on his visits to General Milk's European plants. Once he had finished work, he planned to get in some sightseeing. For this, he needed

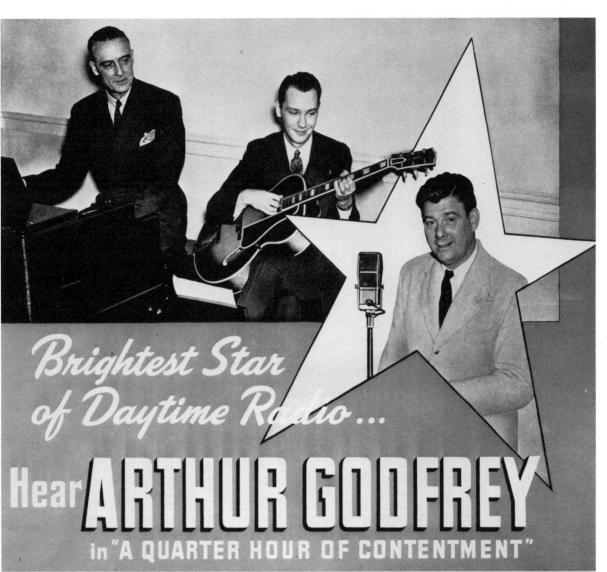

Brightest Star of Daytime Radio...

Hear ARTHUR GODFREY

in "A QUARTER HOUR OF CONTENTMENT"

Enjoy his Songs, Thoughts and Moods

Every Tuesday and Thursday   STATION AND TIME HERE

Irradiated **Carnation Milk**

"FROM CONTENTED COWS"

119

Arthur Godfrey still talks about how he learned to pronounce
"Oconomowoc" when he was sponsored by Carnation Milk in the early forties.

*Elbridge and Evelyn Stuart entertain cattle buyers
at a reception in Seattle in 1965.*

more worldly company. He asked Howard
and Katherine Williams to come along and
show him around.

* * * * *

It was Elbridge's first trip abroad. He was
delighted with London and with the Stuart
homeland. He visited General Milk's plant
at Dumfries, Scotland, and, he reported in
The Carnation (January-February, 1950),
was distressed to find that, because of government regulations, "we are not permitted
to buy such milk as we can obtain at the best
possible price, then sell such milk as we
process at prices people are willing to pay."
Prices were low, he admitted, but to support
them "Britain has had to tax the incomes of
every employed citizen to the fullest extent."

In France, Elbridge was pleased to discover economic controls had been lifted and
"goods were available in the shops at competitive prices." On his tour of the Carentan
plant, he heard stories of its wartime suffer-
ings. Captured intact by the Germans, it had
been sabotaged by the French underground

and so badly mauled during the Allied sweep
across Normandy in June, 1944, that only
one section of the original plant was still
standing when General Milk set about re-
storing the condensery and can factory.

Milk, the visitors were pleased to learn,
was plentiful in France. It also turned out to
be plentiful in Germany and Holland,
despite wartime reports of the slaughtering
of dairy herds to provide meat for German
chow lines. On the contrary, Elbridge was
told, "cows were given very good care because the Germans needed fats for food and
ammunition."

Before the war, General Milk had operated three evaporating plants in Germany.
Now two of them, those at Waren, Mecklen-
burg, and at Allenburg, East Prussia, were
on the Russian side of the Iron Curtain, and
"we can obtain no information whatsoever
about them." The Neustadt-in-Holstein condensery built on the site Phil Kinzer had
selected twenty-five years earlier was "in
excellent condition."

* * * * *

In the 1949 annual report, the first prepared at Carnation's new World Headquarters, net income of 3.16 percent of dollar sales was slightly better than the year before, but below the 1936-41 period, when—with one exception—it had ranged from 3.64 percent to 4.59 percent. It would be difficult to regain this profitable high ground, Elbridge advised Carnation stockholders, because of "the growing tax burden the company has to bear."

Net earnings the following year, $9,484,-113 (3.7 percent of sales), were the highest in the company's history, but federal income taxes had leaped from $4,900,000 in 1949 to $8,500,000. By 1952, due in part to bigger budgets for advertising and selling evaporated milk and to the expansion of the markets on Friskies, Carnation's net earnings dropped to $6,881,363 (2.2 percent of sales). Federal income taxes (after $385,000 credit for excess profits tax "carry back") came to $5,200,000, which represented 43 percent of the company's net income before such taxes.

Elbridge was distressed by the rising cost of government (he had complained about it when Herbert Hoover was in the White House), but in a *Time* article (Oct. 26, 1953)

he struck a characteristically positive note.

"I get tired of hearing all this defeatist talk about how it is impossible for a company to continue to grow under this tax structure," he said, and went on to explain that the difficulties could be offset by "a little extra sweat, a little more guts, and quite a bit more brains."

Now in his mid-sixties, Elbridge needed someone to share his executive burdens. Faced with a similar situation in 1930, E. A. Stuart had come up with a new title, executive vice president, and bestowed it on his son. In 1951 Elbridge created the post of assistant to the president and, to fill it, he picked one of the most popular members of the Carnation high command, Alfred M. Ghormley who, in the words of Dr. E. B. Oberg, retired director of research, "had a way of making anyone he talked to feel important."

"He would come in a plant he hadn't visited in maybe five or six years and call everybody by name," recalls an old associate. "He was badly crippled by arthritis and lived in constant pain, but I never heard him complain and only once did I ever see him get really mad. That was when somebody tried to help him up out of his wheelchair."

121

*This photo of the 1954 board of directors marks the end of
an era. The following year P. G. Kinzer, seated at left, and
W. C. Cross, seated at right, retired from active service. (Kinzer
continued on board until 1965.) Other directors: Seated,
A. M. Ghormley and E. H. Stuart; standing from left, A. P. Herold,
E. H. Stuart, Jr., R. R. Brubaker, Lawrence Arnold, R. H. Fullerton,
H. E. Olson and E. S. Hartwick.*

10
The
Instant
Revolution

*"We're very slow to take up anything new.
But after we have thoroughly
investigated and decided to expand, we
put everything we've got into making
it a success, and we never quit."*
ALFRED M. GHORMLEY, 1954.

ALFRED GHORMLEY KEPT his eighth-floor window closed against the sounds of construction crews working to create additional office space, part of which would be given over to a new test kitchen. In less than five years the company had outgrown its new Los Angeles headquarters. Its net earnings had more than tripled since the war and, despite the continuing decline in the domestic consumption of evaporated milk (down from a 1945 peak of 86,800,000 cases to 54,000,000 in 1953), Carnation Evaporated Milk was still the world's largest single-branded food item sold in cans, and the cans were made by Carnation.

"Carnation has operated without a loss since the depression year 1932," noted the *Wall Street Journal* (September 30, 1954). "During the five years since December 31, 1948, earnings totaling $38,290,000 after income and excess profits taxes have averaged a fat 23.5 percent per year on the common stockholders' equity. In the meantime, net worth has been boosted 82.5 percent from $32,286,000 to $58,957,000, after payment of $11,275,000 in common dividends. With 67 percent of its $107,000,000 total assets in cash, Government securities or other

quickly-realizable forms, the firm has an exceedingly liquid balance sheet."

General Milk, the overseas affiliate with offices on the seventh floor of Carnation's World Headquarters, was operating in France, Germany, Holland, Scotland, South Africa, Mexico, Peru and Australia. Two South African plants were producing sweetened condensed milk exclusively. Natives spread it on bread. In some countries, where fresh milk was plentiful but unsanitary, customers were willing to pay a premium for the safety of evaporated milk. In each of the last three years, a Carnation spokesman pointed out in 1954, "General has paid its owners dividends of $500,000."

"In going abroad," reported *Time* (October 26, 1953), "Carnation has greatly changed dairying in much of the world. In some areas Carnation's aid has boosted milk production as much as 400 percent in a few years, increased land values as much as 100 percent, and caused a drop in fresh milk prices of as much as 500 percent. But Carnation has also run into some troublesome folklore. For example, in Africa and Asia, natives got the idea that drinking evaporated milk caused impotency. Not until World

War II, when Australian and American soldiers conclusively proved this was not true, did the myth die."

At the turn of the century, when E. A. Stuart was selling Carnation Cream from a six-pack sample case, the infant mortality rate in the United States was about 100 per 1,000. Fifty years later, thanks largely to a safer milk supply, the figure had shrunk to 25 per 1,000. Two out of three of the country's babies were drinking evaporated milk and Carnation's medical liaison men and women were working closely with doctors, nurses, hospital staffs and new mothers to make sure that their brand continued to lead the field.

"We never sell any product, new or old, unless we are sure that the quality is right," Alfred Ghormley told an interviewer in 1954. "Through advertising, salesmanship, price and other inducements you can get a customer to try anything once, but you can keep that customer only if your product is uniformly reliable. In considering new products, we try to find things that can be developed for mass marketing, fitting into our existing sales organization and methods. A tremendous amount of goodwill and consumer acceptance has been built up for the Carnation label, and we think it can be profitably transferred to additional products whenever we are satisfied that we want to add them to our line."

To protect the good name of the Carnation label, researchers not only ran tests on the company's various products to see that they came up to Carnation standards, but also worked to find ways to improve them and to create new products. Carnation's research, like its other activities, was dispersed. The headquarters of the Research and Development Department, established in 1940, was in Milwaukee. Additional research was carried out in Oconomowoc and at Carnation Milk Farms.

Plans for a research center had been shelved during the war, and then delayed again while the company looked around for a suitable headquarters site. Finally, on

124

July 22, 1952, ground was broken in Van Nuys, California, for a central research facility. The one-story white building, a half-hour's drive by freeway from World Headquarters, was formally opened on October 8, 1953.

"No one can possibly tell what kinds of new products will be carrying the Carnation-Albers label ten years from now," *The Carnation* (July-August, 1953) noted. "Whatever they are, they will start as ideas and Carnation Research Laboratories will be the key to their practical development."

In their dealings with the eighth-floor of World Headquarters, the company's Bunsen-burner brigade would be represented by Dr. Philip K. Bates, general manager for research. The running of the six laboratories (Engineering, Cereals, Bacteriological, Biological, Processing and Analytical) would be left to Dr. E. B Oberg, director of research,

M. Ghormley, assistant to the
president, speaks at grand opening
Research Laboratories in Van
ys, California on October 8,
53. Seated from left, Lee
bridge, president of the
lifornia Institute of Technology;
C. Cross, vice president; and
Philip K. Bates, general
nager of research.

125

The Research Laboratories, expanded several times to meet
growing needs, looked like this in 1971.

who retired in 1972 after nearly thirty years with Carnation. During that time he had watched its research staff grow "from about seven to about one hundred and seventy."

"Carnation's devotion to research has already led it far from its original pasture," the 1953 *Time* article observed, and quoted Elbridge Stuart as saying that if the company "somehow stumbled on a hair tonic, and it proved to be a good one, Carnation would sell it." The company had spent a million dollars developing a dog food, and it was also feeding, among other creatures, calves, horses, chickens, turkeys, rabbits and hogs, but Carnation still evoked for most Americans an image of red-and-white cans of evaporated milk stacked on grocery shelves and contented black-and-white cows grazing contentedly in the green pastures of Washington's Snoqualmie Valley.

The Carnation Milk Farms was not just a place where the company's top management could assemble every summer to pitch horseshoes, play poker and bend an elbow after the day's work of planning for the com-

ing year. It was a world-famous dairy research center. Star of the Carnation show herd making the rounds of county fairs and livestock exhibitions in the summer of 1953 was Carnation Homestead Daisy Madcap, who, on January 13, had set a new 365-day world's record of 1,511.8 pounds of butterfat.

Elbridge, like his father, was devoted to the farm and equally certain that the future of the dairy industry lay with research, or, as Charles F. Kettering defined the word, with "finding out what you are going to do when you cannot keep on doing what you are doing now." Professor I. A. Gould of Ohio State University's Department of Dairy Technology felt the same way.

"Research needs are all about us," he wrote in *Food Engineering* (October, 1954). "New dairy products await discovery."

*   *   *   *   *

In the fall of 1954 Carnation went to market with a revolutionary improvement on a dairy product the Tartars were using at the close of the thirteenth century.

126

The Research Committee hears Dr. Bates explain a gas chromatograph.
Seated from left, R. D. Kummel, (unidentified), Tom Marquis, Len Sperry, Art
Herold, Will Claus, Mark Shackelford and Jack Bullis. Standing from left, Mark
Matthews, F. B. MacKenzie, Fred Hoover, R. C. Evans and E. B. Oberg.

"When the Service, that is, the Military Service, is distant, they carry but little with them," reported Marco Polo in 1298. "They make a provision of milk thickened and dried to a state of paste, which is prepared in the following manner. They boil the milk and skim off the rich or creamy part as it rises to the top, put it into a separate vessel as butter, for so long as that remains in, the milk will not become hard. The latter is then exposed to the sun until it dries. On going into the Service, they carry with them about ten pounds for each man and of this one-half pound is put every morning in a leathern bottle with as much water as is thought necessary. By their motion in riding, the contents are violently shaken and a thin porridge is produced, on which they make their dinner."*

Nearly six hundred and fifty years later, American soldiers in South Pacific jungles were mixing dried milk with water and forc-

*Quoted by Clarence H. Eckles, Willes B. Combs and Harold Macy in *Milk and Milk Products* (McGraw-Hill, 1943), p. 306.

ing the stuff down. It was lumpy and tasted rather like boiled chalk. On the home front, where milk in any form was scarce and expensive, powdered milk had become such a staple that when the fighting ended, many homemakers continued to use it for cooking and baking. Their purchases boosted production for the family kitchen from 2,400,000 pounds in 1948 to 94,000,000 five years later.

There were two processes for manufacturing dry milk—spray and drum—both using the same general principles. First, part of the water was removed from fresh milk by means of the conventional vacuum pan, and then, in the spray process, this evaporated milk was reduced to powder when hot air was blown at a high velocity into a large drying chamber.

Spray-dried milk was widely used in the manufacture of bread, cookies, cakes and candies, but in the home it was less than satisfactory. It was difficult to dissolve and it still had a chalky taste. Borden, however, was doing well with a dry milk product it called Starlac. In 1952, while Pet was field-

Dr. E. B. Oberg, director of research, explains a lab process to a television reporter.

ing a competitive entry, Carnation was preparing to lay claim to its share of this limited but growing market. As a fringe benefit, the company saw an opportunity to put its skim milk to profitable use, a goal that had occupied its researchers for years.

By the end of 1953, Carnation was about ready to introduce a spray-dried nonfat milk powder. Shortly before Christmas a klatch of advertising and marketing men drove out to the Van Nuys laboratories to hear Research Director Oberg deliver a lecture on the merits of the new product the company was manufacturing in Oconomowoc. He tried manfully to make it appear superior to its competitors already in the marketplace. Paul Willis, working out the advertising campaign with Erwin, Wasey, was no less resourceful in his efforts to confer distinction on the nonfat milk powder. It would be presented as a kitchen convenience that performed well for the home baker.

"We planned to direct our sales pitch toward its cooking uses," recalls Virginia Piper, who had recently taken charge of Carnation's new Home Economics Department. "By adding it to flour, you came up with what was in effect a do-it-yourself dry mix that offered better nutrition at less expense."

While Carnation was preparing to plunge into the market with a conventional powder, a revolutionary nonfat dry milk that dissolved instantly, didn't cake and tasted remarkably like fresh milk had been devised in a Northern California laboratory. Nobody at World Headquarters knew about it, however, until later that winter when one of the company's salesmen stumbled across it in Sacramento, where delighted homemakers were stocking up on bright blue packages of something called Peebles Instant Nonfat Milk.

Samples were sent to Dr. Oberg's researchers at Van Nuys and to Virginia Piper's test kitchen on Wilshire Boulevard, a short walk from World Headquarters. Their reports confirmed what the top brass on the eighth floor had already discovered simply by mixing the Peebles product in cold water, stirring and sipping. Every other kind of dry milk, including Carnation's floor-to-ceiling stockpile in Oconomowoc, was now obsolete.

* * * * *

"He had ten ideas a minute," says Gale Reimer, who worked for David Dart Peebles at Western Condensing Company before joining Carnation's Engineering Department. "He'd come in one day all enthused about a project, and two days later he'd have dropped it and started something else."

In the opinion of J. L. Kraft, the cheese company founder, Dave Peebles "contributed more to the dairy industry than any other single man." When he died in 1965 at the age of 80, he held more than seventy patents on the processing of milk and other foods. Dairy farmers were in his debt for enabling them to turn a profit on whey, historically a waste product of cheese-making. Thanks to a Peebles process, dry whey had bobbed up on the shopping lists of manufacturers of livestock and poultry feeds.

"He had little formal education, but he had a very fertile imagination, and he was always looking around for new processes and new products," says Tom Marquis, a Western Condensing researcher before signing on with Carnation. "The instant milk process came about pretty much by accident. Mr. Peebles had converted a big barn in Petaluma into a pilot plant. It had a couple of driers, some evaporators, and various odd pieces of equipment.

"One day a researcher, using a flour-sifter sort of device, put some dry milk powder in the top of a spray-drier—a large chamber about ten feet in diameter and about twenty feet high, with a cone on the bottom to permit hot air to be brought in to do the drying as fluid milk is sprayed in at the top. In this instance, however, dry powder was coming down, and when the atomizer was turned on, it atomized a little water, which mixed with the dry milk. The dampish powder that collected at the bottom of the chamber was shoveled up and put out in the sun to dry.

"When it was taken over to the lab for

New light Chocolate-Bavarian Cream!

—BECAUSE YOU CAN WHIP LOW-CALORIE CARNATION INSTANT!

Enjoy luscious, rich chocolate flavor like old-fashioned Bavarian Cream—but with wonderful new-fashioned *lightness!*

The secret is *whipped* Carnation Instant Non-fat Dry Milk—*with 2/3 less calories than whipped cream!* Use whipped Carnation Instant in this modern Bavarian...or in any whipped cream recipe to cut down the fat, calories and cost ...or as delicious topping for only 1¢ a serving!

Only Carnation Instant is the "Magic Crystals" Nonfat Milk—delicious for drinking, perfect for cooking, ideal for whipping. Modern way to *all* the natural protein, calcium and B-vitamins of freshest whole milk, without the load of fat calories. Comes in 3, 8 and 14-Qt. cartons and the new package of 5 pre-measured 1-Qt. envelopes. Costs as little as 8¢ a quart.

CARNATION INSTANT LIGHT CHOCOLATE-BAVARIAN
(Makes about 8 servings with only ½ the calories of ordinary Bavarian)

    1 package chocolate pudding and pie filling mix
    1 tablespoon (1 envelope) unflavored gelatine
    ¼ cup sugar
    4 teaspoons instant coffee
    1½ cups liquid CARNATION INSTANT
    1 square unsweetened chocolate
    2½ cups whipped CARNATION INSTANT
    "MAGIC CRYSTALS"

Combine pudding mix, gelatine, sugar, instant coffee and liquid Carnation Instant with chocolate in sauce-pan. Cook over low heat, stirring constantly until thickened. Cool. Whip cooled pudding, then fold into whipped Carnation Instant. Blend well. Spoon into 1½-quart mold. Chill until firm (about 2 hours).

TO MAKE 2½ CUPS WHIPPED CARNATION INSTANT FOR THIS RECIPE:
1. Combine ½ cup ice water with ½ cup Carnation Instant "Magic Crystals" in bowl. Whip until soft peaks form (3-4 minutes). **2.** Add 2 tablespoons lemon juice. **3.** Continue beating until firm peaks form (3-4 minutes longer).

The big little breakfast

Remember Carnation Instant Breakfast when you're out of time for your regular breakfast. All the good, honest nourishment you need in the morning—all in one neat glass. Read the label. Mixed with the substantial nutrition of milk, you get the protein, vitamins, minerals and energy of this bacon and egg breakfast. The big little breakfast. That's Carnation Instant Breakfast.

CHOCOLATE

Carnation instant breakfast

makes milk a meal

Virginia Piper, left, director of the Food Service Center, and Olive Picciano, advertising coordinator, have been promoting Carnation products for more than twenty years.

some routine tests, we discovered that once it was put in water, it didn't float like ordinary spray-dried milk. Instead, it wet immediately and sank. It wasn't in solution, but it wet without any trouble at all. If you let it stand for a few minutes, though, insoluble particles settled out, leaving a glass of curds and whey. Here was the germ of a revolutionary idea. If we could somehow glue those spray-dried milk particles together, so they formed a porous mass, and if, at the same time, we could avoid the development of insoluble protein curd, we would have an instantly soluble dried milk.

"Some months later Mr. Peebles called me into his office one morning and said, 'How would you like to work on a new product?' We worked on it for about six months and found out what conditions had to be avoided to prevent coagulation of the milk protein, and then it took another six months or so to make sure we could manufacture the product consistently.

"We built a pilot production plant in Tulare. We didn't dream that instant milk would ever sell in the volume it later attained, but we could see commercial possibilities in it, so, instead of building a laboratory-size plant, we designed one that could turn out 25,000 to 30,000 pounds a day."

*   *   *   *   *

Mark Shackelford, vice president in charge of the Instant Products Division, was an account executive in the Chicago office of Batten, Barton, Durstine and Osborne when a voluble California inventor burst in one day with the announcement that he had a "revolutionary product" he was going to turn over to the advertising agency. It was something called Peebles Instant Nonfat Milk.

"The office wasn't interested," Shackelford says. "Western Condensing was too small a company for such a large agency to handle profitably. We suggested he go to a smaller agency. But Mr. Peebles was persistent. Bruce Barton came out to Chicago and met with him. They hit it off, so Mr. Barton said, 'I think this thing has a real future and we ought to take it on regardless

Amazing Milk Discovery!
Carnation Instant
Not like any other

Not a powder, not a flake—
only Carnation has

Magic Crystals

that burst into delicious
nonfat milk!

Others claim it...only Magic Crystals can do it...prove it yourself:

DISSOLVES INSTANTLY!
Photographs show powdery "Instant" Brand X, flaky "Instant" Brand Y and new Carnation Instant Magic Crystals poured into glasses of ice-cold water. Brand X floats on top of water, Brand Y only partly dissolves. *Only* new Carnation Magic Crystals dissolve instantly and completely.

CAN'T CAKE OR HARDEN!
Exposed to air overnight, powdery Brand X and flaky Brand Y caked and hardened. *Only* Carnation Magic Crystals do not cake or harden—do not absorb flavor-robbing moisture—*stay fresh and free-flowing from first to last!*

FRESH MILK FLAVOR!
Only Carnation brings you the true, full flavor of freshest pasteurized nonfat milk—*concentrated* in Magic Crystals. Unlike powders or flakes, exclusive Carnation Magic Crystals burst into truly delicious fresh-flavor nonfat milk—*ready to drink immediately!*

All the Protein, Calcium and
B-Vitamins of Fresh, Whole Milk!

And you can prepare new Carnation Instant as rich as you wish! A single extra tablespoon of Magic Crystals per glass gives your family 15% *more* of these important values for strong growth, sound teeth and good digestion. And a richer flavor children love.

Use Carnation Instant for drinking, over cereals, in cooking. No special recipes needed—no need to learn new cooking ways—just use liquid Carnation Instant in any recipe. Discover wonderful Magic Crystals—*new* Carnation Instant in the brilliant red and white package—*today!*

Look for the easy-pour spout

For drinking, cooking, baking—

Save ½ on
Milk Bills!

New—from Carnation...World Leader in Evaporated Milk

"from Contented Cows"

Introductory newspaper ad for Carnation Instant.

of the fact that we'll probably lose money on it.' So I became the account executive and we set out to introduce it in test markets."

In Sacramento, the Peebles product captured 56 percent of the city's total dry milk business in thirteen weeks. Meanwhile, the shiny blue boxes of Peebles Instant Nonfat Milk had turned up on the shelves of Carnation's test kitchen.

"I was delighted and overwhelmed," Virginia Piper said recently, when asked about her first reaction to the product. "The sight of those magic crystals drifting down from the surface of the water and becoming a homogenous product with just a stir or two was phenomenal, like discovering that Christmas was every day of the year."

Once Carnation's eighth-floor movers and shakers had taken a look at Peebles Instant Milk, they were understandably eager to sit down and chat with Western Condensing's president.

"The person in our company who knew Dave Peebles was Jack Bullis," recalls Everett Olson. "We asked Jack if he would bring Mr. Peebles to us, so we could get acquainted with him. He arranged a meeting and Dave took a great liking to Alfred Ghormley. He felt that Alfred was a man of tremendous integrity, someone he could trust, and I think it was for that reason, and that reason alone, that we finally got together with Dave Peebles."

On May 28, 1954, Elbridge Stuart and Dave Peebles, as presidents of their respective companies, signed an agreement to form a jointly-owned subsidiary, the Instant Milk Company, which would manufacture the Peebles product. It would be marketed under the Carnation label. Dave Peebles was to be the chairman of the board of the new company and Alfred Ghormley its president. Its treasurer would be Carnation's financial mentor, Everett Olson.

"Dave Peebles was a very proud man," he says, "and I think he wanted to see that his revolutionary product was marketed in such a way as to receive the response from consumers it deserved."

The name of David Peebles was well-known in the feed business, where the inventor's dry whey had become a staple manufacturing item, but no Peebles label had ever appeared on a grocery store shelf until the instant milk was test-marketed in January, 1954. Carnation, on the other hand, had one or more of its products on sale in ninety-five percent of the country's retail food stores at the time it entered into negotiations with Western Condensing and flashed the word to Oconomowoc to stop production of the original Carnation nonfat dry milk.

"We were left sitting here with a hundred thousand cases of the old powder," recalls a plant official, who will never forget those hectic winter weeks when the plant worked around the clock, even during the Christmas holidays, to pack the conventional product in one-pound glass jars. "We dumped the stuff out of the glass jars, packed it in large fibre drums and sold it to the government. We used the jars for malted milk."

The decision to scrap the inventory accumulated at Oconomowoc was "a very easy one," says Everett Olson, who, on looking back to the dawn of the instant era, is struck by the fortunate timing of Carnation's joint venture with Western Condensing.

"We could have gone to market with our conventional product and then discovered that the entire industry had been revolutionized by this new process," Olson points out. "We hadn't intended to spend a great deal of money advertising our original dry milk. We hadn't thought the industry was large enough to support that kind of a campaign, but coming out with an entirely *new* product, that changed the entire climate. It gave us an opportunity to do something that we couldn't have done before. And, of course, by reason of the features of the new product, the industry grew tremendously for a number of years."

*　　*　　*　　*　　*

Exactly one hundred and one days (and an undetermined number of sleepless nights) after Carnation and Western Condensing announced their agreement "to manufacture and sell certain dry milk solids," Southern California grocers were featuring displays of Carnation Instant Nonfat Dry Milk Solids. It was backed by what *The Carnation* (July-August, 1954) called "the hardest-hitting and heaviest advertising campaign in Carnation's history." It included wide use of newspapers, radio, television and magazines.

Carnation salesmen got their first look at the product on July 30 during simultaneous sales meetings in Los Angeles and Houston. Teams from World Headquarters then fanned out across the West and Southwest, conducting similar meetings. As the plants at Tulare, California, and Watertown, Wisconsin, made more product available, new territories were opened. The story hit the wire services in late August when press releases were handed out in Los Angeles and New York.

"The Carnation Company announced yesterday the successful development and distribution in the immediate future of 'instant milk,' a non-fat dry milk of granular structure which makes it instantly soluble in the coldest water," reported the *New York Times* (August 26, 1954).

A month later, on September 30, the new product prompted a *Wall Street Journal* correspondent to take a long, respectful look at the history of the 55-year-old company.

"Carnation Company's famed 'milk from contented cows' has been evaporated, condensed, made into ice cream, and even sold as is, each time scoring a hit with contented housewives," the article began. "Now the company—world's biggest producer of evaporated milk—is readying a new technique.

"It's bringing to market a granular, instantly-dissolving dry milk with what it hopes will be profit-making advantages over earlier milk powders. . . . The market potential for a product of this type is anybody's guess, but obviously Carnation believes it's substantial. . . .

"Carnation has never sold consumer-use dry milk before. Its new venture is still pretty much in the trial stage. But the way in which the product has been launched illustrates the carefully-considered and meticulously-executed policies that have made Carnation Company successful in a highly-competitive industry."

* * * * *

Research conducted by the American Dairy Association before the introduction of Carnation's Instant Milk showed that nearly three-fourths of the powdered skim milk then on the market was being used for cooking and the rest (27 percent) for drinking. Virginia Piper, who had just moved into her new seventh-floor test kitchen at World Headquarters that summer of 1954, set out to monitor the use of Instant Milk in representative American kitchens by having homemakers turn in weekly menu diaries. The kitchen reporters insisted they were using the new product only for cooking purposes.

"They can't possibly use that much each week," Ginny told the product's advertising and marketing managers, "Unless they're drinking it or taking milk baths."

Once Carnation realized that its kitchen-counter diarists were fibbing about their use of Instant Milk (an earlier generation had been similarly secretive in putting margarine on the table), marketing strategists set out to capitalize on the product's unique advantages by presenting it as a tasty, economical and convenient replacement for fresh milk as a beverage.

"This is the one that's *delicious* for drinking," proclaimed the first advertisement in *Life* (March 21, 1955). In smaller type, the subheadline picked up the instant mixing theme: "Carnation Instant 'Magic Crystals' — secret of *fresh* flavor nonfat milk instantly!"

"The words 'nonfat milk,' at the bottom of the subheadline, were hard to find," Bob Davis, Instant Products Division general advertising manager, recalled for *The Carnation* (February-March, 1962). "There was a question in our minds regarding the use of the word 'nonfat.' Was it negative or positive? Was it a good selling idea?"

Now fresh milk flavor always handy!

New Carnation "Magic Crystals" Milk Discovery

This is the one that's delicious for drinking because this is the one with Magic Crystals. *Only* Carnation Instant is freshest, pasteurized nonfat milk in *actual tiny* crystals... *Magic* Crystals that burst into *fresh* milk flavor instantly, even in ice-cold water! Ready to drink. Ready instantly for cereals, cooking, baking—no special recipes needed! Rich in *all* the protein, calcium and B-vitamins of freshest, *whole* milk.

Discover today how Carnation Instant, the *only* Magic Crystals Milk Discovery, gives you fresh milk flavor—*all* you want, *any* time, *instantly*—at great savings to you!

WITHOUT MAGIC CRYSTALS WITH MAGIC CRYSTALS WITHOUT MAGIC CRYSTALS WITH MAGIC CRYSTALS

Prove the difference yourself!

Only Carnation Magic Crystals mix *instantly*, in ice-cold water, with just a light stir. Powdery concentrates do not.

Only Carnation Magic Crystals mix *completely*. Ready to drink, freshly delicious. No powdery, undissolved residue.

For Drinking, Cooking, Baking...

Saves 1/2 on Milk Bills

In Convenient 3-Qt. and Economical 8-Qt. Sizes

Life ad, September 3, 1956.

As later research proved that it was a positive idea and a strong selling point, copywriters made the words more prominent. They were still a bit timid, however, about stressing one of the clinching sales points—economy. Finally, in a June 2, 1958 advertisement, the message had been boiled down to less than twenty words: "Carnation 'Magic Crystals' Instant bursts into fresh flavor nonfat milk instantly *for as little as 8¢ a quart!*" The subhead restated the theme: "This is the Instant that's delicious for drinking!"

The instant revolution, Mark Shackelford points out, was not an instant financial success.

"We had some awkward moments when we started out. It was a small industry. Its total annual volume when we entered the market was around 80,000,000 pounds. Our 3¼-quart package—the only size we offered at first—added about 15,000,000 pounds. As our volume increased with the introduction of larger sizes, we increased our advertising dramatically. We now have eight sizes."

Everett Olson, who is as frugal with his words as with his company's money, sums it up in a single sentence: "It was a great opportunity and we took advantage of it."

* * * * *

Carnation Instant Milk went to market at a time when the Founder's youngest grandson, Dwight Stuart, was making a name for himself in the Sales Department. The young man had been taken in hand by Henry Arnest, one of the company's Depression recruits who, in 1953, had been appointed general sales manager in charge of national field sales for the newly combined Carnation and Albers sales forces.

"Dwight's father watched his development with intense interest and never let up on him for one minute," Henry says. "He wanted to be sure that his son was earning his progress on his own merit and that I wasn't showing him any favoritism over the other fellows. We traveled together and I was always proud of him. He handled himself well. The Stuarts move with great confi-

dence, but also with humility. There's never been any room at Carnation for cockiness."

Dwight was appointed to the new position of sales promotion manager, Evaporated Milk Sales, in the spring of 1953, and in the fall of the following year, he was moved up to assistant general sales manager, serving as East Central Division manager. He went East to take over his new job just in time to get in on the excitement of introducing Carnation Instant Milk.

"It was like putting on a little magic show," he recalls. "It took everybody by storm."

It also imposed something of a strain on the working relationship between the large international food company and the small California research outfit that had got together to form Instant Milk Company.

"I don't think the people at Western Condensing realized what they were getting into," says Tom Marquis, who moved over to the Carnation payroll in 1954 and retired nineteen years later, after having planned and supervised construction of the company's five instant products plants. "It was fine to own half of something Carnation was enthusiastic about, but the thing I believe Western Condensing overlooked was that in participating in the development and marketing of a new product, you not only participate in the profits but also in the costs. It was quite a shock when Carnation presented a bill for Western Condensing's 50-percent share of the advertising campaign, for instance. There were some long faces at Petaluma the day the bill came in."

"We did, indeed, sustain some important losses," Everett Olson said recently, "and it meant that Western Condensing had to come up with their 50 percent of it, which was a strain on them, and so after a while it was agreed that Carnation Company would take over the entire operation. Shortly afterwards, there was no reason to maintain Instant Milk Company, so it was liquidated."*

* * * * *

Carnation's leadership in the instant revolution had "a great impact on the company,"

134

says Dwight Stuart. "Until then our progress in product development had been concerned primarily with the pet food field, where we'd competed against products that had already proven themselves in the marketplace. It was tough going. With Carnation Instant Milk, it was just the opposite. We went to market with something new, a revolutionary breakthrough. That helped us with our customers, who had pegged Carnation as a somewhat staid old evaporated milk company, and it helped us internally as well. Its success helped make other product introductions easier."

Henry Arnest agrees. "It built confidence within the company. I told Mr. Stuart, 'We've got an organization now. We can sell as long as we have something to take to market.'"

Carnation Company, after gobbling up the dry milk market with its instant product, was like a hometown team that had gone to South Bend and beaten Notre Dame. But, despite its exuberance, its annual reports during the 1950s gave little indication of the dimensions of its victory, especially when net sales and net earnings were compared with the figures of the previous decade. In the 1940s sales rose from $62,714,629 to $245,605,362, and earnings shot up from $2,319,027 to $7,764,599. In the 1950s, however, sales went up more than fifty percent (from $256,325,931 to $396,282,501), but profits stayed on a plateau. They were $9,484,113 in 1950 and $9,981,480 in 1959.

"There was a tremendous marketing expense which was not recovered until years later," explains Dwight Stuart. "The really profitable growth of the company didn't occur until the early 1960s, when we reaped the benefits of the instant process."

Meanwhile, on February 22, 1957, ex-

actly twenty-five years after his election as president of Carnation Company, Elbridge Stuart resigned and assumed the title, chairman of the board, a position that had remained vacant since his father's death in 1944. E. A. had stepped aside as president when he was seventy-five years old. His son was sixty-nine when he came to the same decision.

"Despite the great depression of the thirties, World War II and the Korean War," Elbridge pointed out in his letter to the board of directors, "the company has made steady progress. Its net sales have grown from under $30,000,000 to $358,000,000, and net results have risen from a loss in 1932 of $660,000 to a net profit this past year of over $9,000,000. Such a record could only have been made by a combination of the highest quality products, a sound merchandising policy, and a most loyal and cooperative organization."

Alfred Ghormley, assistant to the president for the last six years, moved up to the presidency, relinquishing his former job to Elbridge's oldest son, E. Hadley Stuart, Jr. Like his father, Hadley had started working for Carnation during school vacations. After becoming a full-time employee in 1940, he had gone on to become a superintendent (1942), director (1945), assistant vice president (1948) and vice president (1953). Since 1956 he had been head of the Can Division.

Hadley and his father, like Elbridge and E. A., had differed at times on company policies, but their disagreements had always been voiced within the bosom of the corporate family. This situation changed briefly, however, in the spring of 1961 when Hadley decided to leave the company and made the announcement at a news conference in San Francisco. The event is still mentioned by the press in stories concerning Carnation, but the Stuart family and company spokesmen choose to consider the defection as a personal matter and prefer not to discuss it. The annual report for 1961 carried the terse announcement that E. H. Stuart, Jr., "had resigned as Vice President, Director and member of the Executive Committee."

135

*In 1955, Foremost Dairies acquired all the stock of Western Condensing, including its half-interest in the Instant Milk Company. Carnation bought this half-interest in January, 1956. Two and a half years later Carnation and Foremost formed Dairy Foods, Inc., as a vehicle for granting other manufacturers nonexclusive licenses under their respective instantizing patents. Carnation sold its half interest in Dairy Foods to Foremost in 1969.

11
What's New?

*"When you start down a corridor,
you never know how many doors are open to you."*
H. E. OLSON

THE INTRODUCTION OF Instant Nonfat Dry Milk was followed a year later by Instant Chocolate Flavor Drink ("NEW! No Need to Add Milk. Complete . . . Delicious With Water"). It turned out to be an idea whose time, unfortunately, hadn't come, but the technology behind it spawned a series of successful instant products, starting in 1956 with a hot cocoa mix.

"The Instant Products Division can happily report that business is booming," announced *The Carnation* (January-February, 1958). Instant products were pouring out of Oconomowoc and Chilton, Wisconsin ("the largest milk plant in the world"), and the Waverly, Iowa, condensery, established in 1921, was being converted to instant operations.

At the same time marketing experts and researchers were shuttling back and forth between World Headquarters and the Van Nuys laboratories, working on new products. One day Ralph Brubaker, vice president in charge of grocery products sales and advertising, dropped in on Mark Shackelford of Instant Products with an idea making the rounds of the eighth floor.

"Ralph said the company was interested in getting into the coffee creamer business," Shackelford recalls, "so I went out to the lab and talked to Dr. McIntire.* In every experimental product he came up with, he ran into

trouble with the butterfat. It oxidized and produced an off-flavor. The problem could be licked by substituting vegetable fat, but, under the federal filled-milk law, no milk product containing vegetable fat was permitted to cross state lines. Finally Dr. McIntire said to me, 'If we really want to make a nice-tasting product, it will have to be non-dairy,' and I said, 'Let's try it.' "

"I talked to the people at the lab about it," Dr. McIntire says. "We'd done some work on a milkless liquid product, so I suggested we take the water out and replace it with corn sirup solids. Lady Luck, we discovered later, was riding on our shoulders. By chance we'd chosen corn sirup because it was an inexpensive carbohydrate with a low level of sweetening. We might just as easily have tried lactose, but since then we've learned that it wouldn't have worked nearly so well.

"In the original formulation of Coffee-mate we had twelve percent protein in the dry product, and here at the lab it worked beautifully, went right into the coffee, but when the plant in Oconomowoc produced it for the first time, it wouldn't disperse readily. We suspected the protein, because it has a great affinity for water and was probably binding up. We decided to cut the protein in half—actually, we went down to five percent—and then we took it back to the plant, and that was it. Worked like a charm."

The development of a non-dairy product to compete with fresh cream touched off

136

*Dr. J. M. McIntire, assistant director of research, succeeded Dr. Bates as general manager in 1967.

Carnation's booth at the Supermarket Institute's 1955 convention in Cleveland. It was staffed by, from left, Bud Nolte, Ruth O'Day, George Catledge, Fred Huber and Dwight Stuart, who helped introduce the ill-fated Instant Chocolate Drink.

some soul-searching on the eighth floor, where it was bound to awaken long-buried memories of the company's experience with Hebe. The product posed a particularly difficult problem for Alfred Ghormley, one of the most highly respected figures in the dairy industry.

"There were many long discussions with Mr. Ghormley," Dwight Stuart recalls, "and in the final analysis he agreed to the test-marketing of the product only on the basis of the argument that if we didn't do it, somebody else might."

Everett Olson sat in on the discussions as Alfred Ghormley's right-hand man. "There

were many questions as to what the reaction of dairymen might be," he says, "but we bit the bullet and went with the product. We knew that more margarine was being sold per capita than butter. So we took the gamble. We had some reaction from dairymen, but it wasn't serious."

Trouble came not from dairymen, but from the laws their state legislators had drawn up for them.

"There was a legal question in many states as to whether the product could be challenged as a filled milk," explains Bob Kummel, Carnation's general counsel. "There are other laws in other states applying to any-

The highly automated Instant Breakfast packaging line in Waverly, Iowa.

thing that purports to be a dairy product. In defending Coffee-mate, we argued that it was a *sui generis* product. It was not an imitation of anything. It was a brand new product and did not purport to be anything other than itself. We had eighteen lawsuits in eighteen different states, and we won them all."

* * * * *

"Carnation Company is currently test marketing a totally new product called Instant Coffee-mate," reported *The Carnation* (February-March, 1961). The editors described it as "a true convenience product, because it keeps fresh in the jar indefinitely without refrigeration, doesn't lump like powdered creams and pours freely." It costs "less than a penny a serving."

"We had many advantages," says Shackelford. "Aside from Coffee-mate's wonderful taste, our product whitened coffee better than the competitive product ounce for ounce, and it was possible for us to make

a substantial investment in advertising. That gave us a tremendous leverage in what was then a very small market. We ran into some problems at first, but in our second year sales shot up 75 per cent."

After creating a new industry with Coffee-mate, the Instant Products Division followed up with another successful innovation. Senior Vice President Henry Arnest, who took the product to market, traces its origins back to an Arthur D. Little Company study.

"Their research showed that the new trends in food would be convenience items that enabled people to get nutrition easily and quickly. Because of postwar schedules, Dad was going one way every morning and Mom another, while the children dashed off to school, so the family wasn't sitting down to have breakfast together as they used to.

"Well, the survey indicated that many of the youngsters and adults were not getting a good breakfast. It was suggested that this was a nutritional problem that we at Carna-

Coffee-mate non-dairy coffee creamer has only 11 calories per level teaspoon. Needs no refrigeration. But most important of all:

Coffee tastes best with Coffee-mate...

no wonder—
it even
whips!

From Carnation

McCall's ad, August 1965.

tion could solve, so being a dairy-oriented company, we said, 'O.K., let's fortify milk,' which wasn't a new thing, but we went one step further. We said, 'Let's fortify it sufficiently to make it equivalent to a well-balanced breakfast.' "

By the end of 1962 Dr. McIntire's men in white had formulated a tasty, nourishing breakfast that could be had simply by tearing open an envelope and stirring the contents into a glass of cold milk. Naming the newborn product touched off a family argument. Some wanted to give it a name that could be registered as a trademark. Their suggestions included ZING, POW and MINI-MEAL. Others held out for a simple descriptive brand name that told consumers what the product was.

"We were introducing a new concept, and by having the name explain its use and its nutrition advantage, we were able to get the idea across more quickly than we might have otherwise," Jack MacDonald, group product manager, points out. "If we had chosen a different name, maybe the product wouldn't have gone over."

Carnation Instant Breakfast was test-marketed in six cities in early 1963. In the fall of the following year, it went on sale in eight Western states.

"For years," Shackelford explained in *The Carnation* (August-September, 1964), "doctors and nutritionists have been telling us that breakfast is our most important meal. Many people worry about the fact that they don't eat a breakfast that is big enough to give them proper nutrition. We've now taken the worry out of breakfast and created something we feel is preferable in taste to the usual hurried breakfast."

In the spring of 1965, Instant Breakfast went into national distribution with five flavors (Chocolate, Chocolate Malted, Coffee, Eggnog and Plain). It was an immediate success. In a matter of months it was selling at the rate of half a billion servings a year.

140

Jack MacDonald, left, the product manager who introduced Instant Breakfast, with Tom Marquis, who helped develop the first truly instant milk, then became general production manager for Carnation's Instant Products Division.

"College kids loved it," Jack MacDonald said recently. "They could mix it and gulp it down in a hurry. Athletes used it for its convenience and its nutrition, and also because it was quickly assimilated. The properties of the product fitted into many different life-styles, and because of the novelty of having a complete, balanced meal in liquid form, we got a great deal of publicity."

A *Life* article on the celebrated heart surgeon, Dr. Michael De Bakey, noted that he started his day by "tossing down a glass of instant breakfast." A magazine for office workers quoted a Cleveland, Ohio, hospital dietician who warned employers that "the office worker who doesn't eat a good breakfast or lunch can't be as productive or have as good a work attitude as the one who does."

Carnation's medical specialists, carrying on their missionary work among doctors and nurses, got a warm response once it was made clear that the contents of a single packet, when added to eight ounces of whole milk, provided one-fourth or more of the minimum

Carnation instant breakfast
Storyboard "NOURISHMENT"

It is - hard to believe - but it's true!

This total amount of nourishment:

A poached egg,

two strips of bacon,

a slice of toast,

and juice

is in this glass of Carnation Instant Breakfast

- for about twenty-five cents, including milk.

When there's no time for regular breakfast.

Read the label. Milk supplies substantial nutrition -

But Carnation Instant Breakfast

Makes Milk a Meal!

Network television has been carrying the message of Instant Breakfast's nourishing ingredients since the product's introduction.

daily requirements of vitamins A, B₁, B₂, C and D, niacin, iron, calcium and phosphorus. The handy new "meal in a glass" also provided vitamins B₆, B₁₂, and copper, along with 25 percent of the National Research Council's recommended daily adult dietary allowance of protein.

In a revised edition of his delightful exposé of American food faddism, *The Nuts Among The Berries* (Ballantine Books, 1968), Ronald M. Deutsch took exception to a Carnation Instant Breakfast advertisement which appeared in *Good Housekeeping* (March, 1966). Deutsch cast a critical eye on the statement: "Each glass delivers as much protein as two eggs, as much mineral nourishment as two strips of crisp bacon, more energy than two slices of buttered toast, and even vitamin C—the orange juice vitamin."

Although the text attributed the nutritional value of the breakfast to "each glass," thus referring to the milk as well as the dry product mixed with it, Deutsch got the notion that the company was trying to convey the impression that the powder alone offered "all the nutrients of a breakfast of eggs, bacon, toast and orange juice." Later, the Federal Trade Commission drew a similar inference, as Bob Kummel explained in a recent interview.

"They raised the issue of the nutritional value contributed by the milk that the consumer supplied as opposed to the mix we sell. We thought that it was commonly recognized that milk is nutritional. It is certainly part of our advertising policy, since we are in the milk business. We thought it was redundant, but we didn't fight it. We were more than willing to acknowledge that milk is, indeed, nutritious."

* * * * *

For some years Carnation had been keeping an eye on products designed for weight-watchers. By 1964 the market had come to be dominated by two brands of canned liquids, Metrecal and Sego, both of which were vulnerable in an important area—flavor. Word went out from the eighth floor to Dr.

McIntire's researchers to develop a product dieters would enjoy using.

Bill Jackson, group leader at the Van Nuys laboratories, was assigned the task of formulating what came to be known as Slender. There were three requirements for the product. It would have only 225 calories when added to an 8-ounce glass of milk. Its flavor must be pleasing. It could be mass-produced.

"That last requirement was the stickler," Bill later told *The Carnation* (June-July, 1967). "It is easy to make a great product here in the lab, but to come up with something that will work for million-pound production is much more difficult. Because we wanted our product to be mixed with whole

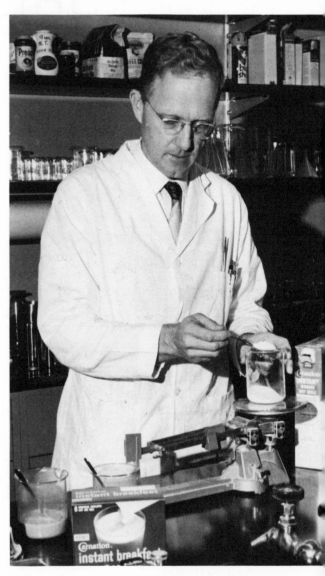

A research team led by Bill Jackson parlayed the company's expertise in instantizing and flavors into such successful products as Instant Breakfast and Slender diet food.

milk, we had to begin our calculations with the calories and components of milk. The difference between the 162 calories in eight ounces of milk and our goal of 225 was 63. We had to add all the necessary nutrients and flavor ingredients without adding more than 63 calories."

To keep the calorie count down, Bill had to eliminate sugar and reduce the amount of nonfat dry milk he would normally use in a high-protein product. Protein in some other form had to be added. There was the rub.

"As you know," he explained, "a powdered product is not an instant product. A substance is instantized by sticking a lot of grains of powder together into a porous, irregular form that will absorb liquid quickly and dissolve easily. Without sugar and the natural sugar in nonfat milk we had a problem."

The problem was worked out and in October, 1966, Slender went into three test markets. At the same time a team of physicians in Phoenix and one in Beverly Hills conducted clinical research on the product. Seventy-three subjects were placed on a diet of nothing but Slender for three weeks. Three dropped out. The weight loss for the rest averaged 12.58 pounds. The study showed that dieters could rely on Slender as their sole

Reader's Digest ad, October 1972.

143

source of calories, drinking it four times a day, without ill effects.

"The surprising feature of this formula was its satiety value," the report added. "Most of the subjects questioned stated that their appetite was satisfied and that they were not hungry during the day."

Mark Shackelford, as manager of the Instant Products Division, and Lee Abramson, as product manager for Slender, carried the good news to the division's Management Committee and finally, with the approval of the Executive Committee, the decision was made to market Slender nationally. Marketing plans were worked out with the sales department and, on March 28, 1967, Carnation's new North Waverly, Iowa, plant started production on five flavors: Chocolate, Dutch Chocolate, Jubilee Cherry, French Vanilla and Wild Strawberry.

Sales representatives were assembled in four cities (San Francisco, Chicago, Dallas, Philadelphia). The hotel meeting room in each city was turned into a simulated ball park—Carnation Park, naturally—with a baseball diamond, bleachers, dugouts, tickets and scorecards. The salesmen were decked out in baseball uniforms and their coaches, similarly costumed, gave them the Slender pitch, filling them in on the product's dazzling earned-run average in test markets and clinical studies.

"We were marketing something that nobody really wants to use," recalls Lee Abramson. "Nobody wants to go on a diet, because nobody wants to give up the things that got them in trouble in the first place. So we stood back and took a hard look at our product and asked ourselves, 'All right, what's going to make people buy it?' We decided not to dwell on the weight-loss aspects, but to put our emphasis on flavor and convenience. Here was something that tasted so good you'd want to stay with it, and you wouldn't have to count calories. Slender had already counted them for you. That, of course, is the key. It's not the product that works, it's the reduction of calories."

Slender was brought to public notice na-

tionally in the pages of *Life* and *McCall's* in June, 1967.

"The first liquid diet that doesn't taste like a liquid diet," proclaimed the headline, and the text played up the product's handiness. The weight-watcher simply opened a packet, dropped the contents into a cold glass of milk, stirred and drank. Together, the milk and Slender produced the minerals and vitamins of a meal on "a mere 225 calories." Moreover, it tasted so good it wouldn't "remind you, with every sip, what a sacrifice you're making." The advertisement ended with a promise: "If you don't find it delicious, we'll cheerfully refund your pounds."

From the day it first went into test market, Slender had the look of a winner. Everything fell into place. Nothing went wrong. It was a different story two years later when canned Slender was about to make its debut and ran afoul of the federal government's ban on the use of cyclamates. The order was handed down on October 18, 1969, and manufacturers were given until February 1 to stop selling products containing the artificial sweetener. Carnation chose not to take advantage of the three-and-one-half month respite. Sales of Slender were halted immediately. The company's researchers, fortunately, were waiting at Van Nuys with a new formula. Non-cyclamate Slender, instant and canned, began to appear on grocers' shelves in January.

* * * * *

The 1960s began with new highs for sales ($417,629,239) and profits ($11,152,358). The decade ended with a sales volume bordering on the brink of one billion dollars ($964,404,077) and a net income of $39,567,801. Much of the credit for this surge in sales and profits belonged not only to the Instant Products Division, the youngest and most glamorous member of the corporate household, but also to Pet Foods, a scrawny stepchild left thirty-odd years earlier on the doorstep of Albers Bros. Milling Company.

From infancy, Instant Products had been the darling of the eighth floor, getting what-

144

...nstant plant in Jacksonville, Illinois, produces and packages Coffee-mate non-dairy creamer.

The only dog food that's

PURE BEEF, NO BY-PRODUCTS.

Only new MIGHTY DOG from Carnation can wear this brand...pure beef. All other canned dog foods contain by-products. But new MIGHTY DOG is pure, tender beef. No by-products. Only his vitamins and minerals added. Wait till you see him eat new, pure beef MIGHTY DOG. Single-serving cans, no left-overs.

Introducing two new reasons why no cat ever walked away from Friskies Buffet

Beef & Liver. Poultry Platter. Two exciting new flavor varieties from Friskies Buffet. Each has the kind of protein cats need and the meat varieties cats love. Each variety is cooked slowly...very slowly...to keep the meat tender and tasty. Delicious. Now there are 17 reasons why no cat ever walked away from Friskies Buffet.

Sunday Supplement ads, September 1972 (upper), and March 1973 (lower).

ever it wanted in the way of new factories and equipment. Pet Foods often had to make do with hand-me-downs. Edwin Ladegaard, general production manager for the Pet Food and Cereal Division, tells the story of Frank Hall's experience in the 1950s, when he was sent to Jefferson, Wisconsin, to convert its venerable condensery to the manufacture of pet food.

"Frank was our construction troubleshooter at that time," Ed says. "The day he got to the Jefferson plant the door was locked, so he kicked it open and went inside. He had a single sheet of paper in his hand. That constituted the entire engineering plan for what he was supposed to do. In 1969, when we began our new plant at St. Joseph, Missouri, we had engineers' drawings a foot high."

So shaky was Carnation's commitment to the national distribution of Friskies that in 1959 the Executive Committee considered withdrawing from the fiercely competitive dog food market in the East. "We weighed the odds," Everett Olson recalls, "and after many meetings decided to stick it out." In the next decade the country's dog and cat population grew three times as fast as the human population. By 1973 pet foods constituted a $1.75-billion-a-year industry and, thanks to the 1959 decision to hang on, Carnation was one of the five companies that controlled two-thirds of the business.* The dollar volume of Carnation's pet food sales in the single month of January, 1974, equalled the total figure for the entire year of 1960.

"Since 1962 we've consistently grown at about double the growth rate of the pet food industry, which has been growing at the rate of about ten or twelve percent a year," says Don Moore, vice president in charge of pet foods.

Don's father, the versatile Merton Moore—calf-salesman, Carnation chronicler and Albers advertising manager—was largely responsible for the successful introduction of

*The other four, reported by *Forbes* (October 15, 1973): Ralston Purina, Liggett & Myers, Quaker Oats and General Foods.

Friskies Cubes in western markets in 1934. The pellets were followed eight years later by Friskies Meal. Both Cubes and Meal sold especially well during World War II, when canned dog food fell victim to the shortage of metals.

"Much thought and serious consideration has been devoted to the feasibility of Friskies taking on a new postwar dress," Erwin, Wasey reported in 1946, when researchers under Dr. E. M. Gildow were working at Carnation Farms on a canned dog food. It was tried out in Washington and Oregon markets in the spring of 1948. Canned dog food, by then, had become the second largest single canned item sold in the United States (evaporated milk was first).

"From all indications the sales of dry Friskies has not suffered in any way by the introduction of canned Friskies," declared Erwin, Wasey in making its 1949 recommendations for advertising the new product in the Pacific Northwest, where it was still in the test stage, its sales running "well ahead of original estimates."

The first national advertising campaign for Friskies was launched in 1953. Six years later the dry dog food was in distribution in approximately seventy percent of the United States, and canned Friskies was being distributed nationally, except for the New York City area. That breakthrough came in 1960, some months after the Executive Committee's decision not to surrender the eastern marketplace.

"Since 1958 our company has introduced nine new Friskies products and increased distribution to include all of the United States on most products and the major part of the country on the rest," reported *The Carnation* in the spring of 1963, the year Pet Foods was split off from Albers and designated a separate division, with Don Moore as its national product manager. Four years later it was combined with Cereals and Don was made its vice president and manager.

* * * * *

The Friskies marketing and research people whipped up an experimental product

145

in the early 1950s, a special food for puppies, small dogs and—the label proclaimed as something of an afterthought—cats.

"We had it in only one market, here in Los Angeles," says Carnation's super-salesman, Henry Arnest. "I'd see people buying it and I'd ask them what they were using it for, and they'd say, 'Well, we have a cat.' I'd ask them, 'Will the cat eat it?' and they'd say, 'He doesn't particularly like it, but on weekends, when we're away from home, we leave it out for him and he eats it.'

"I felt that a product designed for cats, something made from fish, would sell. It was a nutty idea, the company thought, but I'd talked to too many ladies with cats. I kept asking for $2,500 to do some research, and finally Mr. Ghormley said, 'Well, let's give Henry a vote of confidence and let him have his $2,500.'"

Norman Berkness, product manager for canned dog and cat foods, remembers the meeting. It came at a time when Pet Foods was projecting a sizeable loss for the year. Alfred Ghormley listened to Henry's persuasive plea for $2,500 and, as Norm recalls his comment, he said, "We ought to be able to raise that amount of money from our own pockets."

Henry Arnest's bargain-basement survey persuaded the company to take a flier in cat food. An arrangement was worked out with Western Canners, a Newport Beach, California, fish cannery, to provide fresh mackerel which Albers blended with cereals, vegetables and vitamins. It was put on sale in the West early in 1956, and *The Carnation* (July-August, 1957) was delighted with its success during its first eighteen months. "The finest quality cat food on the market today," the editor declared.

As early as 1955 Friskies researchers at the Carnation Farms research cattery had reminded the company's pet food planners that fish was not the only diet that cats enjoyed. A rural cat's smorgasbord included small birds, field mice, gophers and young rabbits. The reminder led in 1958 to the introduction of Friskies Chicken Flavor Cat

146

Life and Saturday Evening Post ad, December 1948.

Two of Friskies' long-time promoters—Vice President Don Moore, center, and Product Manager Norm Berkness, right, who helped the line develop from four products to forty-four.

Henry C. Arnest talked to housewives and the result was one of Carnation's most popular products—Little Friskies for Cats.

The pet food plant at Jefferson, Wisconsin, bears little resemblance today to the condensery it once was.

Food, made from chicken by-products. It was followed by a new concept for cat food, between-meal snacks marketed as "treats."

"The treat food business started only five years ago, so it's fairly new," Don Moore explained in 1963. "In the West treats have succeeded in capturing 38 percent of the cat food market by weight and 56 percent of the dollar volume. So far, 50 percent of all treat business is done on the West Coast, partly because it started there and partly because western families are more willing to try new products. But this popularity is bound to spread."

Unfortunately, however, the product had fallen on lean days by the summer of 1967 when Glynn Morris, fresh from Columbia Graduate School of Business, arrived at World Headquarters in time to participate in the evolution of cat treats to a successful new premium line.

"The treats had been advertised simply as Friskies in a small can," Glynn recalls. "They had no separate identity as a specialty cat food, and they didn't have the palatability of their two leading competitors. They contained cereal, which is fine from the point of view of nutrition, but not palatability. We decided to reformulate into an all-meat product, and that increased our palatability tremendously. We selected the name Buffet, which had a good food connotation, suggesting variety. That gave us our unique identity.

"We had many meetings discussing the possibility of test-marketing the Buffet line. Finally, Mr. Olson asked us one day, 'What's your advertising budget for the next year?' and we said, 'Seven hundred and fifty thousand dollars.' He told us to take the money and spend it during the first two months to roll out the new line as a replacement for the treats and get a high level of new distribution.

"We went into New York first. I'd estimated a sale of 45,000 cases for the introductory period. I asked our district manager what he thought we'd sell and he said 60,000. We ended up selling about 125,000. It was an excellent product, better than anything

else on the market, and the company put money behind it. It took off like a rocket."

* * * * *

Carnation's premium canned cat food was followed in 1973 by the introduction of Mighty Dog, a premium dog food that started out to be a convenience food packed in a can designed for a single serving ("No Left-overs"), but somewhere along the road between the Van Nuys laboratories and World Headquarters the concept switched from convenience to ingredients and it ended up as the first dogfood to be made entirely of pure beef ("No By-Products").*

"Alpo had come out with an all-meat dog food," recalls Don Moore. "It wasn't really all-meat; it was meat and meat by-products, but they'd been very successful with it. We made a concept study on two products. One was for old dogs, the other for small, fussy dogs. The small, fussy dogs won out, and we decided to call the product Mighty Dog."

The Alpo advertising theme carried the message, "All meat and meat by-products. No cereals." Carnation presented Mighty Dog as all meat. Period. No cereals *and* no meat by-products. It was pure beef, and it came in a handy single-serving can.

"It had the advantage for the owner of not having to give the dog half a can, put it back in the refrigerator and then serve a cold, congealed, unpalatable mess the next day," says Hugh R. Chamberlin, new product development manager for Pet Foods. "The dog got a fresh meal every day. From the time we first went into test market, there was never any question of Mighty Dog's success. It's the most palatable dog food on the market anywhere in the world."

No one at Carnation could recall a new product that had generated such an enthusiastic response. Samples of the unsolicited testimonials appeared in the Summer, 1973, issue of *The Carnation*.

"Our terrier has been eating your Mighty

---

*The term, by-products, includes such things as liver, kidney, spleen, tripe, brains and lungs, but not skin, horns, teeth, bones and hoofs.

Bob Bartos, manager of Friskies Research Kennels, with Carnation's Scottish Terrier, Ch. Bardene Bingo, winner of Westminster Kennel Club's Best in Show in 1967. The dog was an English, American and Canadian champion.

Dog beef, and she loves it. I tasted it the other day and now I know why."

"He would eat, at best, every other day (unless he got h-u-m-a-n food). I began to feel guilty! Was it his home life? Was it because he was named Shalom and has to put up with a Catholic mother? But finally we came across your miraculous product. Incredible as it may seem he has eaten regularly for the past month!"

"For five years she ate table food or nothing at all. Since I gave her Mighty Dog she won't eat anything else!"

"My mother thanks you for not having to cook for the dog. My dog thanks you for not having to eat my mother's cooking."

* * * * *

A successful pet food must satisfy both the customer who buys it and the consumer who eats it, but before any new Carnation product goes into test market, it must first satisfy Bob

Bartos, who runs the Friskies Research Center's kennels at Carnation Farms, and Ron Stapley, who runs its cattery.

"Our activity," Bob once told *The Carnation* (April-May, 1963), "is based on breeding and management practices as encountered in everyday life by the average pet owner and large and small breeders in the U.S.A. These studies are correlated with controlled nutrition to produce for the American dog or cat the best possible food for his health and well-being, as well as for the convenience and economy of his master."

"We're here for two reasons, nutrition and palatability," Ron explained to a visitor who recently dropped by the cattery. "If you have a cat food product that doesn't taste good, you can have all the nutrition in the world built into it, but it won't do any good because the cat won't eat it. The reverse is also true, of course. You can have an extremely palatable food without the nutrition built into it, and they'll eat it, but it won't do them any good."

Cats, for example, like fish, but its lack of vitamin E can cause trouble. Dogs like sweets, which get no response from cats. To Mike Aldrich, a group product manager who handles food for both cats and dogs, the cat's ability to detect the most subtle variations in a test product is uncanny.

"A cat can immediately spot the difference in a formula that has 5 percent more liver than another," he says.

* * * * *

By a happy stroke of timing, the spate of new pet foods and instant products streaming out of Carnation's plants came at a stage in the company's development when its updated recruiting and training program was providing the aggressive, professional young sales managers it needed to market its new lines. The man chiefly responsible for building Carnation's present-day sales organization is Senior Vice President Henry Clay Arnest.

"Our personnel program was modernized in 1949, when we moved into World Headquarters," he recalls, "but by 1953 it was apparent that the program wasn't working. I told Mr. Ghormley I'd like to present a program that I thought would fit our long-term needs. I said I'd like to talk to Mr. Stuart. That was a Thursday, I remember, and I said, 'I'll be ready Monday morning, if you'll make a date for me.' Mr. Stuart's reaction, as almost always, was simple and direct. He said, 'I want a training program here and I don't give a damn how you do it. Just do it.'

"I recommended that we continue to recruit young people in the colleges, as we'd been doing, but that we only count that as an initial interview. My feeling was that our recruiters were not operational people. I proposed that after these initial interviews, I'd go out with my associates and interview candidates, and we'd tell the colleges that the people who passed these initial interviews would be selected to go to New York, all expenses paid, for final interviews with top

management. In 1953 very few companies, and none in our industry that I know of, paid the expenses of candidates into New York."

Alfred Ghormley, addressing the San Francisco Ad Club in the spring of 1955, explained Carnation's reasons for overhauling its marketing team as the nation's economy shifted from a sellers' market of wartime shortages to a buyers' market of peacetime plenty. The company needed a team that "would be able to promptly recognize, and promptly adjust its marketing program to the complex, rapidly changing trends of the modern marketing scene, that could come up with better selling, better advertising, better merchandising, new items, improvements in old items, and so forth, to keep pace with the continually increased tempo of modern business."

The team Alfred had in mind would "be able to meet any competition, any time, any place, under any conditions, and make progress." Equally important, the team would have to be "capable of systematically developing potential replacements for top-level, key men in the marketing organization—and in the company."

Bob Stevens, beating the academic bushes to flush out management trainees, had just found one such man at Michigan State. Timm Crull, Class of 1955, had decided to have a chat with the Carnation representative because he'd been favorably impressed by a magazine article written by another of the company's recruiters, Wally Jamie. Timm's interview went swimmingly and he was invited to fly back to New York to meet Henry Arnest, who is now his neighbor on the eighth floor of World Headquarters.

"First time I'd ever been to New York," Timm recalls. "I'll never forget it. The interview was on a Sunday morning at 9 o'clock. They made me an offer then and there. I had a number of offers for jobs, but the reason I decided to go with Carnation was that I felt it was a people-oriented company. I had better offers monetarily, including one from General Motors, but none of them offered Carnation's sort of personal relationships.

The placement director at Michigan State put the arm on me to go with GM. 'Just think,' he warned me, 'if you're successful with Carnation, you'll end up living in Los Angeles, California.' "

Timm and his family have ended up living in one of its posh suburbs, San Marino, and he has been spectacularly successful with Carnation Company. He received five promotions in his first six years and made vice president at the age of 36. He was elected to the board of directors five years later. He had just turned 42 in February, 1973, when he was picked to be one of Carnation's three group vice presidents, with multi-divisional responsibilities.*

"Our sales organization is a home-grown

*The other two were Clarke Nelson and Glen Mitchell.

outfit," Timm says. "Everybody, right up through the vice presidents, has started as a salesman within our organization. We've developed our people. We know them well. They're career-oriented, company-oriented. This is a great strength, as compared with an organization that is continually hiring marketing soldiers of fortune who move from company to company. We have seven general sales managers. Every one of them started with Carnation Company the day he got out of college.

"There's a tremendous *esprit de corps*. This attracts young people, and it holds them. There's a great advantage to being part of the Carnation marketing team, they find. The Carnation name is well known and highly respected in our industry. When that name is on a product, our customers accept

151

Carnation has always trained its own sales force. These 1969 general sales managers include John Thompson, extreme left, now vice president in charge of grocery products sales, and Dick Chaput, second from left, now national sales manager for food service. Others are Bill Matthews, Bill Baar, John Nielsen, Bob Jessel and Floyd Goettge.

it as a quality product that will be strongly promoted and will serve a definite need of the consumer. It's either a product that hasn't been on the market before or an improvement of something already on the market. This has helped our growth tremendously over the last twenty years."

* * * * *

While Grocery Products trained fresh troops to fight the jungle war for shelf space, Distribution streamlined its operations to adjust to the new demands from Sales. In an earlier day, when Carnation was essentially a one-product company as far as grocers were concerned, it could ship evaporated milk by the carload. Once it got into instant products and new lines of pet foods, however, it ran into traffic problems in filling orders quickly and economically.

The solution lay in filling cars off the production line and shipping them to a central point for distribution, thus enabling Carnation customers to buy a mixture of products at carload prices. Before the new system was introduced, products had been piled up in a hundred different public warehouses. Ultimately the consumer had paid for storage and handling and local trucking charges. By the spring of 1962, Carnation had seven distribution centers.

"Everything is shipped in carload lots," reported *The Carnation* (February-March, 1962), "and it costs no more to deliver to the customer's siding than it did to the public warehouses. Since Carnation products are no longer spread out across the country, our total inventory can be much smaller. Because the merchandise moves faster and doesn't lie around on shelves, it is much fresher."

Carnation products travel not only by rail, but also in a fleet of more than five thousand vehicles designed to serve the company's varied needs, which range from the delivery of ice cream and rabbit feed to the transportation of a purebred bull or a 25,000-pound roll of tinplate.

"In the last few years," says Ken Smith, assistant transportation manager, who handles the fleet's hotline to World Headquar-

ters, "we've managed to carry more products in fewer vehicles because they're built of lighter material and that enables them to carry heavier payloads and still meet the load-limit requirements of state highway departments."

* * * * *

By the late 1960s, acquisitions, diversification and growth had confronted Carnation with additional distribution problems. Its twenty-eight plants were turning out two hundred and fifty products for national distribution. To move them to the seven distribution centers and from there to the company's customers required more than 20,000 rail shipments a year and some 200,000 invoices.

"The problem is fascinating because it encompasses not just the traditional aspects of warehousing and transportation," noted *The Carnation* (April-May, 1968), "but inventory control, packaging design, data processing and transmittal, re-order levels and sales forecasting as well."

At a cost of nearly three quarters of a million dollars, Carnation installed an IBM 360/40 at World Headquarters in 1968. The third-generation computer was capable of holding within its mechanical memory everything the company needed to know about the movement of its products from raw material to plant to can and to customer.

"Acquiring a computer like the 360/40 means we have the ability to coordinate operations and to simplify tremendously complex problems—really the essence of good business practice in this day and age," said Vice President Reed Braithwaite, who had been put in charge of data processing. "Simplification means greater efficiency—faster service, fewer errors, fewer customer complaints—and, ultimately, a payoff in dollars and cents."

On a spring weekend in 1974, workmen showed up at World Headquarters to replace the 360/40 with a new IBM 370/145.

"This gives us double the capacity of our old computer," Reed explained. "We can now have larger files, devise new systems

Carnation's distribution centers make carloads of mixed products possible, saving customers time and money.

and handle remote entry and remote printing, which means that we can enter information in the New York sales office, for example, transfer it to Los Angeles, update our files, and pass the relevant material on to a distribution center in Michigan or Pennsylvania."

Distribution's space-age technology, however, has to deal with the antiquated railroads of the 1970s. For nearly twenty years Al Davis, assistant vice president, Transportation and Distribution, has been attending conferences where canned goods shippers weep into one another's Scotches-and-soda about the steady deterioration in rail service which has now achieved the dimensions of a national crisis. The growth of canned goods shipments keeps going up, the availability of cars keeps going down. Meanwhile, to the distress of the shippers, empty cars continue to rattle across the countryside after having made a delivery somewhere.

"How many railroads today have operating departments that follow the philosophy that the movement of empty cars to a point where they are sorely needed will bring additional business to the railroad and give that added leverage which contributes so much to earnings?" Al asked at the 1974 Canned Goods Shippers Conference. "Why the importance of utilization of equipment, loaded and empty, as a contributor to earnings is not included as part of standard operating procedure escapes me."

In conversation a few weeks after the conference, he reverted to the subject of the car shortage.

"The only way we've been able to get by is by raising the volume per car from twenty-six tons back in 1956 to an average of forty-one tons today. We've put up with this deteriorating situation for a long, long time. It's gotten the attention of Congress, and I'm a bit fearful that we may get more of a political than an economics solution."

* * * * *

Carnation's increasing involvement with new products has posed new problems not only for Transportation and Distribution, but also for Purchasing, which must shop for ingredients often in short supply, and Engineering, which must provide plants and equipment, even when a new process calls for unheard-of new machinery. Both departments seem to enjoy the chance to work fresh wonders in buying and building.

"If everything were perfect," says Joe MacBriar of Purchasing, "this would be one of the company's dullest departments."

Joe is a second-generation Carnation employee. His father, W. N. MacBriar, started working for E. A. Stuart in 1910, when he set out to develop his Snoqualmie Valley farm. Joe signed up with Carnation in 1932. He was in Tulsa, working in ice cream sales when he joined the Army in 1942. Four years later, restored to civilian life, he was assigned to Los Angeles as Fresh Milk and Ice Cream's purchasing agent. He was appointed director of the company's purchasing department in 1964.

"Carnation has been fortunate," he told *The Carnation* (Winter, 1973-74), when food companies were grappling with shortages of such commodities as sugar, cocoa, fats and oils. "We have always treated suppliers fairly when it's been a buyer's market. They're human; they remember."

It's up to Joe MacBriar to see to it that Carnation plants get a steady supply of the materials they need to manufacture and package their products, old and new. It's up to Jim Webster and his colleagues in Engineering to see to it that the plants are designed, constructed and equipped to run smoothly and economically.

"Our condenseries were practically a standard item," Jim says. "Starting from the back end, we had the engine room and boiler room, then the fresh milk tanks, the cooking and homogenizing equipment, the evaporated milk tanks, the filling machines and the sterilizing machines. We shipped the finished product from the front end. They were very specialized plants, very efficient, all built of reinforced concrete. We've just sold one built in 1910. It's still a fine building."

When Carnation was caught up in the instant revolution, Engineering converted a couple of old condenseries in order to get cracking on production as quickly as possible, and then the department set to work in Waverly, Iowa, on the first plant ever built solely for the processing of instant products. Among other innovations, Carnation's drawing-board dreamers came up with machinery that made possible the automated packing of Instant Breakfast packettes.

"We're into areas we didn't know anything about a few years ago," Jim adds. "We've had to learn—sometimes the hard way."

The Engineering Department traces its origins back to E. A. Stuart's original condensery in Kent, Washington. He hired carpenters and electricians to refurbish the abandoned plant, and as his company expanded, he rounded up his own engineers instead of turning to outside firms. Carnation was well served by such men as W. N. MacBriar, who built the dairy barn where Carnation cows ran up so many of their world records, and Roy Henszey, whose revolutionary devices became standard equipment throughout the industry.

"Henszey's pioneering method of handling milk so that each item flows uninterrupted from the receiving door to the ultimate carload is now so familiar to American dairy workers that they accept it as a matter of course," *The Carnation* (July-August, 1948) pointed out when he retired after thirty-four years as the company's chief engineer.

Roy Henszey was succeeded by John Forslew, who was interviewed by *The Carnation* in the winter of 1966-67.

"Carnation differs wisely from other companies that may have a few engineers on their payrolls, but which farm out major projects to consulting firms," Forslew said.

154

"Because we are similar to a consulting-engineering firm, we find ourselves evaluating possible sites for construction, designing complete multimillion-dollar operations, supervising the installation of machinery, planning for additions to existing plants and remodeling. Carnation may be our only client, but the company's diversification gives a wide range of engineering activity."

"We know our business best," says Jim Webster, who took over the department in March, 1968, when Forslew retired. "We can produce the engineering work more economically in a shorter time for better results. In areas where we are producing new products, in the instantizing process, for example, we design the equipment and keep all the know-how in the company."

* * * * *

One day shortly before the February,

1963, meeting of the board of directors, Elbridge Stuart called Everett Olson to his office and, with Alfred Ghormley looking on from his wheel-chair, broke the news that Alfred's crippling illness had reached the point where he could no longer shoulder the burdens of the presidency. He was to be appointed vice chairman and Everett's name was to be submitted to the board as his successor. It was a moment Everett had spent more than thirty years preparing for. He was ready.

"When you were named assistant to the president in 1961, you must have known that you were the heir apparent?" a visitor remarked recently.

"Well, yes," Everett replied, "unless I stubbed my toe."

"Or got a knife in the back?"

"No, I didn't expect that. We've had no

Before the condensery in Alberta was built in 1962, the Engineering Department made the model being studied by, from left, Roy Lazar, chief engineer for Evaporated Milk; John Forslew, assistant vice president; and J. W. Webster, director of engineering. Models add an important third dimension, useful in both planning and training.

155

infighting here, no politics. A person is judged on the basis of performance, not relationships.''

Everett Olson's performance over the last three decades had made his succession to the presidency inevitable. In recent years, along with holding down the presidency of Albers Milling Company and serving as a director of the Carnation-Pet foreign affiliate, he had presided over the meetings of the Finance Committee and played a leading role in the work of the Executive Committee and the management committees of each of the company's ten divisions.

"Throughout his years with the company,'' noted *The Carnation* (April-May, 1963), "he has demonstrated the ability to analyze people and problems. In committee meetings he is able to distinguish between what is essential and what is merely important, cutting to the heart of the matter under discussion.''

No important decision had been made on the eighth floor in recent years before it had been analyzed and candidly discussed by Everett Olson at top-level meetings.

"He played a tremendous role in the growth of this company long before he was in the driver's seat,'' says an eighth-floor associate. "He did it through toughness, guts and sound business judgment. He has an exploratory mind. It's open, flexible, objective. Everett made a lot of changes around here simply by seeing a need and doing something about it. He's always been a charger, a go-ahead guy.''

Even before he was given the title, he was doing much of the work of the disabled president.

"I don't think the title makes the man,'' he says. "I think the man makes the title. We haven't built any fences around anyone. Just because a person has a certain title, that doesn't mean he can't go beyond that, do a little searching and be a little aggressive and make a few recommendations even though he may be stepping out of his bailiwick.''

Fifteen years before his elevation to the presidency, when Carnation was settling into its new World Headquarters, Everett occupied a modest first-floor cubicle next door to Maynard Heider, the company's office manager, whose thrift has become legend. Watercooler wits insist he prowled the building after hours, fishing pencil stubs from wastebaskets and straightening bent paperclips. Maynard first got acquainted with Everett in 1948 when he was appointed treasurer, the post Maynard's former boss had held in Oconomowoc.

"I didn't know how we'd get along,'' Maynard recalls, "but I found him a very fair and a very fine gentleman to work for. He's a man of rather few words, speaks directly to the point, and one sometimes misreads a man like that. One gets the impression he's unfriendly, distant, hard to get along with. But he's just the opposite once you get to know him.

"He struck me as a very intelligent man, very hard working and very ambitious. He was always in on the making of management decisions, and so it was easy to see that he was going to move upstairs. Many executives who make it big put their job ahead of their family, but not Everett. His family has always been a very, very important part of his life.

"He's often looked on as aloof and cold, and part of that is the way he walks through the office when he comes to work. He'll speak to two or three people he knows real well, but he'll look past the other people. I don't think they realize how darn many things he has on his mind. He knows more about this company than anybody ever will again. He grew up with it.''

12
Taking Care Of Business

*"The company seemed
to explode about the time
Everett Olson moved into command."*
TIMM F. CRULL, 1974

AT LUNCHEON ONE DAY when plans were being laid for the observance of Carnation's seventy-fifth anniversary, Everett Olson shook a fresh cigarette from the open package always within reach and looked back over his forty-three years with the company.

"I don't think we've had any real heroes," he said. "We've worked pretty hard and fortunately for us and for the company our efforts have paid off. No one man is responsible for the success of a company, but one man can cause the failure of a company. If he insists on carrying out his ideas and his ideas are wrong, he can cause a company to fail, but no man can claim the credit for a company's success. That is the work of a team.

"Possibly the man is somewhat responsible for the team, for its efforts, its direction, and so on, but in my case I think it has to be recognized that I inherited a great organization. Certainly we've made changes over the years. Changes will always take place. We did certain things, made certain acquisitions, but that was not because of my *not* having been in the position of president before. It just so happened that when I *was* in that position, these things did occur and I got the benefit. The years have been good to me since I became president."

Nine months after Everett Olson succeeded to the presidency, Carnation made its first major acquisition since the 1929 purchase of Albers Bros. Milling Company. On September 5, 1963, the company acquired a full line of quality tomato products, peaches and Italian specialties by buying Contadina Foods, an old, well established canning company in Northern California.

"The acquisition enabled us to get into a food area we had not been in before," Olson recalled ten years later. "It was a relatively small, family company, but we knew that with our organization, particularly our marketing organization, we could do a great deal to strengthen and expand the company. It was processing less than 200,000 tons of tomatoes a year when we bought it. Now we're processing better than 500,000 tons.

"The company had distribution in the northeast quadrant of the country. Now the division's distribution is national. We did this through our sales organization. The company had operated through brokers. It used to be constantly beleaguered by the banks when it built up inventories. We knew that with our financial strength we could be considerably helpful to a company like that."

Carnation's milkmen, working with con-

158

Final sorting is still a hand operation in a Contadina plant.

tented cows and year-round production lines, were strangers to the ulcer-inducing seasonal problems and perils of transposing tomatoes from vine to can to supermarket shelf. The business had some of the more unsettling elements of participating in a track and field meet on an abandoned minefield, as readers of *The Carnation* (December-January, 1964-65) discovered in the editor's report on the first Contadina-Carnation "pack."

"There are natural hazards to contend with, such as rain which rots the tomatoes in the fields. There are unnatural hazards—braceros who wage sit-down strikes in the fields when they decide their pay per box should be raised. There are mechanical hazards—machinery subject to breakdown without warning, while 20,000,000 ripe, perishable tomatoes are being unloaded in the yard. There are competitors who must be closely watched lest they flood the market with any one type of product and cause a price drop.

"The men whose companies survive and prosper in this business are the ones who, first, are able to make the right decisions in a hurry, and, second, have an organization flexible enough both mentally and physically to implement the decisions. During 'the pack,' the 3-month production period, there is never time to feed information into an electronic computer to find the best course of action. The right answers have to come instinctively, from a broad base of experience."

Sometime before Christmas each year, more than six months before the start of the next pack, Contadina's production and merchandising managers have to decide how many cases of each tomato product they can sell in the 12-month period following the pack. To arrive at such a figure, they have to consider current sales, inventory, prospects and production facilities, along with the possibility of increasing sales by making improvements in products or packaging.

The number of cases to be produced must then be translated into the number of tons of tomatoes the field men will have to line up for Contadina's four Northern California plants (San Jose, Woodland, Riverbank, Hollister). Once the tonnage is determined, the figure is converted to the number of acres of tomatoes required to supply the division's projected needs. Contadina field men then start knocking at the doors of the growers, lining up both early and late-maturing varieties of tomatoes.

"I never appreciated the true luxury of continuous production until I got into tomatoes," says Don Fuhrman, Contadina group product manager who was transferred to the division from Instant Products in the summer of 1970. "They put me to work on sales estimates. I hadn't realized that with tomatoes you've got about twelve weeks to process

all the product you hope to sell in the coming year. You have to come up with the right amount of peeled tomatoes, stewed tomatoes, puree, paste, sauce, and so on. You just get one shot of the dice, and that's it.

"In Instant Products we'd make sales estimates for each product, month by month. If at the end of a month, we found we'd overestimated, we could have the plant cut back a shift or, conversely, if we'd underestimated, the plant could work overtime. At Contadina I discovered I had to keep reworking estimates continually on almost a weekly basis, depending on the type and quality of the tomatoes that were coming in.

"One of the tomatoes we pack, for example,

Aerial view of Contadina plant, Riverbank, California.

is pear-shaped. If they weren't coming in or if they were coming in but weren't of peelable quality, we'd have to switch to something else, but we still had contracted for a fixed amount of those pear-shaped tomatoes and somehow we would have to manage to pack that many tons.

"When I'd visited our instant plants, probably the largest quantity of finished goods I'd ever seen was about a week's production. Well, at the end of a season with Contadina, we'd have a year's supply on hand. The first time I went to the Contadina plants, I was amazed. Everywhere I looked, *everywhere*, I saw finished goods. Every warehouse was full. They had cases piled on the docks, covered with tarps in case of rain. I shook my head and said to myself, 'Fuhrman, what in the world have you done?' "

* * * * *

Because of the nature of the business, Contadina's top salesman, Jim Matalone, and its production manager, Ray Warren, worked closely together. The relationship ended on a winter morning in 1974 when Jim died of a heart attack while driving to work.

"I took a lot of field trips with him," Ray recalls. "I got to see the great respect our customers had for him. He was a man of his word. If he saw we were running into a shortage of tonnage and would have to prorate our customers, for example, he would notify them before the season ended, so they'd have a chance to go somewhere else and cover themselves. He lived the canning business. Every year you run into a new set of challenges. You have to work with variables and still end up with a product of the same high quality."

Much of Ray's work these days involves programs in Contadina plants to help uneducated and unskilled employees, mostly Mexican-Americans, get some schooling, improve their skills and move up to management jobs. He is also stamping out the last vestiges of the traditional allocation of jobs on the basis of sex.

"There are no more men's jobs or women's jobs, only people's jobs," Ray says, and Vice President Glen Mitchell nods agreement.

"The program that is now being promulgated provides that in each of our five wage brackets, thirty percent of the work force should be women," he explains. "There's some doubt as to whether we can find that many women who want to take those positions, but we are starting a program to identify those who are willing to participate in the training. They have a preferential status over men until that thirty percent is reached.

"If a woman wants to be a forklift driver or a seamer mechanic, that's fine. There's nothing to hold her back. The program takes a lot of promotional opportunity away from men, and we now find men bidding for what used to be women's jobs. Historically, only women worked at the sort tables. Now men are showing up there, too."

Glen Mitchell, a 1952 graduate of the University of Southern California, has made his own break with tradition at Carnation. He is the only member of the company's highest echelon who came in from the outside instead of working his way up the corporate ladder. He had been vice president of the Van Camp Seafood Division of Ralston Purina before joining Carnation in 1968. Five years later, when the board of directors created a new administrative level—group vice president—Glen moved up another rung, along with Clarke Nelson and Timm Crull.

"We have, as a division, extremely ambitious programs for market growth," he said a year after his appointment. "We've been hamstrung by the lack of capacity, but with the purchase of the Hollister plant* and additional money going to our other plants, we will have a very meaningful increase in our pack. As we look at our sales requirements, we seem to have a home for all our products."

* * * * *

*A tomato and spinach processing plant at Hollister, California, was acquired for cash from Royal American Foods in late December, 1973.

160

Old-world tomato paste: thick but often bitter. New-world tomato paste: sweet but often thin.

Contadina: always thick <u>and</u> sweet.

Contadina Tomato Paste is never bitter, never thin. It's made of rich, sweet California tomatoes with 82% of the water removed. Use in recipes requiring rich tomato flavor, like the Italian Spaghetti Sauce below.

ITALIAN SPAGHETTI SAUCE
(Makes about 2½ cups)
¾ cup chopped onion, 1 crushed garlic clove, 1 tbsp. chopped parsley, 2 tbsp. oil, 1 6-oz. can Contadina Tomato Paste, 2 cups water, ½ tsp. oregano, ½ tsp. basil, ½ tsp. salt.
Saute onion, garlic and parsley in oil. Drain off excess oil. Add remaining ingredients. Mix well. Simmer uncovered 20 min. Stir occasionally.

Know the difference between Tomato Sauce and Tomato Puree?
Tomato Sauce is lighter than Paste, rich and lightly seasoned for your convenience. Use with rice, noodles or meat loaf.
Tomato Puree is also lighter than Paste but without seasoning. Makes rich, velvety sauces.
For free, 24-page recipe book, write Contadina Cookbook, Box AH—125, Los Angeles, Calif. 90019.

For free, 24-page recipe book, write Contadina Cookbook, Box LM—125c, Los Angeles, Calif. 90019.

CT-203 Printed in U.S.A.

Contadina ad, 1965

Carnation Farms in 1972, with Friskies kennels (below).

On the morning of January 30, 1965, just three months before Alfred Ghormley would have celebrated the fiftieth anniversary of his humble start with Carnation Company, he lost his long, heroic fight against arthritis. Death not only put an end to his pain, but also spared him the emotional wrench of seeing a workman hoisted high above Wilshire Boulevard on a spring day in 1966 to take down the red letters, M-I-L-K, from the flashing sign atop World Headquarters.

"The removal of MILK from the sign signifies a change which has been taking place in Carnation for many years," reported *The Carnation* (April-May, 1966). "As the company has added new divisions and new products, it has ceased to be solely a 'milk company' and has become a diversified food company."

Carnation had entered the frozen foods field in the summer of 1955 with the purchase of Mrs. Lee's Pies, a Los Angeles manufacturer of frozen cakes, cookie rolls and pies (dessert, meat and poultry) marketed under the "Simple Simon" brand name.

"As a division of Carnation, the frozen pie operation will have the advantage of our extensive food research and development facilities, our nationwide sales and marketing experience and our many trade connections," observed *The Carnation* (Midsummer, 1955).

Carnation, with its traditional insistence on quality, proceeded to set its own standards for the fruit it used in making its pies. Instead of the thirty pits the United States Department of Agriculture permitted for each 30-pound can of peaches, for example, Carnation specified *no* peach pits. When competitors bought pitted cherries, they accepted the usual standard of "five plus one," which meant that for every five pounds of pitted cherries shipped to them, they got one pound of sugar. Carnation insisted on a seven-plus-one ratio and ended up with fresher-tasting cherries.

"The Simple Simon business had been pretty much restricted to California markets," Dwight Stuart reminisced recently.

"We tried to expand into markets east of the Rockies, as far east as Chicago and St. Louis. It was a highly competitive situation. We spent a great amount of time, effort and money trying to establish the line of products, but it didn't work out."

The division never fitted in. For one thing, it required a mode of distribution different from anything Carnation was accustomed to, and it also required a substantial outlay of capital at a time when the money could be plowed more profitably into such fertile

MILK has its ups and downs—up in '49, down in '66.

fields as instant products and pet foods. No tears were shed at World Headquarters in the fall of 1968 when Ward Foods bought the assets of the Frozen Foods Division.

* * * * *

In the meantime, Carnation had become one of the country's major meat canners through its acquisition of Trenton Foods, a food processing company with production facilities at Trenton, Missouri, and general offices in Kansas City. The new division came to Carnation in the spring of 1966 after having racked up sales of $27,900,000 in its preceding fiscal year.

"An excellent addition to Carnation's increasing diversification in the food field," President Olson pointed out.*

Trenton's name was unknown to most of the millions of people who were buying its Vienna sausage, beef stew, corned beef hash, chili, tamales, potted meat and deviled ham. Trenton products carried the name of the meat packers and food companies for whom they were made. Only the initiated knew how to identify a Trenton product. They looked at the USDA shield on the side of a can for the establishment number (EST 705) assigned it as a meat canner. Its poultry products carried the identification, P-260.

Once it became a Carnation division, Trenton acquired a brand of its own, Chef-mate, put up in 6-pound, 10-ounce cans sold for institutional use. The new line had been produced by a process so unusual that it was being described as the first basic change in food canning since 1810, when an ingenious Frenchman, Nicolas Appert, developed the modern method of food preservation by heat in a hermetically-sealed container. A hundred and fifty years later, the conventional method for commercial canning was to fill

162

*Carnation's diversification has never included the sale of any canned or frozen seafoods marketed under the Carnation brand name. Griffith-Durney, Inc., of Los Angeles, is licensed to use the trade mark and to sublicense it to its subsidiary, Seafare Corporation, and to other seafood packers. Carnation Company has no financial interest in Griffith-Durney, its subsidiaries or its sublicensees.

Trenton Foods is one of the country's largest processors of Vienna sausage.

All operations within the pressure chamber are monitored from the control room.

In the Trenton Foods plant, No. 10 cans are filled with pre-cooked food in this pressurized chamber.

Harold Melcher, president of Trenton Foods, runs his Missouri meat-canning operation from offices in Kansas City.

the can, then put it into a pressure cooker until the product in the center of the can reached the temperature required for sterilization.

The method worked satisfactorily for the canned food on sale at supermarkets, but not for food put up in No. 10 cans designed for use in kitchens serving dozens or hundreds of people. Depending on the density of the contents of such a large can, it could take five or six hours for its center to attain the prescribed degree of heat. Meanwhile, the food near the outside of the can had been overcooked.

After spending half a million dollars trying to devise a method of cooking food before it went into the can, Swift & Co. decided to turn the problem over to Harold Melcher and Jack Miller, the founding fathers of Trenton Foods. The pair fitted together as neatly as two bookends. Harold was the salesman and the administrator, Jack the machine-shop genius. His inventions included machinery to pack sausage automatically, to form meatballs and to stuff chopped meat into cans. Jack took a look at the model of a pressurized room Swift had built and set to work. Before he finished, Trenton Foods had run through a million dollars.

"When we went into it, we didn't intend to spend that much," Harold told *The Carnation* (August-September, 1967), "but we knew that somewhere along the road there was a better way of preserving food."

Under the Trenton process, food is cooked by steam injection as it is piped under pressure from mixers to canning equipment. By the time it reaches the cans, it has been sterilized without being overcooked. It takes less than half an hour from the time the product leaves the mixer until it is cooked and cooled. The product is handled so quickly and gently it keeps its original texture, color and flavor.

When food is cooked in the home, unpleasant odors and flavors escape while it simmers on the stove (cabbage comes to mind at once). When conventional canning equipment is used, the unpleasant flavors are hermetically sealed into the can along with the

163

product. The Trenton process, for the first time, enabled canners to achieve a home-cooked flavor.

* * * * *

The Trenton process, like the instantizing process, enhanced Carnation's reputation for being an innovator in the fast-growing food service industry.

"One out of every three dollars spent for food is spent on food eaten away from home," the Food Service-Industrial Division kept reminding the eighth floor during the early 1970s, when food service had become a $22 billion industry.

Carnation's malted milk specialists had been calling on soda fountain operators for years, but not until Instant Nonfat Milk was introduced in October, 1955, did the company begin to tap the institutional market made up of restaurants, hotels, schools, hospitals, company cafeterias and county jails.

"We knew institutional kitchens could use literally tons of Instant Milk for cooking once they learned how," recalls Chuck Brown, who helped open up institutional marketing for the Instant Products Division. "We gathered twenty salesmen into crews and started out city by city to sell Instant Milk. We'd come into a town none of us knew, open up the Yellow Pages and call on any restaurant listed in bold type. That was about the degree of sophistication we had. Each sale required demonstrating the product to overcome the prejudice against old fashioned powdered milks that were hard to dissolve and had a chalky taste.

"It took more than two years to build a successful institutional instant milk market, but once this pioneering was done, Carnation had good contacts and a greater knowledge of what the market needed and would buy. For one thing we knew restaurant operators were always interested in economy and convenience. We looked at the hot cocoa mixes being sold to restaurants and said, 'Aha! Here's something that can be improved.'

"All the products on the market were sold in packettes that contained simply cocoa and sugar. Someone had to take the time to heat milk and then mix it with the contents of the packette by stirring vigorously. The Research Laboratory went to work and developed a dry product that contained milk solids and dissolved instantly in hot water.

"At the same time we realized that we could sell more economical bulk packages to people if we had a dispenser. It didn't take long before we were selling a dispenser and Instant Hot Cocoa Mix in bulk sizes as well as packettes. This upped both our sales and the size of our sales force."

* * * * *

In 1958 Carnation's thoughts turned to potatoes. All of the instant potatoes on the market required the addition of milk and butter. Researchers were given the job of developing an economical, buttery instant potato that needed only the addition of water. They came up with the first basic mix to contain potatoes, milk and a butter substitute. The name selected for this new add-water-and-serve product was Trio, because of its three ingredients and the three carnations on its label.

"Trio was the product that started the whole institutional program moving in a big way," noted *The Carnation* (October-November, 1962), and the article went on to discuss the differences between institutional and retail salesmanship.

"The supermarket owner or manager is interested in a product that has been presold through advertising, one with good consumer acceptance. He is a middleman selling branded package products that have a quick turnover. The institutional operator, on the other hand, is interested in a product from a personal point of view. He wants a good ingredient that he can transform into a menu item *his* customers will like. His business is built on the quality of *his* food rather than on nationally advertised brands.

"The institutional salesman, then, must

164

have an intimate knowledge of the product he is selling because he will be asked how it will perform. How does the flavor compare? How long will it hold on the steam table? Is it convenient? Does it require less labor to prepare? What is the moisture content? What is the yield per package? The cost per serving? Are there portion control advantages? How does it fit into a particular operation?

"Restaurant operators who said they had tasted instant potatoes and wouldn't even consider them, ended up tasting Trio and buying. Carnation's salesmen succeeded in doubling the institutional processed potato market and capturing the lion's share for Carnation."

Seventy-five salesmen were calling on institutional and industrial customers from coast-to-coast by 1963, when Everett Olson became Carnation's fourth president. He established an Institutional-Industrial Department,* with Wally Houde as manager and Chuck Brown as his assistant. The acquisition of Contadina and Trenton Foods swelled Carnation's food service volume enormously and the introduction of the cooked-before-canning Chef-mate line continued to keep the company in the forefront of the present-day kitchen revolution.

"We've been able to unseat long-established competition in some major food service chains simply because our product is better," Product Manager Phil Spada told *The Carnation* (Winter, 1971). "If you need proof, here's a new product evaluation from a restaurant-operator: 'Chef-mate is unquestionably the finest corned beef hash on the market.' That's the shortest product evaluation the man ever wrote."

In its 1973 annual report, Carnation noted that the food service market was "consistently attaining a more important role in the company's operations." John Patten, the division's new manager, presides over a cadre of young, hard-working graduates of

*It became the Food Service-Industrial Division in July, 1971.

the management training program who look forward to a bright, busy future.

"I've seen predictions that by 1980 the food-away-from-home business will be as great as retail sales," John says. "As things stand now, we're the leaders in the canned meat business in the food service industry and we have its second largest direct sales force. We have a quality product and we're providing a quality service. We're working in a real dynamic area."

*   *   *   *   *

Bob Kohls, vice president in charge of processed potatoes, most of which are made for the food service market, is equally enthusiastic about his bustling area of responsibility. John Patten's salesmen handle the marketing of all Carnation potato products except frozen french fries. Bob takes care of them.

"It's a challenging operation," he says, "with potato prices and frying oil prices fluctuating from minute to minute. It keeps us on our toes."

Carnation had been in the potato business in the United States for about three years when, in 1962, it entered into a joint venture in Canada with J. R. Simplot of Idaho, the largest potato-processing company in North America. Carnation Foods Company, Limited, was formed to grow, process and market what *The Carnation* (December-January, 1962-63) called "the most complete line of dehydrated and frozen potato products available anywhere."

Farmers around Carberry, Manitoba, had been growing wheat for a glutted market before Simplot flew over the town and decided to touch down for a look at its old Royal Canadian Air Force training station. Sizing up the production possibilities of the three airplane hangars and the potato-growing potentialities of the area's sandy soil, he bought the buildings and some four hundred and sixty acres of land. Then he talked his new neighbors into planting potatoes instead of wheat. He gave them a million-dollar present when he introduced them to the Russet

Burbank (also known as the Netted Gem).

Carnation acquired Pronto Pacific, a potato-processing company at Moses Lake, Washington, in the fall of 1970 and promptly added a granule plant to its existing facilities for frozen products and dehydrated potato flakes. Three years later Carnation increased its capacity by acquiring Western Farmers Association's plant in Nampa, Idaho.

"One of the newest potato plants in the country," Bob Kohls says, "and it's located in an ideal potato-growing area."

The purchase of the plant of Farwest Foods of Othello, Washington, thirty miles south of Moses Lake, recently added another 120,000,000 pounds to Carnation's capacity.

"It's a fast-moving, fast-growing business," says Jim Stauber, sales manager for the Processed Potatoes Division. "It's tough, but we're having a great time."

* * * * *

Carnation manufactures products for the graphic arts because of a chain of events which goes back to 1939, when Mark Matthews of the Fresh Milk and Ice Cream Division got to studying a map of Los Angeles with a view to the future.

"One day we will need a fresh milk distribution station in this area to serve our customers in the San Fernando Valley," he said, and drew a circle in the general vicinity of Burbank.

In due course Alfred Ghormley entered into negotiations with Dick McGraw and his father, Max McGraw, for the five-acre site where they were doing business as McGraw Colorgraph Company. The son, who owned the land, was willing to sell, but his father, who owned the business, balked at the prospect of having to build a new plant. They worked out a deal whereby Carnation would buy the property and lease it back to McGraw Colorgraph.

In 1953, when young couples with babies were swarming into the San Fernando Valley's new tract homes, Carnation decided it was time to make use of the Burbank acreage

166

Carnation began potato processing in the U. S. in 1971 when it acquired Pronto Pacific's plant in Moses Lake, Washington. The architect's rendering includes buildings added in 1973.

its Fresh Milk and Ice Cream people had shown such foresight in acquiring. The tenants were notified that their landlord would like to cancel the lease. Dick McGraw, by this time, had lost interest in the business and his father was in no mood to relocate. Why didn't Carnation buy him out? he suggested, and Carnation did.

McGraw Colorgraph was doing two things that appealed to the eighth-floor. It was making a quality product and it was making a profit. Not a large profit, but nonetheless a profit. During its first five years as a Carnation subsidiary, however, McGraw failed to grow at a satisfactory rate. In 1959 Reed Braithwaite, its president, and Larry Plotin, its general manager, worked out a plan for growth on an international scale through stepped-up research, sales and production.

"Since then," reported *The Carnation*

Frozen potatoes for the Canadian market are processed in Carberry, Manitoba, the location of Carnation's first potato plant.

(April-May, 1964), "McGraw has been on the move. It has doubled the number of products in its line and has several new ones in the oven. It has developed the strongest sales campaign it has ever had. It has built the most modern plant of its kind in the world and is looking for ways to expand the world markets."

McGraw had two primary markets, the editor pointed out. The $1-billion-a-year rotogravure industry involved such things as wood-grained Formica table tops, food packages and labels, trading stamps and newspaper Sunday supplements. The silk screen business was smaller, but was growing at a faster clip. Greeting cards, billboards, posters and decals used the process, as did the electronics industry which was consuming large amounts of silk screen printing for its instrument dials and printed circuitry.

A European subsidiary was incorporated in 1966, and Vice President Braithwaite was pleased to announce that "we have already obtained as customers some of the most respected gravure printers in Europe." Eight years later, when asked how McGraw was making out at home and abroad, Reed said that sales were expanding and the subsidiary was continuing to show a profit.

"We're a very minor part of Carnation's total activities," he added, "but we've had substantial growth in a narrow field."

* * * * *

From its earliest days, Carnation had made its own cans for its evaporated milk and, as the company spread out across the country, it had sold cans to local producers, usually someone who happened to have a condensery near one of its plants. But not until the company began to buy cans for some of its new products, notably pet foods,

did it begin to examine the wide, green gulf between the cost of manufacturing a can and the cost of buying one.

Toward the close of 1955, taking advantage of an opportunity to make a profitable extension of an existing operation, Carnation decided to go into the can-making business. Ed Leigh, whose delight in tackling and solving apparently insoluble problems had brought him to the attention of the eighth floor, was removed from Industrial Relations and named assistant manager of the new Can Division. Six months later he was its manager. He is still running the division, now as a Carnation vice president.

"It was obvious from the outset that to sell cans we had to be better than our competition," Ed says, "Being just as good wouldn't do it. The only way to outsell them was to have better people. And we do. Our people are highly motivated and they have great pride in what they can do. They seem to enjoy playing David in a business of Goliaths."

For evaporated milk, the Can Division turns out what the industry calls "snap-end cans." They are delivered to the condensery with both ends soldered into place and are filled through a small vent hole in the top

In 1972, the Can Division began doing its own coating and lithography at the can factory in Riverbank, California, above. The first such installation was made in Menomonee Falls, Wisconsin, in 1968.

which is then sealed by a drop of solder. For fruits, vegetables, beverages, pet foods and what not, Carnation's can-makers manufacture an "open-top" can, which the canners fill at their plants and then close.

Up until 1950 two can companies, American and Continental, not only dominated the manufacture of machinery for making open-top cans, but for closing them as well. When a canner bought his cans from either company, he signed a contract agreeing to order a five-year supply at a "quantity discount" and, as another condition of the "total requirements contract," he had to lease his can-closing machine from the same company. The canner was not permitted to buy a machine. He had to lease it on terms set by the can-makers.

These arrangements were outlawed in 1950, when a federal judge in San Francisco, invoking the Sherman-Clayton antitrust laws, put an end to "quantity discounts" and "total requirements contracts," because they left "little room in a competitive sense for the independent small businessman."* It was this ruling that made it possible for Carnation to arm Ed Leigh with a slingshot and point him in the general direction of the canning Goliaths.

Ed started with ten can plants, one attached to a pet food facility, the rest supplying snap-end cans for evaporated milk. He now has twelve plants in the United States and one in Canada, turning out a mind-numbing assortment of open-top cans for Carnation and for the division's outside customers, who look to it for personalized service. The big canners like to sell the kinds of cans they manufacture. Carnation's Can Division obligingly offers to make whatever kind of can a prospective customer happens to want.

"We also maintain a Technical Service Group, made up primarily of food technologists, who are experts in processing, in the physical problems of interaction between contents and can," Ed says. "They work with customers in deciding which

*New York Times, June 23, 1950.

coating and can strength are most desirable for a particular product.

"Canning is a more delicate art than the average person would suspect. If beet cans don't have a special coating on the inside, the beets turn white, and if corn cans don't have a different lining, the corn turns black. Consequently, a canner doesn't say, 'Send me a carload of No. 2 cans.' He tells us what he intends to put in them and we combine the right metals and coatings to create the proper can.

"After we've made the cans, sold them and delivered them, we still have a job to do. A can is not a finished product, you know. The customer has to put the top on it and seal it after it is filled. So we advise and help our customers with their sealing and equipment—either in their plants or, if it needs an overhaul, in our machine shop."

The machine shop is in Oconomowoc, where Carnation has been making cans since 1918. The shop not only handles the overhauling and modernizing of machinery, but also makes production equipment, produces replacement parts for the division's can factories and tinkers with experimental devices.

"The tin can isn't really made of tin," points out Norman Kramer, the division's chief engineer. "It's steel, with a layer of iron-tin alloy, then a thin layer of tin followed by a chemical coating. About four-tenths of one percent will be tin."

The art of canning, as every schoolchild is supposed to know, was developed in France to enable Napoleon's armies to travel on a full stomach. A half-century later, thanks to Gilbert Van Camp, an Indianapolis grocer, Union soldiers supplemented their rations of salt herring, cheese and crackers with crudely canned pork and beans. Today's open-top can didn't make its appearance in the United States until 1900. Two years later, in his best-selling novel, *The Virginian*, Owen Wister lamented the "thick heaps and fringes of tin cans" advancing civilization had left to rust and rot on the Wyoming landscape.

In the ecology-minded 1970s empty tin

The 300,000,000th can Carnation sold to Dr. Pepper was made into a plaque in the fall of 1973 and presented to Dr. Pepper's Tom Hunter, right, by Ed Leigh, vice president in charge of the Can Division.

cans are collected in reclamation bins at each of Carnation's can plants. The money saved by this recycling process is set aside in a special fund for the use of local groups working to improve their community's environment. At the same time, Ed Leigh keeps an eye on "ban-the-can" campaigns. Although they are directed primarily at the beverage cans casually tossed aside in public places, Ed points out that restrictive legislation against canned beer and soft drinks would have the effect of boosting the price of cans made for food.

"The ultimate container is one you consume along with the product, but that isn't here yet," Ed says. "Meanwhile, the lowly can's great packaging advantage is low cost for the greatest product protection from processor to consumer. If we ever lose sight of this, we're all in big trouble."

* * * * *

Ed Leigh gained a congenial friend and an inventive business associate in the fall of 1970 when Carnation acquired Dayton Reliable Tool and Manufacturing Company. Its founder, Ermal C. Fraze, has remained as president of the Carnation subsidary, and whenever Ed splashes down in Dayton, Ohio, the two meet in an atmosphere of mutual affection and admiration. Ernie Fraze has earned a place in the history of food packaging by inventing the easy-open can.

With an engineering degree from Ohio Northern University, a certificate from General Motors Institute of Technology and several years of machine shop experience, Ernie established Dayton Reliable on a suburban street in 1950. By the end of the year, he had more than a dozen men on his payroll. He also had a mechanically gifted 10-year-old son at home, puttering about in a basement workshop. Having served his apprenticeship on airplanes, birdhouses and a boat, the lad was itching to get into something more challenging.

About this time Alcoa came to the elder

Upper left : Ernie Fraze—also known as the pop of the pop-top—with son Mark.
Upper right: The rivet on a Dayton Reliable pop-top is fashioned from the
top itself and cannot snap off.
Lower: Dayton Reliable finds housekeeping just as easy with carpeted floors.

Fraze with a problem and a proposition. The problem: How to develop an easy-open can and make the can-opener obsolete. The proposition: If he could come up with the answer, Alcoa would like to buy the patent and pay him royalties on what would obviously be a highly salable device. Father and son, working side-by-side in the basement, took on the project. They figured out how to develop steel dies for stamping an easy-open lid, but there still remained the problem of how to keep the tab from breaking away from the lid.

"Fraze developed an integral rivet process in which the tab is attached to the can's top with a rivet fashioned from the top itself—and the first easy-open or pop-top can was born," reported *The Carnation* (Summer, 1971).

The writer assigned to do the article was astonished to find freshly vacuumed red carpeting in the jig grinding room and walls hung with framed prints and landscapes instead of the traditional machine shop nude calendars.

"People work better in nice surroundings," Ernie explained, and his longtime friend and chief engineer, Don (Pete) Peters, told how Ernie's joy in tackling seemingly impossible problems and working them out permeated the entire staff. Pete cited the government's pathetic, hat-in-hand plea for a tank range-finder.

"We took on the project of building the range-finder when no other company in the country would touch it. The government couldn't get anybody else to quote a price for building it either. But Ernie quoted them one and we built it. We came out all right, too."

At luncheon one day some three and a half years after the Dayton Reliable acquisition, Everett Olson was asked how Carnation came to buy a tool and die company.

"Mr. Fraze, the owner, had had some business dealing with people in our Can Division," he said, "and while there was no direct relationship between his activity and ours, it seemed to us that this would be another leg under our table. He was a very sound operator and he had a tremendous amount of expertise, not only himself, but also his people, and on the strength of that we acquired the company. Since that time, it has expanded into other fields of dies and tooling, and we are making use of its expertise in certain of our areas."

In describing the working atmosphere at Dayton Reliable, Pete Peters once said, "When we have a problem with a job, we sit down and hash it out. Everybody has a part in it and we work together. We never consider that there might not be a solution. With another boss, it would be different, but that's the way Ernie works. He gives everyone room to think and operate. Consequently, there is a free flow of ideas."

Pete might just as well have been talking about Ed Leigh and the way he operates the Can Division.

"Carnation Can Division is one of Dayton's customers," Ed points out, "and we realize, of course, that Continental Can, Dayton's largest customer, is a competitor of ours. Ernie does a lot of development work for them that they wouldn't want us to know about, and he also does work for us that we wouldn't want our competitors to know about. Ernie's very careful about protecting his customers, and rightly so."

"It's an interesting company," says Group Vice President Clarke Nelson, the eighth floor's liaison with Dayton Reliable. "It's grown every year since we've had it."

13
The World Marketplace

"An Australian," U.S. News & World Report *notes,*
"could easily begin his day brushing his teeth
with Colgate, hurry through breakfast of American
cereal and Carnation Milk, stop his General Motors car . . .
to check his Goodyear tires on the way to work at IBM."—
Leader & Press, *Springfield,*
Missouri, July 24, 1973.

Carnation and Pet Milk Company, ancient rivals at home, had been partners in the overseas operations of the General Milk Company since the end of the first world war. It had been a profitable and, for the most part, agreeable working relationship, with representatives of both companies sitting on the board of the foreign affiliate. The directors met as equals, but Carnation, owning 65 percent of the company, was considerably more equal, and General Milk was run from its World Headquarters. As the two partners diversified and expanded their domestic activities in the early 1960s, each began to consider the advantages of getting a friendly divorce and going it alone in the world marketplace.

"We were heading into areas that could bring about certain conflicts that we had not had before," explains Everett Olson. "I think they felt they had opportunities to go overseas in certain other areas that might present conflicts with General Milk Company, and so they came to us to see whether or not we'd be willing to purchase their 35 percent interest. We were and we did."

On January 21, 1966, Carnation paid $42,000,000 for Pet's equity in General Milk.

"This development substantially increases Pet Milk Company's financial strength and its capacity to expand and diversify in the international field," Pet's stockholders were advised, and the annual report went on to add that study teams were already at work in foreign countries "actively exploring opportunities to increase the scope of Pet's international activities."

Carnation, for its part, acquired a new division with interests in plants in fourteen foreign countries and distribution throughout most of the free world, except the United States and Canada. The new international division was primarily engaged in the dairy business (evaporated, condensed and powdered milk), but it was also manufacturing cans, chewing gum and baby food. It promptly acquired a pet food company in Australia.

"Australians, with the third highest income in the world, have an expanding market," W. F. Kistler, General Milk's vice president and secretary explained to *The Carnation* (October-November, 1966), and went on to add that "pet food sales have increased more than three and one-half times in the past five years and are second only to ice cream as the fastest growing item in food markets."

Glücksklee (Lucky Clover), the German subsidiary, was turning out an assortment of eighty-seven items by 1972, when the General Milk Division had strayed so far from its original pasture that its name was changed to Carnation International. In England, meanwhile, Carnation Foods Company Ltd. had brought out a dry food for dogs and cats. It was called Go Dog and Go Cat, because Friskies conflicted with a prior registration. In France, Lait Gloria had introduced Friskies (*"Repas Complet"*) and in 1970 had purchased a canned pet food line it was marketing under the brand name, Ami Chien and Ami Chat.

"In Paris," noted *The Carnation* (Spring, 1972), "a dog is a member of the family, and pet food advertising is a ticklish matter. People are used to buying fresh meat for their pets and naturally they project their own food preferences to the animal."

The chunks of meat in a can of Ami Chien are redder than they would be in an American product, because the French associate rare meat with a three-star dinner. As for cats, their Ami Chat comes packed with a delicate layer of gelatin on top to suggest pâté.

Carnation International long ago learned to live with the inexplicable differences in the world's tastes. The English pour evaporated mik on fresh strawberries or canned peaches, but rarely use it in coffee. The French begin their day with a mixture of coffee and milk, *café au lait*, so Gloria's Lait Concentré is advertised as *"la crémière à café."* In Australia and Mexico, evaporated milk is used primarily for babies; in the Philippines it is also mixed with water and served cold to grownups. The English like milk in their tea, but seldom drink it by the glass, so when Carnation Instant Breakfast appeared in their tight little island, the natives didn't know what to make of it at first.

174

Above: Gloria canned and instant dairy products have been joined by Friskies, Gourmet and Ami pet foods in French supermarkets, all from Carnation's subsidiary, Gloria, S.A.

Left: Signs on wall remind German workers making baby food in Carnation International's Glücksklee factory that babies are relying on them.

Then somebody hit on the idea of feeding it to elderly patients in hospital. The old blokes loved it.

*   *   *   *   *

Elbridge Stuart served as General Milk's president for nineteen years before he visited the company's European plants on his first trip abroad. Once he got a taste of foreign travel he developed a fondness for it and, as a citizen of the world, came to have a particularly close interest in Carnation's overseas activities. Toward the end of his life, when he was content to leave management committee meetings to younger men, he still presided over the executive deliberations of the international division.

He was a modest man, who shrank from personal publicity, but he was pleased and deeply touched in 1955 when, by decree of the President of France, he was named a Chevalier in the National Order of the Legion of Honor. Notification came from French Ambassador Maurice Couve de Murville in a letter which attributed the honor to "the useful contribution you have brought to the development of the French milk industry, and for the generosity you have shown towards French victims of the Second World War."

In the presence of family and friends, the decoration was presented at Elbridge's home by French Consul Raoul Bertrand, who said of the new Chevalier: "In France he founded

175

Receiving the French Legion of Honor was a proud moment for E. H. Stuart.

two important plants, one at Carentan and the other at Corbie, thus rendering outstanding service to the French people. Moreover, immediately after the war he sent to France large quantities of powdered milk when our children needed it most. This generous gesture moved us very much. We are very grateful to him."

To Elbridge, a collector of Napoleonic material,* the white enamel five-pointed star was especially meaningful because the Legion of Honor it represented had been created by the Emperor in 1802 to recognize outstanding service rendered in any field of human activity. To add an appropriate touch to the ceremony, M. Bertrand arrived at the Stuart home wearing a uniform Napoleon had designed and carrying the sword he had used in knighting an aide-de-camp, Gratien Bertrand, the consul's great, great grandfather.

In the spring of 1957, after relinquishing the presidency of Carnation Company to Alfred Ghormley, Elbridge revisited France on a tour of General Milk's European facilities. At Corbie he was given a stainless steel cigarette box shaped like one of the cans the plant manufactured. Elbridge was delighted with the inscription:

> Believe us, we can make a can,
> Faster, better than others can.
> Fill it with milk we also can.
> Of course you know the French can can.

* * * * *

Elbridge was accompanied on his 1957 trip by Bill Dobson, General Milk's executive vice president. Bill had become Alfred Ghormley's protege in the 1940s while working under him as general sales manager of the Fresh Milk and Ice Cream Division. Alfred had taken a liking to the tall, forceful young man and had gone out of his way to bring him into contact with Elbridge at in-

*The collection was given to Whitman College in Walla Walla, Washington, where it is housed in the Elbridge Hadley Stuart Wing of the Penrose Memorial Library.

E. H. Stuart, right, turned the presidency of General Milk over to Bill Dobson, left, in 1965. Bill Lucas, center, succeeded Dobson in 1972.

formal social gatherings. Elbridge had been impressed.

Bill, like Alfred, paid close attention to people and to details. When he visited a plant, he not only talked to everyone, but he also listened, and he could attend to small details without losing sight of big jobs. Elbridge brought him into General Milk in 1951 and he succeeded to the presidency shortly after Pet sold its minority interest.

"Until I went with General Milk," Bill says, "I thought Alfred Ghormley ran the show, and I really looked up to him, practically worshipped him. Then working with Elbridge Stuart—General Milk was his baby, he spent a lot of time on it—I got to see that he made the major decisions and, believe me, he didn't take any time making them either. I traveled to Europe with him and Evelyn probably eighteen or twenty times, and there was never an evening, never once, that he wouldn't call me up and ask

176

Carnation's condensery and can factory in Querétaro, Mexico, northwest of Mexico City (upper).
Condensery and can factory in Arequipa, Peru, 8,200 feet high at the foot of El Misti (lower).

Looking east, down Wilshire Boulevard toward Los Angeles' central city.
World Headquarters personnel took over two floors of the Avco building in 1974.

if I could have dinner with them. A very gracious man.

"He could be very tough, but he never held grudges on business decisions. He'd insist on approving every job order over $2,000, and would squawk like hell over a $10,000 item, but you could drop a couple of million dollars in Brazil and there'd be no recriminations. He'd simply want to sit down with you and see what could be worked out to resolve the problems.

"Every time we'd have an important opening in one of our major subsidiaries, he'd want to bring in a banker or an accountant. I'd want to bring in somebody from sales, so we'd always have a big fat argument. He felt that a banker or accountant would keep a closer eye on the coffers and hold down expenditures. I'd come up through sales, so I felt that what we needed was sales volume, we could always get somebody to look after the money.

"He had the feeling that our foreign affiliates had been neglected by the general office. 'I want you to go out of your way to ingratiate yourself with these people,' he told me. 'Get better acquainted with them personally.' I got to know every foreman in every plant, every superintendent and assistant superintendent all over the world. We decided to bring our managing directors, our general sales managers and our general production managers and their wives over here for periodic visits to acquaint them with the United States. We'd route them out from New York on dome liners, so they'd get to see something of the country, and we'd arrange to have them come down from Seattle to Los Angeles by car instead of plane, so they'd have a chance to talk to people along the way. We wanted them to become more familiar with this country and more appreciative of it."

* * * * *

Sir Ernest Woodroofe, chairman of the British-Dutch combine, Unilever, Ltd., speaking at an international industrial conference in San Francisco in the fall of 1973,

warned multinational corporations that their economic interests abroad went hand in hand with "social considerations."* He noted that Clemenceau, the French statesman, had once prophesied that the British Empire would founder in India, "not on the rocks of political injustice, but of social insult." Years earlier, in talking with the editor of The Carnation (February-March, 1964), Bill Dobson had addressed himself to the same theme.

"Management in the home office and American management abroad must understand and respect the feelings of people in foreign countries," he said. "Management policies must take into account local feelings of national pride, local customs, and the people's aspirations, sensitivities, traditions, and religious beliefs. American management must make certain that its local employees and company are good citizens by the standards of the people of the country. The company itself must support community activities and bear its fair share of civic responsibility."

When Peace Corps volunteers made their way up into the Andes, they found they had been preceded by General Milk's wholly owned Peruvian subsidiary, Leche Gloria. Not only was it contributing to local church, civic and charitable groups in Arequipa, where the company had a condensery and a can plant, and in Vitor, where it had a milk receiving station and a demonstration dairy farm, but it had also been building schools and apartment houses. It turned out to be a soft touch for the Peace Corpsmen.

"We give them crates and tin-plate pallets that they cut up and make into school desks or lunchroom tables," Barry Barber, the Arequipa plant superintendent, told a visiting journalist who was preparing an article for The Carnation (August-September, 1968).

A girl from the Peace Corps came to the condensery door asking for some old cardboard boxes to help shelter a poor family whose home had burned down. She left with

177

*Los Angeles Times, October 20, 1973.

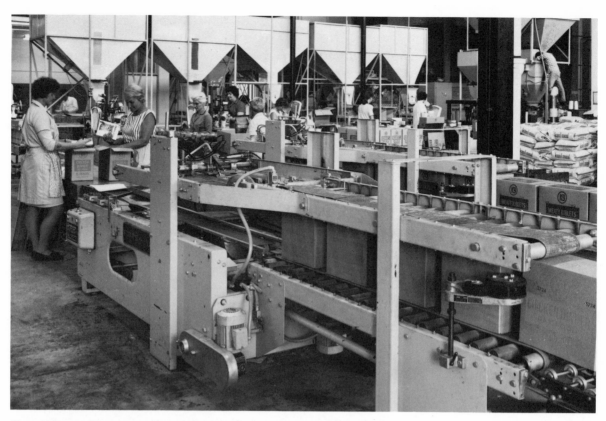

One of the world's most modern dry pet food plants was completed in the outskirts of Sydney, Australia, in 1970 to make Carnation's K-9 line.

a large wooden crate that some equipment had been shipped in. It provided the basis for a new house. A discarded carbide generator that had outlived its usefulness at the plant was carted off to become the start of a wrought-iron business.

In talking to his peer group in San Francisco, Unilever's chairman observed that the multinational corporation often finds itself courted and reviled by foreign governments, "accused of rape by the very people who are trying to seduce it." He suggested that suspicion and hostility could be reduced by giving subsidiaries wide independence within guidelines laid down by the central office. He also recommended that local management be placed in the hands of nationals. Carnation has followed both policies for years.

"A managing director has a great deal of responsibility," says Percy Aubrey (Barry) Barringer, who retired in 1974 after spending thirty-nine years with Carnation, winding up his career as Britain's managing director. "He has to be a very versatile person, because every aspect of the business comes his way and he has to make the final decisions. I'll be involved in advertising one day, possibly passing on a television commercial, and next day I may be presiding over a sales meeting or appearing before a milk marketing board or negotiating a wage settlement. The buck stops at my desk.

"Our French and German companies are rather bigger, but we now have three hundred people in our factories and nearly one hundred in our sales force. We have a board of directors, but the responsibility is mine. Every year the managing directors are flown to Los Angeles to work out our annual budgets and to account for the profitability of our operations. This occurs once each year, but meanwhile we're sending in monthly profit-and-loss statements and quarterly financial budgets, covering marketing expenses and forecasts for the rest of the year. It's like a great many things in life. The degree of trust they have in you depends on your ability and the results you get.

"There was a great change in the relationship with the overseas companies, particularly in Europe, after Elbridge Stuart first visited England and the Continent. He was very fond of England and Scotland, and he was extremely kind to us. We've always had a strong family feeling and we're inclined to boast a bit about not being a big impersonal corporation. Carnation employees in Britain feel this fatherly interest and, consequently, they are very loyal to the company."

* * * * *

In its operations in the world's underdeveloped areas, Carnation subsidiaries have done what the company's Founding Father did at the turn of the century, when his Pacific Northwest condenseries gave neighboring dairy farmers an incentive to increase their production of milk and the company's field men showed them how to do it. Foreign condenseries have also created a demand for fresh milk which has encouraged farmers to go into dairying or, if they were already in it, to call on Carnation to help them improve their methods of production.

Peru was importing milk before the arrival of Leche Gloria in 1942. Twenty years later, when its consumption of milk had more than quintupled, the Peruvian government expressed its appreciation by bestowing the Order of Merit on Elbridge. In December, 1957, when General Milk opened a plant near Manila, the president of the Philippines and his wife showed up for the ceremony. Their country had been spending $20,000,000 a year importing milk at $6 a case. By 1964 locally produced filled milk was saving the Filipinos about $4 a case in foreign exchange.

"A large part of the rural section of Mexico doesn't have refrigeration," says Philip J. McGuire, who manages production and distribution of Leche Evaporada ("*de vacas contentas*") for Carnation de Mexico. "We're

supplying the country with a safe source of milk. Many Mexican mothers today wouldn't think of using anything except Carnation Evaporated Milk for their babies.

"We're also in other products—canned dog food, for one thing—and we contemplate diversification in almost any field that represents a need for the country and an opportunity for us. We feel that it's an obligation on our part to work just as closely as possible with the country itself. The overall economic situation in Mexico needs help, especially in rural, agricultural areas."

When Phil McGuire first went to Mexico for General Milk in 1948, the farmers had no silos and, as a consequence, no feed for their cattle during the dry season. General Milk encouraged them to plant sorghum. Once it was ready, the company lent them a reaper and a chopper. The sorghum was cut up, put in a trench and covered for use in the dry season.

"We still have a long way to go," Phil says, and he is especially disturbed by the relatively low production rate of Mexico's dairy cows, but, he likes to add, "when we built our first condensery, the Queretaro plant, it was designed to reach an eventual capacity of around 250,000 cases of evaporated milk a year. We now have two plants and we're producing 4,000,000 cases a year."

* * * * *

General Milk had been operating in South Africa for a quarter of a century when Carnation bought out Pet and promptly embarked on a diversification program which has put this particular Carnation International subsidiary in the business of canning fruits and vegetables, producing fruit squashes and cordials, and operating the country's oldest pet store. At the same time, its Gold Cross sweetened condensed milk has more than one-third of its market, and its evaporated milk, introduced in 1955, shares its market about evenly with Nestlé.

"One of Carnation's objectives is to reduce our dependence on milk products as a source of profit," Managing Director Ed Baitz ex-

179

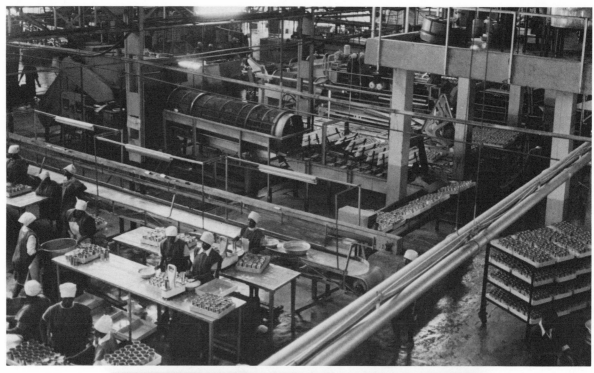

180

*Upper: The Northern Canners plant in Politsi, South Africa,
purchased by Carnation International in 1966,
processes a line of fruits, vegetables and juices.*

*Lower: I. Lopis & Sons, manufacturers of pet accessories
in South Africa, was acquired in 1973, followed Encia
in Italy and Hykro in Denmark, to provide Carnation
International with a new line of products in the pet field.*

plained to Barbara Pederson, editor of *The Carnation* (Winter, 1973-74). "We are too vulnerable with just one main product. We have frequent droughts here and then the cows produce less milk. Some years we have to import to meet market demands and that limits our profit potential."

The company's first South African condensery was built in Bergville, where Zululand sugar cane was within reach, as well as water from the Tugela River and power from the Dundee coal mines. Production of sweetened condensed milk began six months before the bombing of Pearl Harbor. Once the war ended, the company needed more milk supplies. It found what it wanted in the Orange Free State near Harrismith. A condensery was built there in 1950 and now produces four times as much milk as Bergville.

Bill Greve, a South African who ran the company from 1945 to 1968, likes to tell how Mickey Burger, his first field man, tried to get farmers to stop adding water to the milk they were selling to the condensery by the gallon.

"On one occasion," Bill says, "when Burger visited one of the culprits, the farmer was out, but his head man was on duty. Burger said to him, 'You know, the boss must not use the dirty water from the stream to put into his milk.' The man replied, 'He doesn't. He always uses the clean water out of the tap.' "

The processors solved the problem of watered milk when they began buying it on the basis of its butterfat. In the meantime, the Bergville plant's employees had posed another production problem. A Zulu would stay in the compound adjoining the condensery for five or six months at a time and then drift back to his kraal, a small cluster of huts on the veldt. He was allowed to hold onto his job if he sent a replacement, usually a relative.

"We work within the framework of the laws of the country, of course," Ed Baitz said when Ms Pederson asked him about apartheid, "but there are no laws that say we can't improve wages and working conditions, so we are. We are committed to the principle of equal pay for equal work."

Some South African observers doubt that the withdrawal of American capital would bring down apartheid. "More likely," John Blashill wrote in *Fortune* (July, 1972), "the system would be worsened, for an enforced U.S. retreat would almost certainly cause a violent reaction among South Africa's whites. In fact, American withdrawal might be the only thing that could save apartheid in the long run."

"Change is inevitable," says Bill Lucas, who took command of Carnation International in February, 1972, when Bill Dobson retired. "If we can contribute to peaceful change, then that's justification enough for our being there. The unanswered question is whether South African society is sufficiently flexible to allow for fundamental alterations without undue violence and dislocation."

*   *   *   *   *

Canada has never been part of Carnation's foreign operations. The Canadian subsidiary, Carnation Company Limited (Canada), antedates by three years E. A. Stuart's decision to set up shop in England and Europe at the end of the first world war. In the fall of 1966, fifty years after he planted Carnation's flag on Canadian soil with the purchase of a condensery at Aylmer, Ontario, the wisdom of the move was pointed up by the Canadian subsidiary's vice president, Bill Crockett (he was named president a year later).

"Canada with a population approximately one-tenth that of the United States consumes twice as much Carnation Evaporated Milk," he told *The Carnation* (October-November, 1966). "The remote areas of Canada use especially large quantities of evaporated milk. In Newfoundland, for example, practically all the milk consumed is evap."

The Canadian company had grown in its half-century from one plant to six and from one product to thirteen. The most modern

181

evaporated milk plant in North America had been serving western Canada for four years, and salesmen were not only mushing about with Carnation Evaporated Milk, but also Morning Milk (a partially skimmed milk for infants), Coffee-mate, instant skim milk, instant and frozen potatoes, and Carnation Instant Breakfast (*"petit dejeuner éclair"*).

"For forty-odd years Carnation in Canada was a one-product company," Bob Shaw, the subsidiary's vice president in charge of marketing, said recently. "Then in 1959 we introduced Carnation Instant Pasteurized Powdered Skim Milk, produced at our new plant in Alexandria, and we very quickly secured brand leadership. In 1962 we got into potatoes in a big way and the following year we introduced Coffee-mate on the heels of its success in the United States. That success was duplicated in Canada. Then we

came out with Instant Breakfast in the fall of 1966. We had some tough competition for a while, but now we have the market to ourselves. Hot Chocolate came on the scene in the fall of 1972, and has proven to be very successful.

"We still don't have some of the products in Canada that Carnation has in the United States. We have no pet foods, for instance, and no fresh milk and ice cream operation, and we don't market Slender because of the combination of a low market potential and existing competition. We're keeping an eye on pet foods, but breaking into the field now would be rough going. We have everybody in the marketplace here that we're up against in the United States, plus Standard Brands, which dominates the Canadian market.

"Certain aspects of Canadian marketing are a throwback to pioneer days. For ex-

In 1959, when the Canadian condensery in Alexandria, Ontario, was converted to an instant products plant, a cooperative calf untied the ribbon. From left, J. N. Hardy, C. W. Mutchler, Judy McMillan and her calf, Vice President Ted Lang, Mayor George Simon and Vice President W. H. Crockett.

182

ample, some of our sales representatives still make calls by way of coastal steamers, particularly in the important Newfoundland market, where evaporated milk is sold heavily in remote fishing villages. In each port, the salesmen have to scurry around and make their calls before the ship pulls out. For the most part, though, there is little difference in the lifestyle of the two countries."

When Ted Lang was elected president of the Canadian subsidiary in the fall of 1971, he had spent twenty of his thirty years with Carnation in Canada. A native Iowan, with a dairying degree from Iowa State, he had taken charge of the Canadian evaporated milk plants in 1951. He was moved up to vice president four years later. By the time he became president at the age of fifty-two,

he had served as vice president of Canada's National Dairy Council and as chairman of the Grocery Products Manufacturers of Canada.

"They say one always returns to one's first love," Ted once remarked. "I love the people back home in Iowa for their family feelings, their candor, their friendliness, and these are traits I have observed in Canadians for over a generation. I appreciate beauty, and this is a beautiful country, with its lakes and hills and wildlife. My three children have grown up in Canada, married and settled here. I've gotten to know the country and the people, and that's what I love about Canada. You get to know everything and everyone around you, and that way you get to know yourself."

The grand opening of the Canadian plant in Wetaskiwin, Alberta, in 1962, the first all-new evaporated milk plant to be built in North America in thirty years, was a gala affair. Untying ribbon were, from left, Ted Lang, vice president; Paul Baughman, plant superintendent; J. E. Pike, mayor; J. N. Hardy, general superintendent; R. M. Putnam, deputy minister of agriculture; H. A. Moore, member of parliament; and D. H. McCallum, commissioner of dairying.

Carnation's joint-venture condensery in Singapore.

14
Milk
&
Honey

"If a man has good corn, or wood,
or boards, or pigs, to sell, or can make
better chairs, knives, crucibles or church organs,
than anybody else, you will find a
broad hard-beaten road to his house,
though it be in the woods."
—RALPH WALDO EMERSON Journal (1855).

For more than fifty years the world's dairymen have been beating a path to the door of Carnation's Snoqualmie Valley farm. Len Hall, its director of international marketing, enjoys telling the story of how its world-wide reputation was brought home some years ago to Lowell Wilson, a General Milk vice president.

"Lowell was in South America trying to get in to see a minister of agriculture," Len says. "If you've ever traveled down there, you know how this can go sometimes. They promise you he'll see you shortly and you sit around all day, and then his secretary tells you he's gone home, come back tomorrow. Next day you go through the same thing again. Well, Lowell sat there for two full days and never got to see the minister. When he went back on the third day, he clipped his business card to a copy of *Carnation Milk Farms News* and sent it in to the minister. He came bursting out of his office right away, welcoming Lowell with open arms. 'Why didn't you tell me you were connected with Carnation Milk Farms?' he said. 'I never heard of the General Milk Company, but I know all about Carnation Milk Farms. My son is working there right now, learning about Holstein cattle.' The minister took

Lowell into his office and ended up giving him a government car and a driver and sending him on a tour of the country."

Back in 1929, when Holstein aristocrats were content to cross the sea in the hold of a freighter, a Carnation bull calf took to the air, borne aloft on the wings of press agentry to highlight the ground-breaking ceremony for the company's first Texas condensery. The calf flown in from Oconomowoc was Carnation's gift to the local dairymen who would be supplying fresh milk to the plant at Schulenburg. Five thousand spectators turned out to welcome the Flying Bull. Dangling from the red ribbon tied around his neck was a letter from A. J. Glover, editor of *Hoard's Dairyman*, to Governor Dan Moody.

"This calf represents one of the oldest and most important factors for success in the improvement of dairy cattle by breeding," the editor wrote. "Through the inheritance from his ancestors, there is within his veins the potential power of transmitting dairy talent to his progeny—that talent which will economically convert the grain and forage of your fields into milk, our most important food."

Ten years after the chartered tri-motor

In 1968, 18-year-old Lakefield Fobes Delight became the third
Holstein in history to give 300,000 pounds of milk. Carnation Farm
employees who witnessed the historic moment were, from left,
Clarke Nelson, Clarence Okerlund, Reuben Peterson, Duncan
MacKenzie, Leness Hall, Russ Pfeiffer, Al Hay and George Langsjoen.

plane delivered Carnation Badger Aero Lone
Star (ear tag 6201) to Carnation's milk suppliers in South Texas, dairymen began to
hear talk of a simpler, cheaper and better
way to improve their herds. A single collection of semen from a valuable bull could be
frozen and used to breed as many as five hundred cows in barns thousands of miles apart.

Carnation pioneered in the field of artificial insemination in the early 1940s. The
company's Galax, Virginia, condensery was
situated in isolated hill country where no
bull studs were available to neighboring
dairy farmers. Carnation bought a farm in
the community, shipped in bulls from its
Snoqualmie Valley herd, and established
one of the country's first artificial insemination facilities.

The same route was taken in Peru, where
most of the cows in the remote, mountainous
region serving the condensery in Arequipa
were native animals of low productive capacity. General Milk established a demonstration dairy farm at Vitor, the site of its
receiving station, and equipped it with facilities for a modern artificial insemination
stud.

"This is still operating as a very important
service to local dairymen, with Carnation
furnishing all facilities, including one-half
of the bulls, and the Peruvian government
furnishing half the bulls plus the technicians
and veterinary service," George Bulkley
noted in 1963.

Not until the fall of 1965, however, with
the purchase of Eastern Iowa Breeders, a
Cedar Rapids company, and Piper Brothers
of Watertown, Wisconsin, did Carnation
formally enter the artificial insemination
business.

"We are going to do our best to make this
new operation the best bull stud in the coun-

Carnation paid $250,000, the highest price ever paid for a dairy bull, for Paclamar Capsule in 1968. Within five years he had sired more than 250,000 offspring through Carnation Breeding Service. In photo, from left, Ralph Stolle, former owner of Capsule; James Rhodes, Governor of Ohio; Jack Holtzapple, manager of Stolle's farm; and Leness Hall, manager of Carnation Farms Breeding Service.

try," Clarke Nelson, general manager of Carnation Farms Breeding Service, told *The Carnation* (December, 1965). "In addition to offering the best Carnation-bred Holstein bulls, semen is available from top bulls of other dairy breeds, as well as from Polled and Horned Herefords, Angus, Red Angus and Charolais beef bulls."

Carnation set up a Genetics Division seven years later when, in November, 1972, the company acquired Genetics, Incorporated, of Hughson, California. Operating on opposite sides of the Rockies, the two companies had been working together for three years on what they called their Young Sire Program, the establishment of a herd of young dairy bulls with proved ability to pass the desired characteristics along to their progeny.

"The program is expensive and time-consuming and when it appeared that the fastest progress could be made together, we decided to join forces," Vice President Nelson explained to *The Carnation* (Winter, 1972-73). "The name of the game in artificial insemination is having quality bulls. Semen from an average bull sells for $3 an ampule. An excellent bull can command a premium of $10 to $12 over that price. Multiply $10 by the fifty thousand to sixty thousand ampules a year that the good bull produces and you can see that the good bull brings in at least $500,000 a year more than the average bull."

Carnation's breeding service began by breeding 200,000 cows a year. By 1973 it was breeding 1,500,000.

*   *   *   *   *

While the Genetics Division works to improve the breed, Albers Milling Company

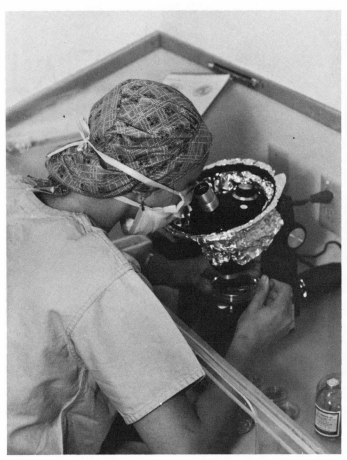

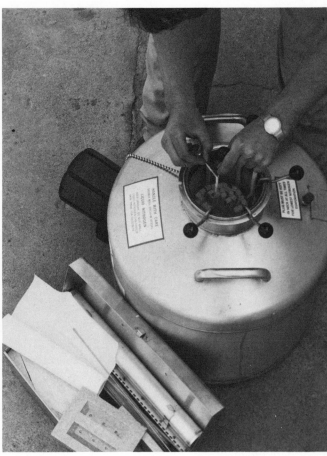

188   *Lab technician at Genetics examines eggs flushed from cow's uterus. The fertilized eggs are isolated and used in ova transfer program.*

Artificial insemination technician removes straw containing frozen semen from liquid-nitrogen holding tank. The "toolbox" in foreground is a do-it-yourself kit for farmers and ranchers.

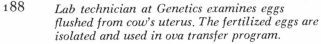

sees to it that the calves will be properly fed.

"Breeding and feeding, it's a winning combination," says Bob Moore, Albers advertising manager. "A farmer can use Carnation-Albers products from conception through production to the end of the line. Research is the key, research as to just what better breeding will do and just what better feeding will do. We've not only got the basic research here at Van Nuys, but we've also got the practical research at the farm."

Years ago, when Bob and his brother Don were playing kick-the-can in the farm's hay barn, their eupeptic father was out on the road, spreading the glad tidings about Friskies and Calf Manna. Albers has come a long, long way since Merton Moore's stray mutts from the streets of Seattle grew sleek on experimental food pellets and E. A. Stuart's record-breaking cows had their picture

taken with movie stars and heavyweight champions.

"In Dad's day," Bob says, "individual cow records made headlines. That day is gone. It's not the record of one cow that matters now, it's the herd average that counts. Those records were made by one man living day and night with one cow. You can't do that any more, not with a herd of five or six hundred cows. Now you take vials of semen and get hundreds of cows that will produce as much as their dams, maybe even more. Individual records lose their meaning in a situation like that. Dad used to say that the advances being made in his time were coming along so fast it was hard to keep up with them. The advances being made now are coming along much faster and they're more important."

As industry spokesmen keep pointing out,

more progress has been made in improving the world's production of milk, meat and eggs in the first seventy years of the twentieth century than in all the preceding years of recorded history.

"Housewives would be paying a lot more for milk, meat and eggs today, if it weren't for research," says G. A. (Buck) Ensminger, president of Albers Milling. "It has increased the amount of milk a farmer gets from his cows, reduced the mortality rate of his calves and cut the cost of feeding his chickens. In the 1950s it took four to four and one-half pounds of feed to produce a pound of broiler meat. Today it takes less than two pounds of feed."

The highly competitive business of formulating, manufacturing and distributing feed for farm animals—the largest single item of expense in the production of milk, meat and eggs—operates on a narrow profit margin. It demands great efficiency to survive.

Albers has survived. It was in its eightieth year in 1974 when it acquired five feed mills and seven company stores from John W. Eshelman & Sons, which traces its corporate roots back to the spring of 1842, when the first John W. Eshelman (1816-1863) established a grist mill in Lancaster, Pennsylvania. A good cow in those days produced one hundred and sixty pounds of butterfat a year and farmers were advised to get more eggs from their hens by plying them with "dough balls covered thickly with lard."

In 1907, when E. A. Stuart was mulling over the idea of creating a model farm to show dairymen how they could produce more and better milk for Carnation condenseries, John W. Eshelman, Jr. (1844-1931) began to manufacture mixed feeds for his flourishing feed store in Lancaster. Twelve years later, when E. A. was getting his first look at his new European milk route, Eshelman and four of his sons formed a partnership. By 1921 they needed a new mill to meet the growing demand for their Red Rose feeds.*

Eshelman in the East, like Albers in the

Albers President Buck Ensminger, left, and Bob Moore, right, advertising manager, with barrelful of entries in an Albers Round-up contest for farmers.

189

West, pioneered in the formulation and manufacture of scientifically balanced feed rations designed, says an Eshelman brochure, to give "the feeder an honest, quality product, one which would yield him a fair return for every dollar invested." The words are the words of Eshelman, the sentiments are the sentiments of Carnation's Founding Father.

*   *   *   *   *

In E. A.'s childhood, when the grandparents of today's young environmentalists were still unborn, water-powered grist mills were grinding the farmer's grain and polluting rivers and streams with waste materials. The formula feed industry sprang from the realization that the millers were throwing away a valuable source of protein for livestock.

*The red rose of England's House of Lancaster was chosen as the Eshelman trademark because of the company's historic association with Lancaster, Pennsylvania, "The Red Rose City."

Thanks to Albers, Eshelman and a few other manufacturers large enough to handle a research budget, today's farm animals are likely to enjoy a more nourishing and better balanced diet than their owners.

"A lowly chicken fed on Albers feeds has as much attention paid to its diet as an astronaut," Dr. W. P. Lehrer, Albers' director of nutrition and research, told *The Carnation* (December-January, 1962-63). "For example, as winter turns to summer a chicken's diet is slowly changed to include fewer calories and more calcium. The ration for hogs is formulated to produce leaner pork, and rations for dairy cattle are being focused toward the gradually increasing demand for milk with higher solids and less fat content.

"Corn, milo, barley, oats and wheat mill feeds are only a few of the ingredients considered and used in Albers feeds. These are sources of energy; however, other nutrients are equally important. We buy fish meal, meat meal, cottonseed meal and soybean meal for protein, which is necessary for growth. We buy vitamins and minerals in carload lots and formulate a diet much more exacting than the average human being enjoys."

While the average human being dines on whatever leftovers the refrigerator may provide on a given evening, the chunks of beef, lamb or pork in the casserole may well have come from animals reared on a diet worked out electronically by a computer. It was Vice President Reed Braithwaite who first recognized the possibilities of developing linear programming to formulate Albers feeds. It took more than three years to learn how to direct the computer to work out mathematical formulae which gave proper consideration to all the complex factors that go into formulating a feed.

Punched cards containing the pertinent data are transferred to tapes which speak to the machine. They tell it what nutrients are necessary for the feed and which ones are available in various ingredients, their palatability, the minimum and maximum amounts acceptable to the animal and its owner, the milling equipment capabilities, the cost of bags and the cost of labor. In a matter of seconds, the computer prints out the formula, listing the correct quantity of each ingredient and stating the cost of the formulation. It may also call attention to ingredients *not* used in the formula, pointing out, for ex-

From this central control station in the Fort Lupton, Colorado mill, a single operator can start, monitor and stop all milling equipment, including a punch-card-controlled mixing system.

ample, that "barley would be a good buy if it cost $8.60 less per ton."

"I have tremendous faith in the future of animal feeds," says Bob McEllhiney, Albers' general production manager. "American agriculture can upgrade the world's eating habits, put milk, meat and eggs on the table. This will create a demand not only for our products, but also for our technology. We still haven't reached the end of the conversion of raw materials into milk or meat or eggs. Use of products we wouldn't have dreamed of a few years ago—bark of trees, wood pulp, waste paper, even manure—may become parts of a balanced feed ration. Somebody will figure out how to do it some day. I don't know what the future holds, but it's an exciting business, exciting enough for me to want to spend the rest of my life in it."

*   *   *   *   *

Evaporated Milk is no longer Carnation's star performer, but the red and white cans designed by E. A. Stuart at the turn of the century continue to dominate a market which, after two decades of decline, still consumes some 20,000,000 cases a year.

"The modern infant feeding for fifty years," proclaimed a mailing piece George Catledge, Carnation's director of medical marketing, recently sent to some one hundred thousand physicians. Unlike the ready-made formulas which have taken much of the infant-feeding play away from evaporated milk, the mailer noted, a Carnation Evaporated Milk formula reaches the baby as nature intended, "with naturally occurring protein and all other nutrients intact." It also has the advantage of enabling a physician to design a formula to accommodate a baby's individual needs and then to modify it to meet changing requirements.

"Evaporated milk will do some things that milk in no other form will do," says Bob Miller, general product manager, and upstairs on the eighth floor Vice President Bob Evans ruefully makes the point, "We have a young generation today that simply can't visualize milk being sold in cans. It doesn't

come across to them that this is one of the best cooking ingredients available for hamburgers, cheese souffles, pumpkin pies, and so on."

Ginny Piper, director of Carnation's Food Service Center, has watched the change from one generation to another.

"Back in 1951, when I started working with the product, its uses were divided equally between baby-feeding, coffee-creaming and cooking," she says. "With the growth of proprietary formulas and the introduction of coffee-creamers, the emphasis has shifted to cooking. Some of the ideas we were using twenty years ago, such as Five-Minute Fudge, are back in use."

Evaporated Milk is like a once-flourishing roadside enterprise that was left to languish when the new state highway struck off in the direction of instant breakfasts, non-dairy coffee creamers, just-add-water mashed potatoes and cooked-before-canning chili. Instead of mooning around with its photograph albums and yellowing newspaper clippings, however, Carnation's senior division has moved with the times. Not content with actively pursuing the doctors, nurses and nutritionists who devise infant formulas, it is also showing up in high school home economics classes and demonstrating the distinctive merits of evaporated milk.

"Our research shows that about 20 percent of the people consume about 90 percent of the evaporated milk sold in this country," Bob Miller points out. "So we've redirected our advertising toward those heavy users in an effort to try to get them to stay with our brand, if they're already using it, and if not, to win them over to Carnation Evaporated Milk. We've added a new ingredient, carrageenan, which 'velvetizes' our product, gives it more smoothness and keeps the butterfat from separating."

In an earlier day, Carnation Evaporated Milk advertisements depicted middle-class homes where domestics in starched white aprons served handsome desserts to handsome white families. Now one set of the one million infant formula guides Carnation

For four generations, we've been raising healthy babies on a budget.

And that's just a start. Babies will thrive on Carnation Evaporated Milk for generations to come because it's good, natural nutrition. The formula has naturally occurring protein and all other nutrients intact. You specify vitamins and carbohydrate according to the baby's individual needs. And the whole formula costs less than any other. But, most important, babies thrive on Carnation Evaporated Milk. That's our past and our future.

Costs less than any other formula.

Carnation Evaporated Milk.® Carnation Company.
Los Angeles, California 90036

Ads in medical journals remind doctors of the superiority of Carnation Evaporated Milk in baby formulas.

sends to American physicians each year has line drawings of a young black mother taking care of a black baby; another is written in Spanish. No product in Carnation's present-day cornucopia has a more loyal following than the young black and brown women whose mothers, and oftentimes their grandmothers as well, relied on Carnation Evaporated Milk because it was both safe and economical.

"After four generations, we're still raising healthy babies," states a 1974 advertisement, which also notes that "the whole formula *still* costs less than any other."

"Sure, there's a lot of excitement in a Coffee-mate or a Mighty Dog," Bob Miller admits, "but this is fascinating, always new challenges, new opportunities. I used to be something of a clock-watcher. I did it in school, in the classes that didn't interest me, and then in jobs I found boring. Once, when I was much younger, I worked at common labor, and it seemed like an 8-hour day was a 28-hour day. Here I'm continually amazed that the day goes so fast."

* * * * *

In Fresh Milk and Ice Cream, General Manager Harold Findlay also works with his back to the clock, his days filled with the complex problems of production and distribution in a time of vanishing dairy farms and burgeoning chain-store competition.

"In the old days, when dairy products were subject to spoilage because of primitive handling procedures, our major cities were ringed by small dairies, which divided up the metropolitan market," Harold says. "As transportation and refrigeration improved, fewer dairies were needed to serve the cities. Many small dairies fell by the wayside because they weren't able to make the capital investment needed to stay in business. Competition required new equipment to squeeze more volume from a single plant.

"Today we think nothing of moving fresh milk from Los Angeles to San Diego, or from Tulsa to Dallas. From Seattle we serve a customer in Kodiak who takes delivery from a barge every two weeks. He never runs out of milk and it never sours on him.

"The milkman on residential routes used to come to the door every day. During World War II he changed to every other day, and now it's twice a week. Meanwhile, he's become an independent contractor. He owns his own truck, buys his milk from our dock and distributes it to his customers. As a man in business for himself, he is more flexible than in the past, when he followed a set course on a fixed schedule.

"As for the chain stores, they now have their own plants, and they have an obvious advantage over us in distributing their dairy products to member stores. We have to sell the chains on our product and our service. They don't. They simply notify a store manager that they will show up at a certain hour with a certain shipment, and they can couple milk and ice cream with all of their deli items—their cheeses, dressings, and so on."

Harold, in the summer of 1974, was

shaken by the discovery that today's average dairy farmer is pushing fifty.

"Young people don't want to go into dairying," he says. "They'd rather grow grain. You don't have to crawl out of bed on a cold winter morning and go milk the wheat."

"The situation is changing," says Vice President Bob Evans. "The industry has gone through a revolution of automation. Farmers are making use of the milking parlor concept which Carnation helped instigate. The cow simply walks into a barn and mounts a platform, where she is automatically washed, milked and fed. The small farmer, with herds of ten to fifteen cows, is going out of business because costs have reached a point where it is no longer economical, but younger fellows are going into dairying with fifty to seventy-five cows, and their earnings are increasing substantially."

* * * * *

In 1963, the year of Everett Olson's eleva-

In the mid-fifties the Fresh Milk and Ice Cream Division had a crowd when it assembled all of its sales managers. From left, front row: Walt Betts, Joe Hunt, Hiram Roe, Dick Izzard, Ross Mainwaring, Jim Bryant, Jerry Aakhus, Forrest Nelson, Joe Breckel, Rex Phillips. Center: Gus Haveman, Mac McKelvey, Ross Leone, Don Moore, Ray Jones, Al Rosburg, unidentified, Les Ludwig, Herb Magnusson, Wilbur Bottjer, unidentified, Mac Walker. Back: unidentified, Fred Abelee, Dale Trinkle, C. W. Fields, Ernie Lehman, unidentified, Harry Wisby, unidentified, Joe Fournier, Bruce McCroskey, Ralph Kirscher.

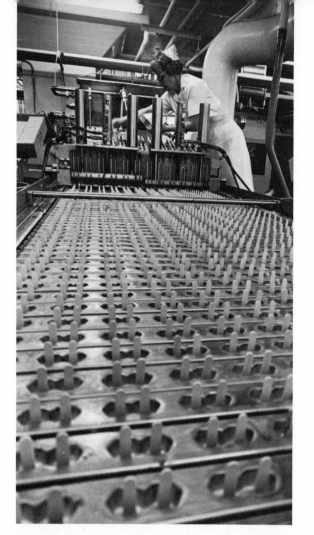

Frozen novelties are big business for the Fresh Milk and Ice Cream Division. In Oakland, Lucille Olson loads wooden sticks into machine that drops them into rapidly-freezing twin popsicle molds.

tion to the presidency, there were forty-nine companies in the United States with annual sales of $1 billion or more. Ten years later there were 127, one of which was Carnation. During this period, as corporations grew larger and more complex, the executive next in importance to the president came to be the chief financial officer.

"Typically," Arlene Hershman reported in *Dun's Review* (March, 1973), "he has become the Number One man in dealing with commercial and investment bankers, brokerage houses, securities analysts and Washington bureaucrats. He is the president's prime ally in acquisitions. Usually, he holds sway over expensive and crucial computer installations. He holds the reins that guide the corporate stock portfolio and its pension plan. And finally he more often

than not is awarded a membership on his company's board of directors."

Chuck Todd, Carnation's executive vice president and treasurer, has been on the board since 1965, when he was elected vice president for finance. A droll, chain-smoking workhorse, Chuck created something of a stir in international financial circles in 1973 when he captured the lowest bond rate ever recorded on the Eurodollar market.

"Todd was ready to sell $25,000,000 worth of the convertibles last fall," the Hershman article noted, "but held back and watched as Gillette waltzed into the bond market in December and paid a very reasonable 4¾ percent for its money. What Todd was waiting for was a strong bounce in the U.S. stock market, which would lure European dollars into American equities. It came in January; Todd went to market with his bond, and came up with a record-low 4 percent coupon. To ice the cake, Carnation's stock was selling a shade within its all-time high, and the Europeans shelled out a 15 percent premium above the current conversion value of each bond."

Chuck Todd is another of the eighth-floor tenants recruited by Al Hartwick when he was building up Carnation's Corporate Department. Chuck took his bachelor of arts degree at the University of Indiana in 1935, got a law degree from Kent College in 1940 and was well on his way to becoming a certified public accountant in 1944 when Al ran onto him.

After the war, when Elbridge Stuart was reorganizing the company's overseas operations, he picked Chuck to be General Milk's vice president and secretary. Working with Elbridge, Chuck was impressed by his ability to read a financial statement like a C.P.A. and to glance at a column of figures and spot an error immediately. For his part, Elbridge was struck by the young lawyer's restless, far-ranging mind, his attention to detail and his incredible memory. Elbridge was also amused by Chuck's lively sense of fun.

"Oldtimers," recalled *The Carnation* (June-July, 1965), "still laugh about the time an associate we'll call Mr. Smith bought a new hat. Mr. Todd and Al Halgren went out and bought the same hat one-quarter of an inch larger. When Mr. Smith hung his new hat on his rack, they switched them. Mr. Smith suddenly realized his new hat was too big, so he carefully lined it with paper and wore it to work the second day. Halgren and Todd put the paper lining in the smaller hat and switched them again. This time Mr. Smith's hat rode merrily on his head, inches above his ears. He removed the lining and another switch dropped the hat onto his ears. The joke went on and on."

Nowadays stainless steel carts move from floor to floor at World Headquarters every morning and afternoon, dispensing coffee,

tea, hot chocolate and cold fruit drinks. Twenty-five years ago, when Carnation first moved into its new home, however, there were no coffee breaks. Chuck and Joe Parrett, his sidekick from the insurance department, used to slip across Wilshire Boulevard for a cigarette and a cup of coffee. Elbridge spotted them from his eighth-floor office and complained to Al Hartwick, who passed a warning along to the pair.

That Christmas, when the seventh-floor members of the corporate family assembled around their Christmas tree to exchange gifts, Joe Parrett received a large, beautifully wrapped package, the contents of which have passed into company legend. Chuck Todd, having drawn Joe's name, had gone

195

Walt Disney came by to welcome Carnation to Disneyland on opening day in July, 1955 and got a ride in the company's delivery truck. The 1890-style ice cream parlor is one of the "Main Street, USA" attractions.

to a war surplus store and bought a helmet liner and several yards of camouflage material used to conceal military supplies in a combat zone. Joe's present turned out to be a custom-tailored cape of the camouflage material. Chuck had also camouflaged the helmet liner and topped it with a miniature palm tree. No one got a bigger laugh out of the gift than Elbridge Stuart.

* * * * *

Elbridge was in his eighty-fourth year when, on February 18, 1971, he resigned as Carnation's chairman of the board. His father had founded the company and shaped its character, but it was Elbridge who had taken it over in the depths of the Depression, when sales were less than $33,000,000, and turned it into a diversified, multi-national corporation. Sales in 1970 crossed the billion-dollar mark for the first time and profits of almost $46,000,000 set a new record in a year characterized by faltering business growth.

"For us," reported *The Carnation* (Winter, 1970-71), "it was a vigorous, active year. We kept our enthusiasm and we worked hard—thinking, planning, producing and selling."

Pet food sales had put such a strain on production facilities that a new complex was taking shape in St. Joseph, Missouri. The can plant in Mansfield, Texas, had outrun its original capacity and another line was being added. Coffee-mate had moved into a new, highly-automated plant in Jacksonville, Illinois. Carnation Hot Cocoa Mix was off to a fine start in national distribution and Trenton Foods had high hopes for its new product, the Spreadables. Overseas, work had been completed on a pet food plant in Australia and construction had started on a Coffee-mate processing plant in Scotland.

"The progress Carnation Company has made under your leadership makes a most phenomenal story," the chairman of Whitman College's board of overseers wrote to Elbridge, who had received a doctor of laws degree at Whitman's 1964 commencement exercises.

From San Francisco came a letter signed by the shaky hand of P. G. Kinzer, who had taken Elbridge under his iron wing sixty years earlier when the young man graduated from Yale and came home to work full-time for Carnation.

"You have done a most wonderful job of directing the company since 1932," P. G. Kinzer wrote, "and are to be complimented in building the company to its present condition."

Bill Cross was dead, but his son, a Milwaukee businessman, read about Elbridge's retirement in the *Wall Street Journal* and wrote him a reflective letter.

"It wasn't until shortly before my father's passing that I finally understood a little of what made him the way he was by reading the book written on the history of Carna-

Carnation completed new facilities for dry pet food production in St. Joseph, Missouri, in 1970.

tion.* It contained so much of the essence of 'The Old Man,' your father. Suddenly it was clear. . . . My dad, as a young man, had come under the influence of your father and patterned his life, his way of doing business and his dealings with people upon that of his teacher and leader, E. A. Stuart.

"You too had the same teacher and, as an only son, must have been even more influenced as has been shown in the success of your company since taking over in 1932. Carnation still has the highest reputation in its industry for quality, for integrity, for good management and all around excellence. I know you are leaving it in good hands and that 'The Company' will carry on in the same tradition that father and son have both so carefully nurtured over the years."

* * * * *

*Elbridge A. Stuart: Founder of Carnation Company, by James Marshall, privately printed (1949).

Elbridge's three sons had grown up under the watchful eye of a stern, demanding and often disappointed widower whose time with them had to be shared with what the boys were reared to think of in capital letters as The Company. Dwight, the youngest, was the prodigal son who had left The Company and come back to find his métier in Grocery Products. Now, as Everett Olson's executive vice president, he was next in line of succession. "Fully" was vice president in charge of Engineering and Purchasing. Elbridge and his oldest son had not exchanged a word in the ten years since Hadley had decided not only to leave The Company, which might have been forgiven, but also to call a press conference and publicly criticize his father's management of it, which had not been forgiven.

The three boys had given Elbridge trouble, but the two daughters he acquired late

Open-top cans in Mt. Vernon, Missouri, ready for sale to fruit and vegetable canners.

in life had given him nothing but joy, and he adored them. As girls, of course, he asked less of them than of the boys. They were not expected to devote their lives to The Company, starting by swabbing a cold condensery floor and rising by pluck and hard work to an office on the eighth floor. Instead, to his delight, they married two young men whose interests, education and experience fitted them for increasingly important responsibilities in the two areas of The Company which had the strongest hold on Elbridge's affections, the international division and the Snoqualmie Valley farm.

Herbert L. (Bill) Lucas, a Princeton history major (Class of 1950), who took his masters in business administration at Harvard, married Ann Stuart in 1959 and went to work for General Milk in Hamburg, Germany, in 1963. His previous experience had included two years with an international banking and investment company, three years in mortgage banking and six in management consulting. He and Ann lived in Germany until 1965, when he was brought to World Headquarters as General Milk's executive vice president.

"American companies abroad often have the reputation of being tough, hard-nosed, with no feeling of loyalty toward their employees," he remarked one day in 1973, a year after he succeeded Bill Dobson as president of Carnation International. "Carnation is different. It has a sort of patriarchal character, which makes it more understandable to many non-Americans. They feel more comfortable with it, more at home."

Clarke Nelson, who grew up on his father's ranches in Montana and Oregon ("I hated milking cows"), met Betty Stuart at Stanford, when both were undergraduates. After majoring in Far Eastern History, Clarke went to Harvard Graduate School of Business Administration for his M.B.A., and in 1958, nearly three years after his marriage, he started with Carnation as a management trainee. He was assigned to Albers.

"He did damn near all the jobs in the mill," an associate recalls, "and since he was just a new kid, we often gave him the dirty jobs."

Clarke moved into sales in 1959 and the following year became staff assistant to the division's president. His flair for figures had given him a reputation for being able to turn out instant analyses of profit and loss statements. In his new job, he was put to work analyzing new projects and reports on existing operations. In 1962 he was made executive director of Carnation Farms, where he spent summer evenings with his father-in-law.

"We enjoyed many of the same things," Clarke recalls. "We both liked to play gin rummy and backgammon, and we got in some trap-shooting. He was always very fair in everything he decided as far as business was concerned, but if you told him something, it better be right. He had a great memory and could come back six months later and say, 'You told me such-and-such, and it should have been thus-and-so.'

"He overruled some of the recommendations I made in regard to the farm, and I think he was probably right in most of those decisions, but if you had a good case for a program, you could always sell it to him. I think that was one of his management abilities, a willingness to listen and to change course."

Russ Pfeiffer, who took over as general manager of the farm in 1946, remembers an illustrative incident.

"We wanted irrigation, because the months of July and August often get very dry, and this land dries out quick. I made a proposal for the irrigation of twenty acres, and he said, 'What do you need irrigation in this country for? You get fifty-two inches of rainfall in this valley. It's foolishness!' I tried a couple more times after that and finally he said, 'No, and don't bring it up again.'

"So I decided to prove my point to him. I took a piece of ground down below the cattery and put in twelve trial plots. Six we left alone, six we hand-watered with hoses. We

198

hand-cut those plots all during the summer. One day in the late fall, when Mr. Stuart was feeling pretty good, I went to see him. I handed him a sheet of paper and I said, 'Mr. Stuart, I want you to read this and please don't get mad before you finish it.' So he read it and then he read it again, and he said, 'Are you positive your figures are right?' and I said, 'I am positive, Mr. Stuart,' 'Well,' he said, 'why are you fooling around asking me for twenty acres? Why don't you figure on a hundred acres?'

"He approved a hundred acres that year and another hundred the next. That's the kind of man he was, tough but fair and reasonable. And he loved this farm so much, especially during the last years of his life. 'My father was responsible for that,' he used to say when we'd walk around the farm. Once when I started talking to Clarke Nelson about building a new dairy barn, Mr. Stuart got furious. 'Are you intimating that you're going to tear that building down?' he said, and I told him, 'It's fully depreciated and it's costing a lot of money.' He stopped me right there. He said, 'It will never be torn down as long as I'm alive.' "

Elbridge died in his eighty-fifth year, September 16, 1972, comforted by the knowledge that the farm his father cleared in the Washington wilderness would be in good hands. Within a year, Clarke Nelson and Russ Pfeiffer were directing a million-dollar expansion program, which included a new dairy complex and modernization of the kennels and cattery.

"He loved the old buildings," Clarke says. "He liked to walk around them, knowing everything was where it had always been. We plan to keep the big barns and use them for calf-raising, storage, garage and maintenance facilities. The new dairy will be completely modern and automated, but the big dairy barn and the big hay barn will still be there, where his father put them."

In 1968 the Board of Directors was made up of (standing, left to right) C. G. Todd, R. C. Evans, H. C. Arnest, L. M. Arnold, W. D. Dobson, A. H. Gordon, D. L. Stuart, E. S. Hartwick, S. A. Halgren. Seated: L. L. Austin, W. D. Mertz, C. A. Nelson, E. H. Stuart, R. F. Stuart, H. E. Olson.

Pluck Wins!

Pluck wins! It always wins! though days be slow,

And nights be dark 'twixt days that come and go.

Still pluck will win; its average is sure,

He gains the prize who will the most endure;

Who faces issues; he who never shirks;

Who waits and watches, and who always works.

Sincerely

E. A. Stuart

1941

A favorite verse of Mr. E. A. Stuart, President of the Carnation Company. A framed copy has for many years hung in his private office.

15
The Cow Jumped Over The Moon

"On the moon flight the Apollo 11 astronauts ate sandwich spreads prepared by Carnation."
—The Carnation *(Fall, 1969)*

In its first seventy-five years, Carnation has gone from the Yukon, where turn-of-the-century sourdoughs tamed their bitter black coffee with milk from E. A. Stuart's red-and-white cans, to the surface of the moon, where two young Americans, in 1969, lunched on sandwiches filled with ham salad made by Trenton Foods' cooked-before-canning process. The company has diversified, grown prodigiously and spread to the most remote reaches of the earth, but World Headquarters is still dominated by the spirit of a Founding Father who combined the practice of such old fashioned virtues as thrift, honesty and hard work with a child's delight in such newfangled gadgets as automatic can-fillers, homogenizers and horseless carriages.

"Take care of the little things and the big things will take care of themselves," E. A. used to say, and his eye for little things still sticks in the memory of his leading cowman, George Bulkley.

"One time at Carnation Farms we were walking back from the barn on a winter evening, he and Alfred Ghormley, who was the farm manager at that time, and myself. We got up on the hill, part-way to Mr. Stuart's bungalow, and at that point we

were just above the mess hall. There were probably seventy-five or eighty men in there eating supper. Mr. Stuart stopped and stood there, looking at the boys in the mess hall, we thought. We waited, and when he didn't say anything, I broke the silence by commenting on how nice it was to see men enjoying a meal at the end of a hard day's work. 'Yes,' he said, 'it's fine to see them eating, but I was looking over the roof of that mess hall at the bunkhouse down there where those fellows live. Every cussed window shows they haven't turned off the lights.' "

The multinational corporation he brought to life in the McKinley era has a space-age computer to keep track of the manufacture and movement of the various products it sells each year for $1.5 billion, but if the head of a division, who may be responsible for the expenditure of millions of dollars on raw material and new equipment, wants to give a stenographer a $20-a-month raise, the proposal must go to E. A.'s successor on the eighth floor for approval.

"A lot of people don't realize how big we are, and maybe we don't either sometimes," says Group Vice President Timm Crull. "As we continue to grow, we're going to have to

201

work very hard at remaining a little big company.''

It seemed a big company to E. A., who had watched sales shoot up from $1,000,000 in 1905 to $30,000,000 in 1932, the year he relinquished the presidency to his son. During Elbridge's years as president and chairman, sales more than tripled, but he too ran Carnation like a small family operation, keeping an eye on the most minute details.

"When I first went to work for him in Milwaukee in 1939," recalls Marsh Bostwick, his secretary, "I was given a stick pen. I asked the office manager for a fountain pen, and he went to Mr. Stuart, and Mr. Stuart said, 'No, buy him a stick pen and a bottle of ink.' ''

E. A. and Elbridge not only watched out for the company's pennies, but for its people as well. E. A. was visiting a condensery one day and found a familiar face missing. The man had been fired, the plant manager explained.

"Why?" E. A. asked.

"He couldn't handle the job."

"How long has he worked here?"

"Seventeen years."

"Why did it take you so long to find out he couldn't handle the job?" E. A. asked, and ordered the man reinstated.

A generation later Elbridge used to say, "If you employ a man for fifteen or twenty years, you'd better find some means to keep him employed until he retires." When his father died, Elbridge chose to honor his memory by creating a trust fund which would provide scholarships in his name to give "aid and assistance in securing an advanced education for the children of the employees of the company."

* * * * *

A few years before his death, Elbridge Stuart was interviewed by Glenn Thompson, Carnation's archivist.

"Did your father ever take a vacation?" Glenn asked at one point, and Elbridge shook his head, and then got to talking about E. A.'s distressing habit of calling Saturday morning business meetings in Seattle.

"We would spend the morning discussing business matters, go out to lunch at noon, and then come back to the office for further discussions in the afternoon. I liked to play golf on Saturday afternoon and sometimes I would tell Father that I couldn't come back in the afternoon. 'Why can't you?' he would say. 'Well, I have a date to play golf this afternoon.' 'Well, do you have to do it? Can't you postpone it?' I would answer, 'No, I have agreed to play in a foursome at two o'clock with. . . .' and then mention certain businessmen in Seattle I was to play with.

"Father would grumble a bit and say,

Carnation's archivist Glenn Thompson, left, and Dick Kearns were 12 years old when Pacific Coast Condensed Milk gave this calendar to customers in 1905. Both men retired from Carnation in 1963; Thompson after 41 years in advertising and Kearns after 36 years in fresh milk sales.

'All right, if you have to.' And he usually added the comment that he didn't see why I couldn't take more interest in the business. Many years later, after Father had practically retired from the company, I was visiting with him and he said, 'Son, I realize now that I was wrong in asking you to give up your golf and take more interest in the business. That was your recreation and you needed it. I didn't play golf, but I know now that I got my recreation by going out to the farm whenever I wanted to get away from business responsibilities. That was my 'golf,' and I shouldn't have asked you to give up yours.''

Now, a generation later, on an Indian summer afternoon when the harried president of a large, successful company might be expected to duck out of the office for a leisurely eighteen holes, Dwight Stuart's green sports car can be found parked near the back door of World Headquarters. Recently, chatting with a visitor, he explained why there are no weekday defections from the eighth floor to Los Angeles Country Club.

"When Carnation moved to Los Angeles in 1949, Jack Bullis had been working here for ten years as production manager in Fresh Milk and Ice Cream. He was a very special person, with many, many friends throughout the company. Jack was a member of Los Angeles Country Club, and he was the kind of a guy who believed that whatever he was involved in was the greatest thing in the world, so everybody else ought to be in on it.

"Well, within a couple of years Jack had sixteen or seventeen Carnation people in the club. One weekday he prevailed on The Boss, as he always referred to E. H., to join him in a round of golf. They went out to the club for lunch and E. H. discovered that all of the other Carnation members were also there that day. He was very upset. 'What are the people down at the office doing today,' he wondered, 'when all the decision-makers are out here, taking the afternoon off!'

"I don't know whether he played the round that day or not, but he made up his mind then and there that nobody at Carnation would play golf on a weekday again and tie up all the people in the company who weren't able to get away from their desks. For the rest of his life he stuck to that. There's always been a certain toughness in the men who've run this company, from E. A. to Everett Olson, but there's also been something else, a rather humble feeling of fairness."

In September, 1972, a week after Elbridge's death, Senior Vice President Al Halgren, who had worked closely with him on company and family foundations, flew east to take part in the dedication of a new dormitory, Elbridge H. Stuart House, at Phillips Academy in Andover, Massachusetts, which young Dwight Stuart had left somewhat abruptly after taking a swing at one of the teachers.

Al was introduced by Frederic A. Stott, dean of administration and development, who told of his two meetings with Elbridge. The first, in 1948, was at a luncheon in Los

203

Senior V.P. Al Halgren presented the 1971 Golden Carnation Award to Carol Voshall, Phoenix Gazette *food editor, for superior nutrition coverage in her newspaper. Carnation began an award program in 1970 to promote better stories on nutrition in U. S. and Canadian newspapers.*

Angeles attended by fifteen alumni. El-bridge at that time was still a bit miffed with Andover for having expelled his youngest son, but, Dean Stott said, he was willing to "put aside personal disappointment to take a fresh, objective look at the school." At their second meeting, in 1969, the dean caught a glimpse of one of Elbridge's most conspicuous traits, his thoughtfulness.

"As a former resident of Los Angeles," Stott said, "I thought I knew my distances, but I badly misgauged and ended up close to being on time only by running the last five blocks. Ushered into Mr. Stuart's rather formal and spacious office, with the sweat streaming from my face, I apologized for my tardiness, but at the end of the first sentence he most considerately broke in to let me recover while telling me about one of the Carnation Company directors, a former track star, who often arrived at meetings in the same condition, since it was his practice to run from the airport into town."

Al Gordon, the redoubtable head of Kidder, Peabody & Co., Carnation's investment broker, is the director whose story Elbridge told to put his guest at ease. Actually, Al doesn't run from Los Angeles International Airport to World Headquarters, a distance of twelve miles, but he does walk it at a brisk pace. He has also walked from airports to the downtown districts of New York, Baltimore, Cleveland and Salt Lake City. When he attended Carnation's first board meeting of 1974, he was late in leaving his west-end hotel and, to his embarrassment, covered the five miles to Carnation's offices in a cab. He was seventy-two years old at the time.

* * * * *

Looking back on the 1960s, the editor of *The Carnation* (Spring, 1970), sized up the decade as "a time of scientific achievement, social upheaval, and the realization that the human race is well on the way toward making its planet unfit for habitation." Americans landed men on the moon, but were powerless to prevent the assassination of President Kennedy, his brother Robert and Dr. Martin Luther King.

"In the last half of the decade protest was contagious—protest against the war in Vietnam, against unequal civil rights, pollution, organized religion and the treatment of Biafrans. Wearing long hair and short skirts, young people everywhere demanded freedom. Freedom to be ugly, to take dope, to avoid the draft, to lose themselves in a world of flashing lights, crashing sound and psychedelic color. We had sit-ins, love-ins and happenings on every corner. Movies made sex a spectator sport.

"Many felt the youth of the world had reached new levels of irresponsibility. And there were times when it looked like it. But for every hippie who dropped out, there were a hundred young people who became more involved in the world about them than their parents had ever been. Better educated, and with the necessities of life more easily attainable, young people of the Sixties had more time to think in terms of the non-material things of life. They developed different goals, unrelated to personal success and financial security. They were more concerned about the people who had less than they did and they tried to help by joining the Peace Corps, Vista and other organizations concerned with social welfare."

In 1970, speaking to the winners in the Dairy Foods program at the National 4-H Club Congress in Chicago, Al Halgren paid tribute to the young people who will be the old fogies of the twenty-first century.

"For many thousands of years man has struggled to produce food, clothing and shelter. This struggle to provide just the bare necessities of life has dominated men's lives through most of history. Now, within one lifetime, have come all the technological breakthroughs that have changed all of that. Before, when we needed housing, we cut down the trees. We needed tractors to do the work of horses, so we built huge factories to produce them and other equipment. We drilled oil wells to produce crude oil, and built refineries to make it more usable. When we needed land, we cleared and plowed it, or used it for whatever need we had. We were not doing, in our opinion, anything bad. We were solving our immediate problems in the struggle of man against nature.

"Now we wake up to realize that in the process of 'conquering' nature we are, in fact, destroying it—and destroying part of our own lives with it. For years we have been saying, 'You can't stand in the way of progress.' Now there's a new generation that is saying, 'The hell you can't.'"

Carnation stockholders, accustomed to an annual report which covered sales and income, dividends, changes in assets and liabilities, acquisitions, capital expenditures, organizational changes and a review of the year's sales, products and marketing activities, discovered that something new had

been added in 1970—Social Responsibility.

"Involvement in social concerns is not new for Carnation," stockholders were reminded. "The company, its management and employees have for many years been deeply involved in giving manpower and financial assistance to hospitals, health organizations, youth programs and organizations dedicated to improving the quality of life. We also constantly strive to increase the job opportunities within our company for members of minority groups.

"Because we see improved education as one important path to a better life, we have increased our already considerable support in this field. In addition to a company-established foundation which gives financial assistance to more than one hundred indepen-

205

There was no more enthusiastic member of 4-H than Senior Vice President S. A. Halgren, shown with the national winners in the 1968 Dairy Foods Program. Carnation has sponsored this program since 1948.

Pledging cooperation at the kickoff meeting for the 1973 United Negro College Fund's Southern California campaign were, from left, Willie Davis, ex-All-Pro Green Bay Packer, now director of Schlitz; Dwight Stuart, president of Carnation and chairman of UNCF's 1972 campaign; E. W. Abner, president of Motown Recording Co.; and Dennis Stanfill, chairman of Twentieth Century-Fox.

206

dent colleges and universities, the company makes sizeable annual contributions to many minority colleges, and we have recently initiated a program of Teaching Incentive Awards to education majors who agree to teach in center-city schools when they graduate. . . .

"Safeguarding our natural resources as well as nurturing our human resources are continuing responsibilities. Every Carnation plant across North America is regularly inspected for possible sources of pollution. We have borne a large share of the cost of improved and enlarged municipal sewage and waste treatment facilities in many communities where we have plant operations, and in others we have built our own water treatment or sewage plants.

"We are in the final stages of converting from coal to gas or oil-fired boilers in all plants. In our vegetable canning plants, we have built the necessary facilities to recirculate and re-use water, as part of a more comprehensive water-management program. We have installed cyclones and separators in our larger mills to eliminate dust emission and a sewage interceptor in our meat-canning plant. Many more projects are on the drawing board to keep Carnation current with developments in the field. Our objective is to continue to earn the respect of the public for responsible stewardship of our resources, life support systems and total earth environment."

* * * * *

Elbridge Stuart's working relationship with Al Halgren in dispensing foundation funds gave rise in the mid-1950s to a new department.

"We'd been contributing to various charities for years," Al recalls, "and Mr. Stuart thought we ought to have a department to coordinate that activity and take a look at what we were doing in the communities where we had plants."

In response to an eighth-floor request for recommendations, Personnel Director Wally Jamie drafted a 15-page memorandum which defined public relations not as a black art bent on deception, but as "a state of the corporate mind." The memorandum suggested a program designed "to interpret the special corporate personality which sets Carnation apart," and concluded with the comment that "PR is not something we say, it is something we '*are.*'"

The Public Relations Department was established in the summer of 1955, with Jamie as its director. The department won the 1969 Silver Anvil Award of the Public Relations Society of America for a product publicity program that included the *Friskies Research Digest*, a professional quarterly journal for breeders and veterinarians, and two paperback books, *The Dog You Care For* and *The Cat You Care For*. A second Silver Anvil Award was won for promotional activities on behalf of Carnation's new diet food, Slender, in 1971.

Three years later, when Halgren and Jamie were about to retire, Gordon Jeffers was appointed director of corporate relations, and given responsibility not only for public relations, product publicity and *The Carnation*, but for equal employment opportunities and foundation matters as well.

A graduate of the University of Southern California, with a law degree from Stanford (1948), Jeff had served a twelve-year stint in Al Hartwick's Corporate Department before being bundled off to Washington in 1967 to set up a Carnation listening post. On his return to World Headquarters in the spring of 1974, he found a Public Relations Department operating smoothly under the leadership of two newly promoted assistant directors, George Wilkins and Eddie Atkinson.

George, a past president of the Los Angeles chapter of the Public Relations Society, is a former newspaperman (*Milwaukee*

Wallace Jamie, right, Carnation's indefatigable PR director, with Congressman Edward Roybal from Los Angeles. For almost twenty years Jamie has served as Carnation's ambassador to the world.

Pet care books published by Carnation promote responsible pet ownership, and Friskies Research Digest provides veterinarians and breeders with reports on what is new in their field.

Journal), who came to Carnation in 1961 as a public relations supervisor. A low-key, articulate professional, he is in charge of product publicity for, among other things, Instant Breakfast, Slender, the Contadina line, processed potatoes and food service products.

Eddie, who handles community and ethnic relations, joined the department in 1966. He compiled and edited *Black Dimensions in American Art*, a survey of black American artists which won a "Business in the Arts 1970 Award" from *Esquire*. He also worked with Al Martínez on a 1974 Carnation paperback, *Rising Voices: The Inspiring Stories of 52 Outstanding Spanish-Speaking Americans*.

Both the company and its house organ, *The Carnation*, have done a lot of growing since September, 1920, when the Nampa, Idaho, plant reported in the first issue of *Carnation Family News* that "Mr. George Brunington, our sterilizer processor, has just finished threshing his wheat." Under Marilyn Smith, who is now the company's supervisor of publications, and Barbara Pederson, its present editor, *The Carnation* has become a highly professional publication.

208

Public relations at Carnation is so muted that *California Business* (March 7, 1974) has referred to the company as "that sentinel of silence . . . where the cows are contented and the management curt." In the same article, however, the writer noted that in 1973 the company had quietly "squeezed out earnings and sales higher than in any udder year in its seventy-four years in business." Earnings had amounted to $64,871,351, sales $1,472,198,191.

*   *   *   *

As 1973 drew to a close, Carnation completed negotiations for its most important acquisition of the year, the purchase of Herff Jones, Indianapolis-based producer of class rings, yearbooks and various other products related to graduation.

"We're involved in the memory-making business," President Jim Hackl told *The Carnation* (Spring, 1974). "We're involved with beautiful things at happy times in people's lives."

The 48-year-old company had been floundering in 1968 when Jim was asked to take it in hand. He organized a strong manage-

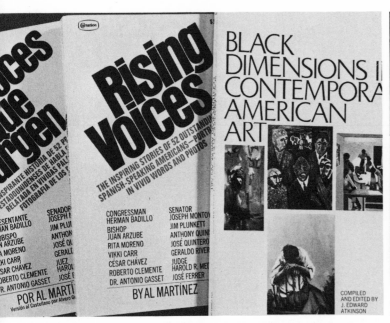

Books to foster pride in the accomplishments of blacks and Spanish-speaking Americans have been published and widely disseminated by Carnation.

Mary Blanding holds check she received from Carnation in 1971 as part of the Teaching Incentive Award Program. Scholarship awards are given to teacher-candidates who agree to teach in center-city schools. With Mary, from left: Rex Phillips, assistant general manager of Carnation's Los Angeles milk plant; Sister David of Marymount College; and J. Edward Atkinson, assistant director of public relations for Carnation.

Products for the youth market make up the major portion of the Herff Jones line.

ment team, plugged some holes in its line of products and embarked on an acquisitions program designed to lessen the company's dependence on class rings, medals and pins. By the time it merged with Carnation, Herff Jones was also turning out yearbooks and diplomas, maps and globes, and graduation pictures, announcements and invitations. Its 1973 fiscal year closed with sales of $43,000,-000 and earnings of $2,000,000.

"Herff Jones came to us through Kidder, Peabody, our investment brokers," explains Chairman Olson. "While it had no relationship to anything that we were in, it appeared to us that it would be a good diversification for Carnation Company. We are both selling products to consumers. It's an excellent company, fine management, good growth record."

"Until Carnation came along," Hackl says, "we had been trying to attract more stockholders by making Herff Jones more successful and giving it more visibility. The chance to merge with Carnation looked like

Jim Hackl, president of Herff Jones Co., acquired by Carnation in 1973.

a good move for our stockholders, and the fact that Carnation was such a fine company made it a good move for our employees."

Shortly before the merger, Herff Jones had acquired A. J. Nystrom Company of Chicago, the country's leading manufacturer of maps and globes for school use. It had recently become engrossed in the production of multimedia learning systems.

"Nystrom deals with the inner as well as the outer world," reported *The Carnation* (Summer, 1974). "Supermachine is their life-size, life-like human torso with removable organs to help elementary school children study physiology, health, hygiene, first aid and physical fitness. The more advanced torso, the kind used in NASA's Space Center to teach the first astronauts about the human

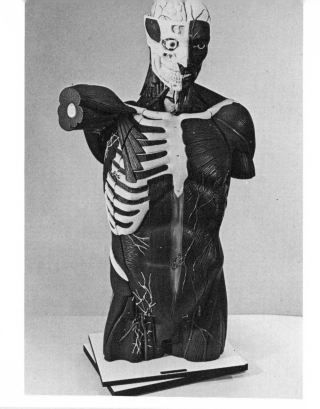

Lower: The country's oldest manufacturer of maps and globes for school use, A. J. Nystrom, was acquired with Herff Jones. Upper right: Vinyl torsos with removable parts are popular teaching aids from A. J. Nystrom.

body, has twenty-six separate parts and can be changed from male to female by substituting the necessary pieces from a suitcase of interchangeable extras."

Along with its ninety salesmen and its forty-eight office-workers, Nystrom has seventy-two employees in its three plants. General Manager Gordon Nelson, *The Carnation* reporter noticed, called each of them by name, and they seemed to enjoy "commenting on the dancing style he had displayed at the company party the previous week-end." The reporter felt very much at home with the new members of the corporate family.

* * * * *

Every spring Carnation's past and present come together when alumni show up for the annual stockholders meeting at World Headquarters. Once the 1974 business session had ended, the company's guests repaired as usual to the reception room on the ninth floor. The gathering had something of the air of homecoming day at a small-town college. Over cookies and coffee, oldtimers swapped stories of the Kinzer-Cross days (evaporated milk's Camelot) and took sobering note of the gray in Dwight Stuart's hair. Only yesterday, it seemed, he had been pleading with

his mother to let him stay up and watch his father trim the likes of Howard Williams and Al Hartwick at the poker table.

Howard, in his eighties, still wore the watch Elbridge had bought for him on one of their visits to Paris. Chatting with Dwight, now in his fiftieth year, Howard was reminded of the time years ago when a sudden illness had brought Elbridge's youngest son to the brink of death in a Boston hospital. Howard had flown east to keep his friend company, and when the boy was reported out of danger, the two men had ducked into a hospitable watering hole for a night neither of them was ever likely to forget.

Al Hartwick, at 71, had been gone from the eighth floor only a little over three years, but already he had become a figure of legend. Young lawyers crept close to see if flames spurted from his nostrils. They found him in a charming mood, the Cary Grant of corporate law.

"One of my favorite people," says Jule Kvamme, vice president and assistant general counsel.

When *The Carnation* visited the Corporate Department in 1965, the editor called attention to the *Wall Street Journal's* recent

211

Above left: Howard Williams, right, long-time head of Carnation's advertising agency, chats with Bill Lucas, left, and Bob Kummel at 1974 stockholders meeting. In photo at right, Chuck Todd jokes with old friends after meeting.

discovery that a rising number of American corporations were finding "faster, cheaper and more effective solutions to many legal problems by beefing up inside law staffs and assigning them tasks formerly handled by private law firms." Carnation had been practicing that kind of corporate law for thirty years.

"Back in the 1930s, when Al Hartwick went to work for the company," Jule points out, "corporate legal departments served as a funnel through which management passed its legal problems along to outside attorneys. To Al, it was a wasteful way of doing business, and he put a stop to it."

"Our legal department is in effect a law firm within a corporation," explains Bob Kummel, Hartwick's mild-mannered, soft-spoken successor. "We do not have outside counsel. It is not only less expensive to operate this way, it is also more efficient. A lawyer who is an employee of the company, working for it full-time, has a much better appreciation of its problems than an outside attorney."

"Exactly," Jule agrees. "You're continually educating outside attorneys as to just what the company is, its functions, its philosophy, its characteristic products, its way of doing business. You spend more time acquainting them with the company than with the problem you're paying them to work on."

Carnation's lawyers tend to be generalists, but one has come to be an expert on patents and trademarks; others have made a specialty of food and drug regulations, antitrust, real property and tax law. Jule assigns day-to-day problems to the lawyer he considers best qualified to handle them, but over the years some of the divisions have established a camaraderie with a particular attorney and may simply drop by his office when they want a bit of advice.

"The legal department is a service center and the product people are in profit centers," says Robin Robinson Claud, one of the department's recent acquisitions. "We're here to make their job easier. Our product is service."

Mrs. Claud, a 1966 graduate of the University of Southern California law school, was working for the American Broadcasting Company in Los Angeles when she was interviewed by Carnation in the summer of 1972. She was charmed and impressed by Bob Kummel and Jule Kvamme, but put off by the austerity of the department's offices. The glass-enclosed cubicles reminded her of a newspaper city room.

"I left with the feeling that I'd love to work for them, but I couldn't leave ABC, where everything was so plush, and the pace so much faster," she says. "Then I went back for another talk with Mr. Kummel and decided to trade the plush offices and the glamour for the peace of mind these people have. In some respects the place reminds me of a convent. You get the impression at first that the people are a little naive about the outside world, but once you've dealt with them for a while, you find they're real sharp. You come in wondering how the mother superior can talk about weddings and prostitution and murders, and then you find she's well-read, she keeps up with things."

*　　*　　*　　*　　*

"We try to select young people we'll enjoy working with," says John Thompson, a graduate of Duke University (Class of 1958), who achieved a corporate vice presidency before he turned forty. "Young people today ask a lot of questions. You can't snow them. They've got to respect the people they're working with."

"We spend nearly half of our time at the field level, working with first-line management," points out his assistant vice president, Fred Hull. "I don't think there's a supervisor anywhere in the country that John and I don't know."

Thompson nods agreement. "As you get larger, you must spend more time with your people. That's how Carnation succeeds in maintaining a people-oriented atmosphere in a computer age."

Management's eye is on the sparrow, as a black youth named Leroy Westbrooks discovered when he was given a temporary job in the mail room at World Headquarters one Christmas. The first morning he reported for work, he was agreeably surprised to find there were no time-clocks to punch. Around ten o'clock a pleasant, middle-aged woman showed up in the basement with a stainless-steel serving cart. His ten-cent cup of coffee was fresh and hot. It was the same coffee served the chairman of the board.

At noon Leroy repaired to the employees' cafeteria next door and ate a three-course hot meal for less than a dollar. At three o'clock that afternoon the cart was back with hot and cold drinks. At four-thirty the hundreds of people streaming out of the building parted in a flurry of friendly small talk. They waved good-bye to the elevator operators, calling them by name.

When Leroy's job ended with the holidays, he went to see Kathy Rossignol, World Headquarters personnel director, and asked if there were any openings for a full-time job. "Can you drive?" Kathy asked, and he said yes, but he was from out of state and had no California license. "You'll have to get a license," Kathy said, and when Leroy pointed out that he couldn't take the test because he had no car, Kathy opened her purse, removed the keys to her own car and handed them to him, along with a ten-spot to cover the cost of the license.

"It seemed the simplest way to handle the situation," Kathy says.

Bureaucratic status symbols are not obtrusive at World Headquarters, but young executives know they have reached a significant plateau in their careers the day they first line up for a midday buffet in the ninth-floor dining room. An employee's rank is indicated by the number of windows in his office, and by its location. A corner office with three windows is comparable to the flag of a three-star general. Upper- and mid-management offices line the walls, leaving junior executives out in the open, separated from stenographers and file clerks only by sheets of glass.

Once in a while a status-sensitive marketing manager goes over the hill, defecting to a walnut-paneled sanctuary in some other corporate headquarters, but most stay on, putting up with the lack of privacy at Carnation because the working arrangements offer opportunities a young M.B.A. doesn't find in large companies where management adheres more closely to the operating guidelines set forth in graduate school textbooks.

"My contemporaries here often make the comment that Carnation has a refreshing management style," says young Dwight Stuart, Jr., the Founder's great-grandson, whose job as product manager of dry cat food rates a one-window office on the sixth floor. "We get the job done by working closely together on a friendly, informal basis."

"It's a clean, straightforward place to work," agrees Hans Reifer, who came to Carnation in 1971 as director of new product development. "Because of our short lines of communication, the people at the decision-making points have the opportunity to share essential information with the people at the points where the information is generated.

"In other companies, it doesn't always work that way. There are jealousies, politics, bureaucratic barriers. Information doesn't flow freely from one jurisdiction to another. Here the management committees have created a healthy climate. They aren't afraid to take risks. They know how to win and how to lose. That's extremely important in the development of new products. Some companies get a winner, and then fail to make the most of it or they turn it into a loser. At Carnation, we don't brood over our failures, and when we get a winner, we know what to do with it."

In developing new products, Hans not only draws on the collective wisdom of the eighth floor, but also on a research and development staff at Van Nuys trained in such varied fields as biology and bacteriology, food and dairy technology, agricultural and chemical engineering. "According to a chemist who has seen both," noted the *Los Angeles Times* (August 21, 1970), "Carnation Company, Los Angeles, has a more sophisticated laboratory than Rocketdyne, the

A new dog food gets the attention of three Ph.D.s at Carnation's Research Center: from left, Milo Nielsen, manager of pet food product development; J. M. McIntire, general manager of research; and Lloyd Miller, director of pet food product development and research.

Canoga Park subsidiary of North American Rockwell."

By the time a new product has left the lab and gone into test market, Hans has carried it across virtually every departmental boundary line at World Headquarters. He has worked with Advertising, Sales and Marketing Research, and if it's something to eat, he has run it past the kitchen professionals at the Food Service Center. Along the way, he may have checked the wording of the proposed label with Bud Daily on the seventh floor and dropped by Joe MacBriar's office to see what Purchasing is paying for a key ingredient.

"It's a multimillion-dollar throw of the dice," Hans says, "but the management committees are very calm in their deliberations. I doubt that there is any other company in the United States that is more willing to pioneer a truly new product."

Carnation is understandably secretive about products still in the laboratory stage, but at the March, 1973, stockholders meeting, Chairman Olson made news when he re-

sponded to a question from the floor about contraceptives in pet foods. Yes, he said, the company was involved in such research. Next day, when a Carnation executive in Kuala Lumpur picked up a copy of *The Straits Times* (Malaysia), he was struck by the front-page headline:

LOVE WITHOUT THE PILLS
—OR THE PUPPIES

"The Carnation Company," he read, "is looking into the possibility of marketing puppy-preventing dog food for pet owners who want to put their female animals on the Pill."

"These products are still in the test stage," the company noted in its 1974 annual report, and referred stockholders to the American Humane Association's estimate that $100,-000,000 is spent each year disposing of unwanted pets.

* * * * *

"It's trite to say it," Everett Olson remarked at luncheon one day shortly before

Pilot plants at Carnation's Research Center in Van Nuys, California, allow study of all production processes.

the company took note of its seventy-fifth anniversary, "but it doesn't seem possible that twenty-five years have gone by since we dedicated this building on our fiftieth anniversary."

The company, in those days, rented out space. Now the Can Division, Carnation International, Albers and Fresh Milk and Ice Cream have spilled out of World Headquarters and are tenants in nearby buildings. Back in 1949 Elbridge Stuart's strong-minded youngest son had walked out on the company after giving it a one-year trial. Twenty-five years later he is installed on the eighth floor as president and his 28-year-old son, Dwight, Jr., is hard at work in Pet Foods.

"We rarely talked about the company when I was growing up," young Dwight says. "Dad's only concern was that I do something that was interesting to me. He didn't want my brothers and me to feel that we *had* to go to work for Carnation. It's no longer a family company. It's a large, publicly-held corporation run on Stuart principles."

Change comes slowly, but it comes. Old-timers still recall the fuss Elbridge Stuart

made when he discovered that the traditional can of Carnation Evaporated Milk had been dropped from the cover of the 1965 annual report. The can belonged on the cover. It had been there for twenty-eight years.

"We don't seem to go through radical and rapid changes," says Dwight Stuart, Sr. "They evolve gradually. Month by month, year by year, nothing seems to change, but when we look back five or six years, we can see that things have changed a great deal, and they'll continue to change. A few years ago, we had only six or seven divisions. Now we have sixteen. That means sixteen different areas to explore and exploit.

"We're making certain plans for the future, based on what seem to us reasonable assumptions, but we're going to remain flexible. The life of a corporation, like the life of an individual, can't be fitted into a master plan. You have to adjust to new conditions. You have to deal not only with the unexpected crisis, but also with the unforeseeable opportunity. If you get a technological breakthrough like the instantizing process, you have to be ready to run with it."

Group Vice President Timm Crull con-

216

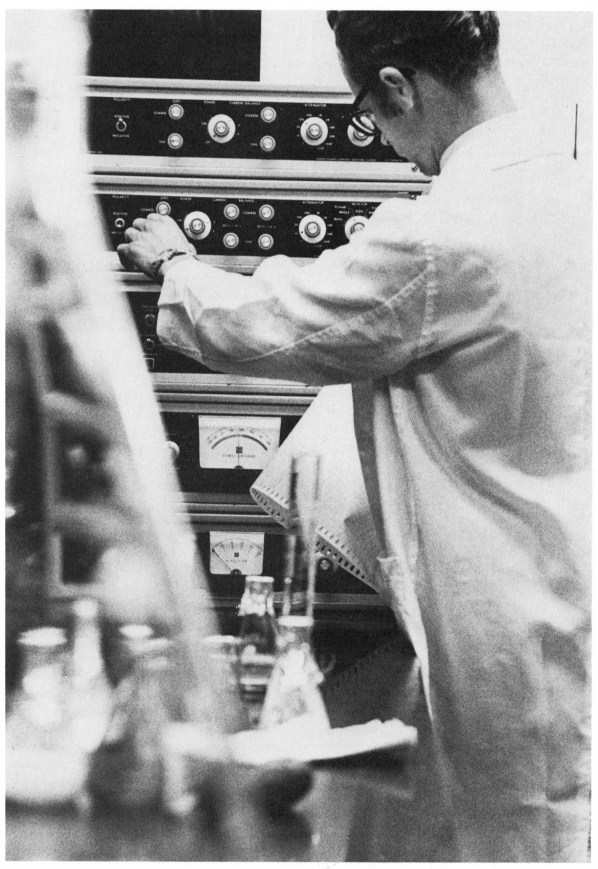

*Research—the big factor in the company's past growth—has plans for
tomorrow with dozens of new products in various stages of development.*

curs. "When we look back on our past," he says, "it's not to revel in our successes, but to use the past in making decisions regarding the future. That's one of our great strengths. So many people here have been with the company for long periods of time. We can draw on their experience at our management committee meetings."

"With a hundred years of experience seated around a table, you're bound to get good results," Dwight Stuart says. "Look at Coffee-mate. No one person at Carnation can take credit for that product. It was a team effort, a lot of different people working closely together, bringing it along, step by step. In many companies our size, the product people have trouble getting to see the president of their own division, much less the president of the company or the chairman of the board. Here it's not just the younger fellows who find it helpful to meet with top management. Senior officers also like to get together for a discussion with their peers."

"We have excellent channels of communication," Timm Crull likes to point out. "In our sales organization, for example, there's never any reticence on anybody's part to criticize a program, to try to improve it. If we didn't have people on the firing line telling us just what the problems are, we'd never be able to take the necessary steps to deal with them. Had we been operating through a network of brokers during the explosive years of the instant revolution, I doubt that we would have received the kind of information that was so important to our growth.

"We have a pretty tough organization. When we came out with Instant Breakfast, we had statistical proof that it would move better if it were in the center of the cereal section at supermarkets. That meant fighting for shelf space occupied by Kellogg's and General Foods. We had quite a battle for about eighteen months, but we demonstrated to the grocer that our product was profitable for him and it offered his customers excellent nutrition. It was a brand-new market. The people who bought Instant Breakfast hadn't been starting their day with corn flakes or oatmeal. They'd been skipping breakfast.

"In my opinion, we're on the threshold of another big spurt of growth. We're working on new products and we're looking at all sorts of things we might be able to move through our distribution system at a profit, but, even more important, we've got a lot of young people dedicated to long-term careers with Carnation. During the next decade or two, the companies that grow and prosper are going to be the ones with strongly-motivated employees, not clock-watchers and job-hoppers. To me, that is Carnation's most valuable asset, its people."

"They made this company," says Chairman of the Board Olson, "and they will determine its future. There are as many opportunities now and there will be as many ten, fifteen and twenty years from now as there were twenty years ago or ten years ago. It's just a matter of having the right people in the right places to recognize those opportunities and take advantage of them."

At the turn of the century, when consumers were campaigning for pure food legislation, Carnation Milk saved the lives of countless babies by offering their mothers a safe, economical alternative to the unsanitary milk delivered to their doors. Two generations later, operating as a multi-product, multi-national company in a world where more than a billion men, women and children (five times the population of the United States) go to sleep every night aching with hunger, Carnation faces even greater challenges and even greater opportunities in serving the members of the human family whose hands reach out to share the earth's abundance.

Dwight L. Stuart   Charles G. Todd   H. Everett Olson

Robert D. Kummel

Henry C. Arnest   *Herbert L. Lucas, Jr.*

Clarke A. Nelson
R. Fullerton Stuart
Albert H Gordon

Norman Barker, Jr.
Walter D. Mertz
Frederick G. Larkin, Jr.

Robert C. Evans
Timm F. Crull
Glen R. Mitchell

Chronology

1899

EAS and Thomas E. Yerxa establish the Pacific Coast Condensed Milk Company, with EAS having "full charge and control of said business" (Aug. 5). The Kent, Washington, condensery converts 2,744 quarts of fresh milk to 55 cases of evaporated milk on opening day (Sept. 6), and a few weeks later EAS hits on the brand name, Carnation. Operations at the end of the year show a loss of $140,000.

1900

A foreman devises a machine to fill the 16-ounce cans of Carnation Cream. Company opens an office in Seattle. Business is incorporated as a Washington corporation (Dec. 31).

1901

EAS acquires his first can-making machinery and on May 27 buys out his partner, assuming his share of their $65,000 debt.

1902

A second evaporated milk plant is opened at Forest Grove, Oregon, with EAS nephew, Harry Stuart, as superintendent. Sanipure, a food for infants, is developed and marketed. Company moves into California with Carnation Cream, bucking heavy opposition.

1903

EHS goes to work at the Oregon plant during his summer vacation. Company turns a profit of $100,000.

1904

Borden's is rumored to have offered EAS $1,000,000 for his company.

1905

Manufacture of Sanipure is discontinued. Carnation Cream is exhibited at Lewis and Clark Exposition in Portland, Oregon. EAS pays A. Gaulin of Paris $2,000 for a machine designed "to prevent the rising of the cream on milk and the transformation of said cream into butter" (Dec. 30). Net sales: $1,138,088.

1906

EAS takes delivery of his French homogenizer (March). Three condenseries are added in Washington (Chehalis, Ferndale, Mount Vernon). EAS adopts the slogan, "Milk From Contented Cows." Federal food and drug law is signed by President Theodore Roosevelt (June 30). H. Everett Olson is born in Chicago (Nov. 1).

1907

New pure food and drug law goes into effect (Jan. 1), and the name of the company's product is changed from Carnation Cream to Carnation Milk to meet its requirements. EAS buys his first automobile, a four-cylinder Pierce Arrow. W. C. Cross takes charge of the newly acquired plant at Hillsboro, Oregon.

1908

EHS is graduated from Phillips Academy at Andover, Massachusetts, and enters Yale University. P. G. Kinzer joins the company's production department (Oct. 1).

1909

EAS buys 260-acre farm in Washington's Snoqualmie Valley. Carnation Milk is exhibited at the Alaska-Yukon-Pacific Exposition in Seattle. Company operates at a loss for the first time since 1900.

1910

EAS incorporates Carnation Stock Farms, capitalized at $100,000 (Jan. 7), and acquires 480 additional acres. Negotiations for the sale of the company are broken off after EAS consults EHS. Pacific Coast Condensed Milk Company, originally incorporated in Washington, is incorporated under the same name in Maine (Dec. 31).

1911

EAS buys a registered Holstein bull and five cows for his Snoqualmie Valley farm. M. J. (Jack) Norton is put in charge of the company's new midwestern plants, three in Wisconsin (Berlin, Richland Center, Chilton) and one in Oregon, Illinois. EHS is graduated from Yale in June and starts work at the Forest Grove, Oregon, plant under P. G. Kinzer (Aug. 1).

221

1912

EHS is transferred to the Mount Vernon, Washington, plant as foreman, and then to Everson, Washington, as supervisor. Segis Pietertje Prospect ("Possum Sweetheart"), Carnation's first world champion cow, is born (April 10). EAS buys 84 registered Holsteins (July). Carnation Stock Farms increased to 1,200 acres. Big feed barn and three milk barns are ready at the farm (Dec.).

1913

EHS is shifted to Berlin, Wisconsin, to serve as Jack Norton's assistant in the Eastern Division. P. G. Kinzer is named general superintendent of plants in the Western Division. Net sales reach $8,529,-592.26.

1914

EHS is promoted to general superintendent of operations. W. C. Cross becomes assistant general superintendent in the Western Division. The Eastern Division moves its main offices to Oconomowoc, Wisconsin (October).

1915

A large farm near Oconomowoc is purchased and designated the Eastern Farm (Jan. 13). EHS is moved back to the Seattle office. A. M. Ghormley is hired as a day laborer at Carnation Stock Farms (April 21). EAS buys a herd of purebred Holsteins and for an extra $5 acquires a priceless old bull, King Segis Tenth. Carnation Milk is displayed at Panama-Pacific International Exposition in San Francisco. Company buys the patent rights and production facilities for Hebe, a filled-milk product (Dec. 15).

1916

Pacific Coast Condensed Milk Company becomes Carnation Milk Products Company, a Maine corporation (Feb. 5). EHS marries Nan Fullerton (June 22). A ton of Carnation Milk is hauled from Seattle to New York in the first transcontinental shipment by truck (July 10-Sept. 9). A Canadian condensery is acquired at Aylmer, Ontario (Nov. 27).

1917

E. Hadley Stuart, Jr. born (July 12). EHS is elected vice president (Nov. 28).

1918

New can factory at Oconomowoc begins operations (March 8). EAS pays $106,000 for a bull calf (June 8). Because of increased sales in the East, general office is set up in Chicago.

1919

EHS transferred to Chicago headquarters. Carnation and Helvetia Milk Condensing Company (the name was later changed to Pet) agree to form an overseas affiliate, the American Milk Products Corporation (April 4), and EAS goes to Europe to set up its offices. A second son, Reginald Fullerton Stuart, is born to EHS and Nan (Dec. 4).

1920

A. M. Ghormley is named superintendent of Carnation Stock Farms. Carnation Milk Products Company becomes a Delaware corporation (July 13). Board of directors sets up a three-member Executive Committee (July 27). First issue of *Carnation Family News* published in Seattle (Sept.). Segis Pietertje Prospect sets a world record, producing 37,-381.4 pounds of milk in one year (Dec. 17).

1921

Jack Dempsey visits Carnation Stock Farms (April 8). Harry Stuart killed in an accident (April 16). EHS returns to Seattle office. Sale of Hebe is discontinued when federal government bans interstate shipment of filled-milk products.

1922

Board of directors votes to move Chicago general office to Oconomowoc (Aug. 17). Executive Committee decides to buy Malt-A-Milk Company of Kansas City, Missouri, which manufactures a chocolate malted milk product sold under the trade name, Cho-Cho (Aug. 17). A. M. Ghormley marries Elizabeth MacLean (Oct. 28).

1923

The Eastern General Office is moved from Chicago to Oconomowoc (April 30). American Milk Products Company decides to buy a creamery business in Carentan, France (Oct. 26), and P. G. Kinzer is sent over to convert it to a condensery and can-making plant.

1924

EHS becomes assistant to the company's general manager, dividing his time between Oconomowoc and Seattle. Name of Carnation Stock Farms changed to Carnation Milk Farms. Company celebrates its twenty-fifth anniversary (Sept. 6). Dwight Lyman Stuart born (Sept. 27).

1925

L. R. Hardenbergh resigns as executive vice president (Jan. 13). Segis Pietertje Prospect dies (March 14). American Milk Products Company decides to establish a condensery at Neustadt, Germany (Aug. 19). P. G. Kinzer returns to Seattle from Europe and is put in charge of Western Division sales (Oct.). Paul R. McKee is elected vice president and secretary (Dec. 29).

1926

Jack Norton becomes general manager (Jan. 1). Company enters the fresh milk and ice cream business in Seattle with the purchase of six dairies (April 21). Production starts at the Neustadt plant (May 1). EAS celebrates his seventieth birthday (Sept. 10). Jack Norton resigns and EHS is named executive vice president (Oct. 31).

1927

EAS inspects American Milk Products plants in France, Germany and Holland. H. E. Olson is graduated from Northwestern University (June). Carnation common stock is admitted to unlisted trading privileges on the American Stock Exchange (Nov. 16). Production of Carnation Malted Milk begins at Ferndale, Washington (Dec.).

1928

W. C. Cross is named general superintendent. Statue of Segis Pietertje Prospect is unveiled at Carnation Milk Farm (July 31). An attempt to consolidate Carnation and Pet Milk fails (Nov.).

1929

A. M. Ghormley is transferred to Seattle office to become P. G. Kinzer's assistant (Aug. 1). Board of directors approves sale of Eastern Farm to A. C. Oosterhuis (Aug. 7). Carnation buys Albers Bros. Milling Company (Oct. 19). Carnation Milk Products Company changes its name to Carnation Company (Nov. 16) and issues its first printed message to stockholders.

1930

EHS elected president of American Milk Products Company (Jan. 20). Carnation enters the fresh milk business in Houston, Texas, with the purchase of Harris Cream Top Milk Company (June 25). Carnation executive offices moved from Oconomowoc to Milwaukee (Dec. 1). American Milk Products changes its name to General Milk Company (Dec. 26). For the first time Carnation publishes its net annual income: $1,411,632.

1931

Carnation's Sunday evening Contented Hour introduced on Pacific Coast network of NBC (April 26). Company enters the fresh milk business in Los Angeles with the purchase of Henry Creamery Corporation (June 16). H. E. Olson joins the company at Oconomowoc as assistant controller (Dec. 28). Net earnings: $1,383,512.

1932

Contented Hour airs nationally from NBC studios in Chicago (Jan. 4). Henry C. Arnest goes to work for the company (Feb. 5). EAS resigns as president and is succeeded by EHS (Feb. 22). Paul R. McKee dies (Dec. 4). EHS hopes "the worst of the depression is behind us" and reports a net loss for the year of $660,609.33.

1933

To further centralize executive operations, P. G. Kinzer and J. F. Douglas are transferred from Seattle to Milwaukee (Jan. 1). A. M. Ghormley elected vice president and director (Feb. 23). Production of malted milk shifted from Ferndale, Washington, to Oconomowoc. A. M. Ghormley is elected president of Albers Milling Company (Aug. 28). A Wisconsin Alumni Research Foundation license permits Carnation to enhance Vitamin D potency of its evaporated milk by ultra violet ray treatment (Nov. 1). Net earnings: $1,078,511.

1934

Dionne quintuplets are born near Callander, Ontario (May 28), and placed on Carnation Evaporated Milk formula (Nov. 27). Carnation begins irradiating its evaporated milk (June). Friskies, a dry dog food, is introduced in western markets. Annual report shows net sales of $37,401,304 and net earnings of $1,057,027.

1935

EAS and wife celebrate their golden wedding anniversary at their Los Angeles home (Nov. 13). Net sales: $44,939,354; net earnings: $1,140,211.

1936

H. E. Olson is transferred from Oconomowoc to Seattle as controller for Albers Milling Company (Jan. 18). Carnation Ormsby Butter King sets a world record at Carnation Milk Farm, producing 38,606.6 pounds of milk yielding 1,402.02 pounds of butterfat (the equivalent of 1,752.5 pounds of butter) in a 365-day test period (Feb. 12). Sale of Friskies moves into the Middle West. Directors establish a vacation plan for all Carnation employees (Oct. 1). Annual report calls attention to large sums of money being spent on research and development, and cites success of Calf Manna, which is on sale throughout the United States and in many foreign countries. Net sales: $52,275,243; net earnings: $1,904,038.

1937

H. E. Olson is elected treasurer of Albers Milling Company (April 8). Albers begins manufacture of corn flakes (May). Mrs. E. H. Stuart dies (Aug. 21). Net sales: $58,565,071; net earnings: $1,810,391.

1938

A. M. Ghormley becomes general manager of the Fresh Milk and Ice Cream Division. Net sales: $53,742,502; net earnings: $1,968,825.

1939

Mrs. E. A. Stuart dies (June 13). Cho-Cho, a frozen malted milk, is introduced. Friskies showing "a fine growth." Net sales: $54,618,181; net earnings: $2,508,095.

1940

EAS loses most of his eyesight, starts growing carnations in nutrient solution at his Los Angeles home. Carnation Research Laboratory, under F. B. MacKenzie, begins operations in Milwaukee (May 1) and EHS advises stockholders, "We are carrying on this research because we feel this is a field where results can be secured which in time will prove very beneficial to your company." Net sales: $62,714,629; net earnings: $2,319,027.

1941

Production of sweetened condensed milk begins at Bergville, South Africa (June 9). EAS celebrates his eighty-fifth birthday (Sept. 10). EHS makes a brief talk on the five hundredth broadcast of the Contented Hour (Sept. 29). Annual report notes that the company has been "called upon to supply large quantities of evaporated milk to our government and to the Canadian and British governments." Net sales: $84,060,505; net earnings: $2,564,450.

1942

A new world record is run up at Carnation Milk Farm when Carnation Ormsby Madcap Fayne produces 41,943.4 pounds of milk in one year (May 21). Carnation has 1,030 employees with the armed forces in various parts of the world. Arthur P. Herold elected president of Albers (Dec. 21). Net sales: $112,719,268; net earnings: $2,546,654.

1943

Albers cereal mill at Oakland, California, is destroyed by fire (Feb. 28). Construction of a new mill begins in April. Company reports record sales of $130,045,124, but price ceilings on evaporated milk and other products keep net earnings to $2,234,321.

1944

EAS dies (Jan. 14). New Albers mill begins operations in Oakland (March). Company now has 1,569 employees in military service. Net sales $148,277,799; net earnings: $2,236,038.

1945

EHS marries Mrs. Evelyn Clark Ruble, a widow with two daughters, Betty and Ann (Feb. 24). Carnation Company Scholarship Foundation, to "make possible many successful business and professional careers for the youth of Carnation families," is established as a memorial to EAS (Dec. 29). EHS reports "a successful year under trying conditions." Net sales: $168,827,627; net earnings: $2,447,480.

1946

First postwar year, EHS reports, "has not been an easy one." Net sales: $186,929,951; net earnings: $3,211,985.

1947

Directors decide to build World Headquarters in Los Angeles (Feb. 17). Net sales: $231,339,460; net earnings: $4,283,387.

1948

Ground is broken for World Headquarters (Jan. 15). Annual report notes that "all of our executives and most of our key personnel have moved to Los Angeles." Logistics of the move handled by H. E. Olson, Carnation's new treasurer (Sept. 9). General Milk completes construction of a condensery at Querétaro, Mexico. Annual report shows net sales of $260,027,447 and net income of $5,768,383.

1949

By spring, company has moved into World Headquarters, but waits until its fiftieth anniversary (Sept. 6) to conduct dedicatory ceremonies. Net sales: $245,605,362; net earnings: $7,764,599.

1950

General Milk completes a sweetened condensed milk plant at Harrismith, Natal, South Africa, and starts work on a sweetened and evaporated milk plant at Merrigum, Victoria, Australia. S. A. Halgren is elected secretary of the company and C. G. Todd assistant secretary (April 10). H. E. Olson elected to the board of directors (Nov. 30). Net sales: $256,325,931; net earnings: $9,484,113.

1951

A. M. Ghormley is appointed assistant to the president (May 28). The Albers mill at Jefferson, Wisconsin, formerly a Carnation Evaporated Milk plant, produces its first can of Friskies Dog Food (June 1). J. F. Douglas retires as chairman of the Finance Committee and is succeeded by John M. Reily (Dec. 31). Net sales: $297,729,394; net earnings: $6,927,168.

1952

Work begun on a research laboratory at Van Nuys, California (July 22). J. F. Douglas dies (Nov. 29). Carnation Foundation established to enable the company to more effectively carry out its philanthropic activities (Dec.). Net sales: $317,986,772; net earnings: $6,881,363.

1953

Carnation Homestead Daisy Madcap racks up a world record of 1,511.8 pounds of butterfat from 36,414.1 pounds of milk in a 365-day test period (Jan. 13). P. G. Kinzer retires as vice president in charge of evaporated milk sales and advertising, but remains a director and a member of the Executive Committee (June 29). Work begins on an addition to World Headquarters. David D. Peebles applies for a patent (serial number 370,420) relating generally "to methods for the manufacture of dry powdered products from liquid lacteal material like skim milk" (July 27). Net sales: $317,647,209; net earnings: $7,232,199.

1954

Carnation buys McGraw Colorgraph of Burbank, California, manufacturers of products for color photography and the graphic arts (May 25). Carnation and Western Condensing Company organize the Instant Milk Company to manufacture and market instant dry milk products made by the Peebles process (June). The first such product, Carnation Instant Non-Fat Dry Milk Solids, is introduced (Sept. 1). Net sales: $310,037,852; net earnings: $7,746,826.

1955

EHS is made a chevalier in the French Order of the Legion of Honor (Feb. 10). H. E. Olson resigns as treasurer and is named head of Financial Department (Feb. 11). National distribution of Carnation Instant Non-Fat Dry Milk Solids is completed (March 1). Carnation enters the frozen food business with the purchase of Mrs. Lee's Pies, Inc., located in Los Angeles (June 18). The Carnation "Gay Nineties" ice cream parlor is opened at Disneyland, California (July). New products include Carnation Instant Chocolate Flavored Drink, put in national distribution; a kibbled and biscuit dog food introduced in the Western states; and Friskies Cat Food, test-marketed in three areas. Peruvian government bestows Order of Merit on EHS (Oct. 27). W. C. Cross retires (Dec. 31). Net sales: $329,248,299; net earnings: $8,070,373.

1956

P. G. Kinzer retires from Executive Committee but remains on the board of directors (Jan. 1). Net sales: $329,248,299; net earnings: $9,028,086.

1957

Alfred M. Ghormley becomes Carnation's third president when EHS resigns and is elected chairman of the board (Feb. 22). By-laws amended to increase the number of directors from eleven to fifteen (March 27). New Seattle fresh milk and ice cream plant is formally opened (July 22). Albers milling and pet food plant at Oakland, California, is severely damaged by fire (Sept. 16). Net sales: $368,639,947; net earnings: $9,517,096.

1958

Dwight L. Stuart elected assistant vice president (Feb. 21). Waverly, Iowa, plant has been converted to the production of Instant Nonfat Dry Milk. Carnation Farm developing a herd of Polled Herefords. Net sales: $378,591,525; net earnings: $9,842,312.

1959

Carnation Instant Nonfat Powdered Milk introduced throughout Canada. Friskies Canned Dog Food is now in distribution throughout the United

States, except the New York City area. Friskies Meal and Friskies Cubes are in distribution in approximately 70 percent of the country. Friskies Canned Cat Food, made with a fish base, expands its market east of the Rockies. Research Laboratory at Van Nuys develops Trio instant mashed potatoes for institutional use and annual report notes that the company is developing "a strong sales force" for this field. Can Division is now operating ten plants. Decade ends with the most successful year in the company's history. Net sales: $396,282,502; net earnings: $9,981,480.

1960

Dwight L. Stuart is elected to the board of directors (Feb. 19). H. E. Olson becomes president of Albers Milling Company (April 1). Friskies Canned Dog Food achieves national distribution by moving into New York City. Carnation Grocery Products and Albers sales divisions are merged. Net sales: $417,-629,239; net earnings: $11,152,358.

1961

A new product, Coffee-mate, a non-dairy coffee creamer, is marketed. H. E. Olson is appointed assistant to the president (March 29). E. Hadley Stuart, Jr. announces his resignation as vice president, director and member of the Executive Committee (May 23). Net sales: $430,050,310; net earnings: $12,189,220.

1962

Canadian Division completes work on a new condensery at Wetaskiwin, Alberta (April) and, after entering into a joint venture with J. R. Simplot Company of Idaho, begins marketing a full line of frozen and dry potatoes (Nov.-Dec.). Friskies Puppy Food is introduced in western United States. Net sales: $437,184,664; net earnings: $12,736,197.

1963

I. E. Olson is elected president, succeeding A. M. Ghormley, who becomes vice chairman of the board and replaces EHS as chairman of the Executive Committee (Feb. 18). Carnation Instant Breakfast is test-marketed in six cities. Five varieties of cat "treats" are placed on sale in the West. Coffee-mate makes its Canadian debut. Sale of recombined evaporated milk begins in the Philippines (May 20). The Institutional-Industrial Division is created (July). Carnation acquires Contadina Foods, a

Northern California processor and distributor of tomato products (Nov. 15). Net sales: $435,354,221; net earnings: $13,969,074.

1964

EHS receives an honorary degree from Whitman College (June 7). Carnation Instant Breakfast goes on sale in the West (Aug.). Ralph R. Brubaker, vice president-marketing, retires (Dec. 31). Net sales: $477,282,206; net earnings: $16,472,067.

1965

A. M. Ghormley dies at the age of sixty-eight (Jan. 30). EHS resigns as president of General Milk and is succeeded by W. D. Dobson, with H. L. Lucas serving as executive vice president (Feb. 19). H. E. Olson is elected chairman of the Executive Committee (Feb. 26). Carnation Instant Breakfast goes into national distribution (May). Carnation Farms Breeding Service acquires Eastern Iowa Breeders, Cedar Rapids (Oct.), and Piper Brothers, Watertown, Wisconsin (Nov.). Fresh Milk and Ice Cream Division arranges with Favorite Foods of Fullerton, California, to market flavored yogurt (Sept. 17). Net sales: $539,924,018; net income: $20,484,189.

1966

Pet Milk Company's 35 percent interest in General Milk Company is purchased for $42,000,000, and the overseas affiliate is made a division of Carnation Company (Jan. 21). Carnation becomes one of the country's major meat canners with the acquisition of Trenton Foods (Sept. 1). To handle its growing volume of sales throughout Europe, McGraw Colorgraph establishes a subsidiary in Antwerp, Belgium (Sept. 16). Carnation Instant Breakfast is introduced in Canada (Oct. 9). Slender, a 225-calorie diet food, is tried out in three test markets (Oct.). Distribution of Friskies Canned Cat Food in chicken, liver and fish flavors is extended to eastern markets. Net sales: $812,907,754; net earnings: $28,028,019.

1967

Slender goes into national distribution (June). Carnation introduces a newly formulated cat food, Buffet, and, for institutional use, the Chef-mate line of canned meat, cheese and pasta products. Dwight L. Stuart is elected senior vice president and assistant to the president (Nov. 8). Net sales: $879,167,-395; net earnings: $31,773,464.

1968

Carnation acquires 100 percent ownership of Fullerton, California, yogurt operation, which was previously 50 percent owned (May 6). Work begins on a new instant products plant at Jacksonville, Illinois (April). Ground-breaking ceremonies for a new pet food plant at St. Joseph, Missouri (Nov. 1). Research facilities at Van Nuys laboratories are being expanded. Net sales: $929,878,748; net earnings: $35,542,017.

1969

The Spreadables, sandwich spreads in aluminum casserole-type containers, are test-marketed, along with five new Chef-mate products. Carnation closes the decade and the seventieth year of its history with record highs in both sales ($964,404,077) and profits ($39,567,801).

1970

Executive Committee is expanded to include three new members, Henry C. Arnest, Robert D. Kummel and Clarke A. Nelson (August). Carnation acquires Pronto Pacific, a Moses Lake, Washington, potato-processing business (Sept. 10) and Dayton Reliable Tool and Manufacturing Company, Dayton, Ohio (Oct. 30). Net sales: $1,053,358,436; net income: $45,883,009.

1971

Carnation Hot Cocoa Mix is introduced into retail markets nationally (Jan.). EHS resigns as chairman of the board and is succeeded by H. E. Olson, with Dwight L. Stuart moving up to the position of executive vice president (Feb. 18). A new marketing group for processed potatoes is established at World Headquarters (May). The name of the Institutional-Industrial Division is changed to the Food Service-Industrial Division (July). Friskies Dinners, a new dry dog food, replaces Friskies Mix. Coffee-mate is being produced in Scotland at the new plant in Dumfries, and Go-Cat, a dry cat food, goes on sale throughout the United Kingdom. Ted E. Lang succeeds William H. Crockett as head of Carnation's Canadian subsidiary (Oct.). Net sales: $1,148,155,929; net earnings: $50,239,838.

1972

H. L. Lucas becomes president of General Milk when W. D. Dobson retires (Feb. 25). Carnation buys Miller Brewing Company's half-interest in Containers, Inc., the joint Carnation-Miller can-making company with facilities at Menomonee Falls, Wisconsin (March). Carnation's foreign division, General Milk, changes its name to Carnation International (May 12). EHS dies at the age of eighty-four (Sept. 16). New Genetics Division is formed as Carnation acquires Genetics, Inc. of Hughson, California (Nov. 17). Net sales: $1,249,313,748; net earnings: $55,854,252.

1973

Board of directors elects Dwight L. Stuart president, Charles G. Todd executive vice president and Clarke A. Nelson, Timm Crull and Glen Mitchell group vice presidents (Feb. 22). Mighty Dog, a single-serving premium dog food, is introduced nationally (Feb.-March). Carnation Instant Breakfast Bar goes into test markets (July). American Stock Exchange approves Carnation's listing application (July 5). Company acquires Herff Jones, an Indianapolis-based producer of graduation accessories and related products (Nov. 8). Contadina adds to its production capacity by purchasing a tomato and spinach processing plant in Hollister, California (Dec. 11). Net sales: $1,472,198,191; net income: $64,871,351.

1974

Carnation acquires two additional potato-processing plants, one at Nampa, Idaho (Jan. 2), the other at Othello, Washington (Feb. 22). P. G. Kinzer dies at the age of ninety-six (Jan. 15). Albers expands its production into the East and South with the purchase from John W. Eshelman and Sons of five feed mills and seven feed stores (Jan. 25). Board authorizes an additional $50,000,000 long-term debt (Feb. 22), and Carnation becomes the sixth company to be given both Moody's and Standard & Poor's triple-A rating (April 18). Earnings for second quarter are reported at a record high, $18,530,000, on sales of $445,706,000 (Aug. 13). World Headquarters goes quietly about its work on the company's seventy-fifth anniversary (Sept. 6).

227

Carnation Company Facilities

WORLD HEADQUARTERS
Los Angeles, California

RESEARCH LABORATORY
Van Nuys, California

SALES OFFICES

United States

Atlanta, Georgia
Baltimore, Maryland
Birmingham, Alabama
Boston, Massachusetts
Buffalo, New York
Charlotte, North Carolina
Chicago, Illinois
Cleveland, Ohio
Columbus, Ohio
Dallas, Texas
Denver, Colorado
Detroit, Michigan
Honolulu, Hawaii
Houston, Texas
Indianapolis, Indiana
Jacksonville, Florida
Kansas City, Missouri
Los Angeles, California
Memphis, Tennessee
Milwaukee, Wisconsin
Minneapolis, Minnesota
New Orleans, Louisiana
New York, New York
Omaha, Nebraska
Philadelphia, Pennsylvania
Phoenix, Arizona
Pittsburgh, Pennsylvania
Portland, Oregon
St. Louis, Missouri
Salt Lake City, Utah
San Francisco, California
Seattle, Washington
Spokane, Washington

Canada

Edmonton, Alberta
Halifax, Nova Scotia
Montreal, Quebec
Saint John, New Brunswick
Toronto, Ontario
Vancouver, British Columbia
Winnipeg, Manitoba

Carnation International

Athens, Greece
Bangkok, Thailand
Barcelona, Spain
Brussels, Belgium
Copenhagen, Denmark
Durban, South Africa
Esbjerg, Denmark
Hamburg, Germany
Johannesburg, South Africa
Kuala Lumpur, Malaysia
London, England
Manila, Philippines
Melbourne, Australia
Mexico City, Mexico
Paris, France
Rotterdam, Holland
Singapore
Tokyo, Japan
Udine, Italy

ALBERS PLANTS

Location	Operation	Starting Date
Seattle, Washington	Cereal and Feed Mills *(Closed 1961)*	1929
Portland, Oregon	Feed Mill	1929
Oakland, California	Cereal and Feed Mills *(Feed mill section destroyed by fire 1957)* *(Trans. to Pet Foods & Cereals 1967)*	1929
Los Angeles, California	Feed Mill *(Closed 1960)*	1929
Peoria, Illinois	Manufactured Calf Manna and Friskies *(Closed 1955)*	1936
Hillsboro, Oregon	Dry Friskies Plant *(Trans. to Pet Foods & Cereals 1967)*	1947
Sullivan, Wisconsin	Feed Mill *(Closed 1955; building trans. to Carnation for General Stores)*	1947
Kansas City, Missouri	Feed Mill	1950
Fort Lupton, Colorado	Feed Mill	1956
Beaumont, California	Feed Mill	1957
Fresno, California	Feed Mill	1958
Eugene, Oregon	Feed Mill *(Destroyed by fire 1968; not rebuilt)*	1958
Santa Rosa, California	Feed Mill	1958
McMinnville, Oregon	Feed Mill *(Changed to Feed Store 1967)*	1958
Honolulu, Hawaii	Feed Mill	1959
Red Bluff, California	Feed Mill	1959
Ft. Smith, Arkansas	Feed Mill *(Closed 1970)*	1960
Twin Falls, Idaho	Feed Mill *(Closed 1968)*	1961
Tacoma, Washington	Feed Mill	1961
Bellingham, Washington	Feed Mill	1961
Stockton, California	Feed Mill	1967
Chamblee, Georgia	Feed Mill	1974
Circleville, Ohio	Feed Mill	1974
Klamath Falls, Oregon	Feed Mill	1974
Sanford, North Carolina	Feed Mill	1974
Tampa, Florida	Feed Mill	1974
York, Pennsylvania	Feed Mill	1974
Brighton, Colorado	Poultry/Egg	1961
Logan, Oregon	Poultry/Egg	1961
Tenino, Washington	Poultry/Egg	1963
Honolulu, Hawaii	Poultry/Egg	1964

Location	Operation	Starting Date
Henderson, Colorado	Poultry/Egg	1965
Ewa, Hawaii	Poultry/Egg	1965
Waianae, Hawaii	Poultry/Egg	1966
Mt. Angel, Oregon	Poultry/Egg (Closed 1973)	1967
Auburn, Washington	Poultry/Egg (Closed 1974)	1969
The Dalles, Oregon	Poultry/Egg	1974

CAN FACTORIES

Location	Operation	Starting Date
Oconomowoc, Wisconsin	Open-top Cans	1918
Maysville, Kentucky	Evaporated Milk Cans	1929
Gustine, California	Evaporated Milk Cans	1933
Mt. Vernon, Washington	Evaporated Milk Cans	1935
Mt. Vernon, Missouri	Evaporated, Open-top Cans	1938
Cambridge Springs, Pennsylvania	Evaporated Milk Cans	1939
Waupun, Wisconsin	Open-top, Beverage Cans	1947
Aylmer, Ontario, Canada	Evaporated Milk Cans	1951
Hillsboro, Oregon	Open-top Cans	1954
Nampa, Idaho	Open-top Cans	1961
Riverbank, California	Open-top Cans	1963
Menomonee Falls, Wisconsin	Beverage Cans	1966
Mansfield, Texas	Open-top, Beverage, Aluminum Cans	1969
St. Joseph, Missouri	Open-top, Aluminum Cans	1970

CANADIAN OPERATIONS
Carnation Company, Ltd.

Location	Operation	Starting Date
Aylmer, Ontario	Condensery	1916
Sherbrooke, Quebec	Condensery	1939
Kerwood, Ontario	Receiving Station	1943
Waterloo, Quebec	Receiving Station	1947
Fordwich, Ontario	Receiving Station (Sold 1956)	1951
Alexandria, Ontario	Receiving Station (Converted to dry milk plant 1959)	1951
Wetaskiwin, Alberta	Condensery	1962

Carnation Foods Co. Ltd.

Location	Operation	Starting Date
*Carberry, Manitoba	Potato processing	1962
*Taber, Alberta	Potato processing	1966

*Joint Venture

CARNATION FARMS

Location	Operation	Starting Date
Carnation, Washington	Registered Holstein Farm, Albers Research Farm, Dog Kennels and Cattery	1910

CARNATION INTERNATIONAL

Location	Operation	Starting Date
Australia		
Merrigum	Condensery	1952
Sydney (Blacktown)	Pet Foods	1966
Melbourne (Blackburn)	Pet Foods	1973
Brazil—*Joint venture sold in 1971*		
Itaperuna	Powdered Milk Plant	1959
	Can Factory	1959
Governador Valadares	Pre-condensing plant	1965
Itapetinga	Powdered Milk Plant	1967
*Cuba—*Factories expropriated by Government in 1960*		
Bayamo	Condensery	1931
	Can Factory	1931
Sancti Spiritus	Condensery	1938
Denmark		
Esbjerg	Pet Accessories	1974
Dominican Republic		
*Santa Domingo	Condensery	1971
France		
Carentan	Condensery	1923
	Can Factory	1924
Corbie	Condensery, Can Factory	1955
Vire	Butter	1960
Bricquebec	Powdered Milk	1962
Marconnelle	Powdered Milk	1970
	Pet Foods	1972
Guingamp	Pet Foods	1972
Germany		
Neustadt i/Holstein	Condensery	1926
	Can Factory	1931
	Butter Factory	1968
**Waren, Mecklenburg	Condensery	1937
**Allenburg, East Prussia	Condensery	1937
Bad Essen	Condensery	1952
	Can Factory	1952
	Baby Food	1960
Marktbreit	Condensery	1958
	Can Factory	1958
Gnissau	Creamery, Cheese Factory	1967
Holland		
Schoonhoven	Condensery	1927
Gorinchem	Condensery	1928
	Can Factory	1928
Tricht	Receiving Station	1938

231

*Joint venture
**Not under Company operation; in communist-occupied territories.

Location	Operation	Starting Date
Meerkerk	Cheese Factory *(Converted to Pet Accessories warehouse 1974)*	1948
Italy		
Udine	Pet Products Plant	1973
Jamaica		
*Kingston	Condensery	1939
Malaysia		
*Kuala Lumpur	Condensery	1965
	Can Factory	1966
Mexico		
Querétaro	Condensery	1948
	Can Factory	1952
Durango	Condensery	1956
Lerdo	Pre-condensing Plant	1968
Panama		
*Panama City	Condensery	1937
	Can Factory	1962
*Chiriqui	Dairy Products	1970
Peru		
*Arequipa	Condensery, Can Factory	1942
*Vitor	Pre-condensing Plant	1945
Philippines		
Manila	Condensery, Can Factory	1957
Scotland		
Dumfries	Condensery	1935
	Can Factory	1966
	Coffee-mate Plant	1967
Aberdeen	Pre-condensing Plant	1957
*Singapore	Condensery	1967
South Africa		
Bergville	Condensery	1941
	Can Factory	1949
Harrismith	Condensery	1949
Afrikaskop	Cheese Factory	1965
Politsi	Food Processing Plant	1966
Durban	Food Processing Plant	1973
Johannesburg	Food Processing Plant	1973
	Pet Products Plant	1973
Spain		
Barcelona	Food Processing Plant	1969
Gijón	Food Processing Plant	1972
Valencia	Food Processing Plant	1973
Thailand		
*Bangkok	Condensery *(Sold 1971)*	1970

232

*Joint venture

CONTADINA FOODS

Location	Operation	Starting Date
Riverbank, California	Canned Tomato Products	1963
San Jose, California	Canned Tomato Products	1963
Woodland, California	Canned Tomato Products	1963
Hollister, California	Canned Tomato Products	1973

DAYTON RELIABLE TOOL & MFG. CO.

Dayton, Ohio		1970

DISTRIBUTION CENTERS

Rochelle, Illinois		1967
Stockton, California		1968
Elwood, Kansas		1969
Fort Wayne, Indiana		1969
Mechanicsburg, Pennsylvania		1969

EVAPORATED MILK PLANTS

Location	Operation	Starting Date
Kent, Washington	Condensery Can Factory *(Closed and later sold 1934)*	1899
Forest Grove, Oregon	Condensery *(Closed and sold 1929)*	1902
Chehalis, Washington	Condensery *(Sold 1925)*	1906
Mt. Vernon, Washington	Condensery	1906
Ferndale, Washington	Condensery Converted to Rec. Sta. 1916 *(Closed 1958)*	1906
Hillsboro, Oregon	Condensery *(Transferred to Albers 1947)*	1907
Monroe, Washington	Condensery *(Closed and sold 1940)*	1908
Everson, Washington	Condensery *(Closed and sold 1934)*	1909
Stanwood, Washington	Condensery *(Closed and sold 1933)*	1910
Berlin, Wisconsin	Condensery *(Closed 1955. Destroyed by tornado 1956)*	1911
Richland Center, Wisconsin	Condensery *(Closed 1967)*	1911
Oregon, Illinois	Condensery	1911
Chilton, Wisconsin	Condensery *(Transferred to Instant Products 1954)*	1911
Jefferson, Wisconsin	Condensery *(Transferred to Albers 1952)*	1916
Oconomowoc, Wisconsin	Condensery *(Transferred to Instant Products 1953)*	1916

Location	Operation	Starting Date
Sedro Wooley, Washington	Condensery (Closed 1924. Destroyed by fire)	1917
Hartland, Wisconsin	Receiving Station (Closed and sold 1953)	1917
Nampa, Idaho	Condensery (Closed 1961. Converted to can factory)	1918
Sullivan, Wisconsin	Receiving Station (Closed 1949. Became general stores 1954)	1918
Sparta, Michigan	Condensery Converted to Rec. Sta. 1956 (Closed and sold 1961)	1920
Cambridge Springs, Pennsylvania	Condensery	1921
Corry, Pennsylvania	Receiving Station	1921
Deansboro, New York	Condensery (Closed and sold 1933)	1921
Waverly, Iowa	Condensery (Transferred to Instant Products 1958. Discontinued patron milk 1970)	1921
Fort Lupton, Colorado	Condensery (Closed 1953)	1921
Johnstown, Colorado	Condensery	1921
Loveland, Colorado	Receiving Station (Closed 1940)	1921
Gustine, California	Condensery	1921
Cattaraugus, New York	Condensery (Closed 1953)	1923
South Dayton, New York	Condensery	1923
Mt. Vernon, Missouri	Condensery	1924
Tupelo, Mississippi	Condensery (Closed 1971)	1927
Murfreesboro, Tennessee	Condensery (Discontinued patron milk 1974)	1927
Bell Buckle, Tennessee	Receiving Station (Closed 1962)	1927
Watertown, Tennessee	Receiving Station (Closed 1974)	1927
Maysville, Kentucky	Condensery	1928
Northfield, Minnesota	Condensery (Closed and sold 1962)	1929
Lonsdale, Minnesota	Receiving Station (Closed 1954)	1929
Baldwyn, Mississippi	Receiving Station (Closed 1971)	1929
Manchester, Tennessee	Receiving Station (Closed 1974)	1929

234

Location	Operation	Starting Date
Neosho, Missouri	Receiving Station (Closed and sold 1965)	1929
Schulenburg, Texas	Condensery (Trans. to FM&IC 1951)	1929
Hillsboro, Ohio	Receiving Station (Closed 1970)	1934
Coshocton, Ohio	Condensery (Converted to soy protein production 1968)	1934
Crows Landing, California	Receiving Station (Transferred to FM&IC 1946)	1934
Hillsboro, Wisconsin	Condensery (Converted to receiving station 1956. Sold 1966)	1935
Bellville, Ohio	Receiving Station (Closed and sold 1968)	1935
Rogers, Arkansas	Receiving Station (Closed and sold 1962)	1935
Sugar Creek, Ohio	Receiving Station (Sold 1942)	1935
Owen, Wisconsin	Condensery (Sold 1945)	1936
Castalia, Iowa	Receiving Station (Sold 1967)	1936
Wrightstown, Wisconsin	Receiving Station (Closed and sold 1956)	1936
Sulphur Springs, Texas	Condensery	1936
Mt. Sterling, Kentucky	Receiving Station	1936
Okolona, Mississippi	Receiving Station (Closed 1953)	1936
Gratiot, Wisconsin	Receiving Station (Closed 1970)	1936
Ava, Missouri	Receiving Station	1936
Seymour, Missouri	Receiving Station	1936
Mohicanville, Ohio	Receiving Station (Closed 1956)	1936
Rushville, Ohio	Receiving Station (Closed 1968)	1936
Turlock, California	Receiving Station	1936
West Concord, Minnesota	Receiving Station (Sold 1962)	1936
Galax, Virginia	Condensery	1937
Statesville, North Carolina	Condensery	1939
Riner, Virginia	Receiving Station	1939
Albemarle, North Carolina	Receiving Station	1939
Shelby, North Carolina	Receiving Station	1940
Clarksburg, West Virginia	Condensery	1940
Cameron, West Virginia	Receiving Station	1940
Oakland, Maryland	Receiving Station	1940

Location	Operation	Starting Date
Jamestown, Michigan	Receiving Station (Sold 1961)	1941
Reeman, Michigan	Receiving Station (Closed and sold 1955)	1941
Spruce Pine, North Carolina	Receiving Station (Closed and sold 1953)	1941
Sparta, Tennessee	Receiving Station (Closed 1974)	1941
Lowell, Wisconsin	Receiving Station (Closed and sold 1954)	1943
Maxwell, California	Receiving Station (Closed 1961)	1943
Chico, California	Receiving Station (Closed 1972)	1943
Scottville, Michigan	Receiving Station (Closed and sold 1953)	1943
East Bristol, Wisconsin	Receiving Station (Closed and sold 1953)	1943
Oconto Falls, Wisconsin	Receiving Station (Closed 1954)	1943
Dadeville, Alabama	Receiving Station (Sold 1961)	1943
Harrison, Arkansas	Receiving Station	1943
Anderson, California	Receiving Station (Closed 1959)	1944
Wellsville, Utah	Condensery (Sold 1967)	1946
Sunnyside, Washington	Condensery (To FM&IC 1957)	1946
Hazleton, Iowa	Receiving Station (Closed 1961)	1946
Campbellsville, Kentucky	Receiving Station	1946
El Dorado Springs, Missouri	Receiving Station	1946
Monroe, North Carolina	Receiving Station (Closed 1973)	1947
Ontario, Oregon	Receiving Station (Closed 1958)	1947
Rosendale, Wisconsin	Receiving Station (Closed and sold 1950)	1947
Waupun, Wisconsin	Condensery (Closed 1958)	1947
Randolph, Wisconsin	Receiving Station (Closed 1953)	1947
Morrison, Illinois	Condensery Converted to Rec. Sta. (Closed 1970)	1947
Sheridan, Michigan	Condensery	1947
Girard, Kansas	Receiving Station (Closed 1969)	1947